Reduced worktime and the management of production

Reduced worktime and the management of production

CHRIS NYLAND
The University of Wollongong

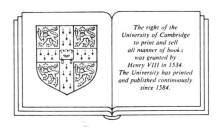

The right of the
University of Cambridge
to print and sell
all manner of books
was granted by
Henry VIII in 1534.
The University has printed
and published continuously
since 1584.

CAMBRIDGE UNIVERSITY PRESS

Cambridge
New York   New Rochelle   Melbourne   Sydney

658.542
N 995

Published by the Press Syndicate of the University of Cambridge
The Pitt Building, Trumpington Street, Cambridge CB2 1RP
32 East 57th Street, New York, NY 10022, USA
10 Stamford Road, Oakleigh, Melbourne 3166, Australia

© Cambridge University Press 1989

First published 1989

Printed in the United States of America

Library of Congress Cataloging-in-Publication Data
Nyland, Chris.
Reduced worktime and the management of production / Chris
Nyland.
p. cm.
Bibliography: p.
Includes index.
ISBN 0 521 34547 2
1. Industrial management. 2. Labor productivity. 3. Work. I. Title.
HD31.N93   1988
658.5'42 – dc19   88–16852
                                                                  CIP

British Library Cataloguing in Publication Data
Nyland, Chris
Reduced worktime and the management of production.
1. Reduced working hours.
I. Title
331.25'7
ISBN 0 521 34547 2

To
BERENICE

Contents

Preface

Between 1870 and 1980 total annual paid working time in the major nations of the industrialised capitalist world contracted by approximately 40 per cent. This book attempts to explain how it is that this dramatic development occurred. A general discussion of the worktime issue is opportune because this topic traditionally becomes a major political and economic issue in times of high unemployment. During periods of economic crisis the labour movement invariably puts forward the argument that standard times should be reduced in order to spread the available work amongst as many individuals as possible. The ongoing crisis that has emerged following the end of the "long boom" has proved no exception to this general rule. An examination of the worktime issue is necessary, moreover, because the contemporary worktime debate is still dominated by the belief that the primary reason time standards have contracted to the extent they have is the rising incomes workers have enjoyed through the last century. Despite some limited attempts to widen the debate as unemployment has increased since the early 1970s, this basic hypothesis remains the core of modern worktime theory.

The central theme in this volume is that the changing nature of worktime is not primarily explained by worker preferences for income and leisure. Rather, it is argued, the primary causal factors bringing about this development have been the changing nature of the capitalist production process and the changing nature of the demands this process places on the psychophysiological capacities of human beings. The work shows that this hypothesis is not an original contribution to the worktime debate but rather that it has a lineage dating from the late eighteenth century and that, indeed, in the first half of the present century it was considered a virtual truism.

To explain how and why twentieth-century standard worktimes have contracted to the extent they have it is necessary to understand the nature of the economic revival experienced by capitalism in the years immediately after the First World War. It is argued in this work that the regeneration that occurred at this time is primarily explained by the rapid expansion of the processes associated with rationalisation or scientific management. The major changes to worktime that occurred during the 1920s and subsequently were an integral element in the development of this new science. It is further argued that the nature of scientific management has been seriously misunderstood by the overwhelming majority of contemporary scholars. Few have been willing to acknowledge the enormous contribution to society's capacity to eliminate poverty the development of this science made possible. Fewer still, outside the socialist nations, have recognised the potential its further development has for enabling human beings to throw off the dominance of the invisible hand of the market and to give people the ability to direct their own history.

This work then is concerned with the issues of working time, the rationalisation of production and the long-term viability of capitalism. The argument makes the following substantive points:

1. Worktime is not merely a function of income, as is claimed by both marginalists and many radicals. The theoretical underpinnings of the income argument are criticised and shown to be little more than unsubstantiated assertion.

2. It is suggested that Marx's understanding of capitalist competition, human capacities and the inverse relationship between working time and intensity led him to conclude that capitalist societies would be characterised by a tendency to reduce the length of time workers normally spent at their place of paid employment.

3. The science of management pioneered by Frederick Taylor was not merely a tool available to employers for increasing the exploitation of workers. It was a double-edged sword that could be and was utilised by the labour movement to advance its interests. The workers thus played a positive role in bringing about the rationalisation and further development of the forces of production.

4. An explanation is provided for what has long appeared the greatest weakness in Marx's economics, that is, the

apparent invalidation by history of his prophecies concerning the rate of profit, cyclical crises and the immiseration of the working class. It is suggested that this seeming failure is explained largely by the rise of scientific management, which gave birth to a new capitalist epoch; further, that the present period of decay into which capitalism appears to have fallen may well signal the end to this stage of development.

Acknowledgements

In the preparation of this volume I have received assistance and a great deal of critical comment from many friends and colleagues. Of special importance in this regard was Tom Sheridan, whose doubt and insight constantly acted as a goad compelling me to challenge my assumptions and as a restraint ensuring I did not drift too far from the material world. For kind assistance I am also indebted to D. Atkinson, M. Beresford, J. Jose, D. Kelly, G. Lehman, D. McEachern, J. Pincus, B. Smith, G. Snooks and K. White.

For technical assistance I should like to thank M. Baker, P. Huxtable, R. Kamenjarin, D. Kuss and B. Triffett. Thanks also to the staff at Flinders University Library and particularly to those who have staffed the inter-library loans desk.

Finally I owe thanks to the School of Social Sciences at Flinders University for granting me a visiting research fellowship and thus enabling me to complete this work.

CHAPTER 1

The history of worktime thought

The development of capitalism has been accompanied by major changes to the length of time the direct producers normally spend at their place of employment. Through the two centuries 1500 to 1700, for example, British worktimes tended to increase. Since this period these times have progressively contracted with sporadic reductions in time standards tending to characterise the labour market overall (Bienefeld 1972: 9). As traditional worktime patterns began to change in the fourteenth century, a debate arose as to why the time workers normally labour should tend to be subject to widespread and sustained variation. The debate has continued to the present day. This work will begin by examining the major theoretical contributions that have been put forward to explain this phenomenon. Because of the leading role formerly held by British economic theorists, the survey will primarily utilise the experiences of that nation.

Prior to the middle years of the eighteenth century those individuals who wrote on economic topics, with very few exceptions, took it as given that the direct producers were innately slothful. They invariably insisted that working people would not labour longer or harder than was necessary to satisfy those minimal wants to which they aspired, unless they were forced to by hunger or terror. The essence of their belief is encapsulated in Arthur Young's maxim that "everyone but an idiot knows that the lower classes must be kept poor or they will never be industrious." The claim that workers would reduce their supply of labour power if its price was increased was irrational in terms of the supply-and-demand analysis economic writers tended to find attractive even before the rise of classical economics. For the overwhelming majority of economic observers, however, this irrationality caused little disquiet as long as market forces remained inadequate, by themselves, to ensure that employers' needs for labour power were satisfied.

For over two centuries mercantilist scholars simply ignored

the problem of irrationality and openly endorsed the interests of the employers vis-à-vis their employees. They argued that where the former could not find adequate supplies of labour power at the subsistence price they were willing to pay, the state should adopt policies that would enable this situation to be remedied. This was justified on the grounds that the nation must have a positive balance of trade. If working people restricted their work effort, costs would rise and the competitiveness of the nation's industries would be undermined. Workers, consequently, must not be allowed to freely choose the extent to which they laboured. Where such individuals showed any marked preference for leisure over income, it was insisted, the state had a duty to take steps to ensure that direct producers were made to work. The prescriptions the economists put forward to attain this objective included the state fixation of wages, the expansion of inward migration, enclosure of common land to eliminate economic independence and manipulation of the supply of food in order to drive up its price. In essence all these proposals aimed to lower the standard of living of the working people in order to compel them to work harder and longer. If high incomes lowered the willingness of the labourers to work, it was reasoned, low incomes should have the opposite effect.

The assertion that it was necessary to maintain the income of the working population at subsistence level in order to increase normal worktimes went largely unchallenged until the early years of the eighteenth century. From this period, however, an increasing number of observers began to voice some doubt as to the validity of this claim. It became increasingly common for economic writers to concede that not all workers were idle and dissolute and that whereas it was true that many still were, this was often for reasons beyond their control. These questioners of mercantilist orthodoxy also argued that depressing the working people's living standards might even be counterproductive. High wages, it was suggested, could act as an inducement that would encourage workers to undertake a greater expenditure of effort. David Hume (cited by Coats 1958: 40), for example, emphasised the need to provide incentives in all areas of economic activity: "It is a violent method and in most cases impractical, to oblige the labourer to toil, in order to raise from the land more than what subsists himself and family. Furnish him with the manufactures and commodities and he will do it of himself."

Prior to 1750 those writers who were sympathetic to this perspective were few in number. In the third quarter of the century, however, it gained much more support, the culmination of which was to prove a major transition occurring in 1776 with Adam Smith's *The Wealth of Nations*. Smith argued that nature had imbued human beings with a desire to improve their lot and that for most people this innate drive was sufficiently strong to more than offset their "natural sloth."

Some workmen, indeed, when they can earn in four days what will maintain them through the week, will be idle the other three. This, however, is by no means the case with the greater part. Workmen, on the contrary, when they are liberally paid by the piece, are very apt to over-work themselves, and to ruin their health and constitution in a few years. (Smith 1964: Vol. 1, 73)

Smith's belief that most people would strive to improve their lot led him to reject the economists' traditional approach to worktime. He also opposed their support for state manipulation of the labour market, arguing that individuals must be given the freedom to buy and sell labour power in an unrestrained market. Given the desire of most human beings to improve their condition, he argued, it was not necessary to coerce them to increase their work effort. Provide them with sufficient economic inducement and they would do this of their own accord.

The belief that an acquisitive and hedonistic spirit was innate in human beings and that workers would increase their labour effort if offered the chance to increase their income was to become part of the orthodoxy of classical economics. Pollard (1978: 97) has argued that it was the humanism of the classical economists that led them to abandon the mercantilists' labour policies. His interpretation of this major change in economic thinking, however, must surely be considered overly generous. To begin with, the changed perspective was not applied to all workers, for it certainly did not include the Irish. The latter continued to be considered so dissolute there was no choice but to compel them to work. Pollard's assessment also fails to consider a point he has well made elsewhere, namely that in the four centuries prior to 1750 the working people of Britain were subjected to an unprecedented remoulding as the working class was being "made." The enormity of this change cannot be overstated, for it involved the transformation of the very nature of the labouring population: "Men who were non-accumulative, non-acquisitive, accustomed to work for subsistence, not for maximisation of income, had to be made obedient to the cash stimulus and obedient in such a way as to react precisely to the stimuli provided" (Pollard 1965: 160–161).

By the second half of the nineteenth century, Thompson (1967) has suggested, capitalist wage incentives were becoming widely effective. This is not to argue that the transition was complete by this period. Simply getting the workers to show up regularly for work remained a problem for employers well into the nineteenth century. Skilled workers, who managed to retain a high degree of bargaining power throughout the industrial revolution, created particularly severe difficulties for employers in this regard. Nevertheless, it is the case that the attitudes of working people did change and changed to a form that was more acceptable to the employers and to the economists. It is this change in the material world, rather than any newfound humanism on the part of economists, that surely better explains this major shift in their thinking. Finally, Pollard's kind interpretation also fails to consider a further point he has correctly stressed elsewhere. Through the eighteenth century population growth and the development of the enclosure movement greatly increased the number of workers seeking employment within the British labour market. There was, moreover, an increase in the rate of population growth around 1740, and a second burst of acceleration in the 1780s. The vastly increased number of workers this development flooded onto the labour market from 1750 onwards greatly enhanced the employers' ability to determine conditions of employment in many trades. Many workers and particularly those in the newly emerging textile factories were driven to labour at a daily rate which all but totally ignored their long-term interests, with worktimes often being brutally extended and intensified.

It is in the context of this major shift in bargaining power in the employers' favour that one needs to assess both the economists' newfound belief that workers would respond positively to the chance to gain greater income and their insistence that the state should allow the labour market to operate freely. The first factor enabled them to explain, in a manner favourable to the employer, why workers were increasing their work effort. When buyers and sellers of labour power entered the market, it was argued, they did so as free agents each seeking, in their partnership, to improve their lot. Where workers increased the amount of work they undertook, this was clearly a manifestation of a free decision on their part to take advantage of the opportunity offered to them by the employers to satisfy their desire for greater income. In other words, the workers were increasing their work effort because of their innate desire to improve their lot, not because they had no real choice in the matter. The second factor in the economists' argument was equally an exercise in apologetics. To argue that the state should adopt a noninterventionist economic policy, treating the buyer and seller of labour power as equals, when the market is skewed heavily in favour of one side or the other, is clearly to favour the stronger protagonist. Such an argument, however, had the advantage that it enabled the economists not only to continue actively promoting the employers' interests but to do so while maintaining the pose that they were unbiased scientists.

The classical economists, then, remained as assuredly committed to the interests of the employers as the mercantilists had been. It was not their humanism that led these individuals to revise orthodox theory. Rather, it was the fact that the labouring population had changed and that they were provided the opportunity to obscure, even from themselves, both the class nature of the relationship between capital and labour and their own class bias under the facade of market freedom.

To argue that Smith's support for an unrestricted labour market was in fact a defence of employer interests is not to claim that this scholar made no objective and substantive contribution to worktime theory. His insistence that humans will strive to improve their material wellbeing remains a central tenet within modern economic theory. He also made a most important contribution when he attempted to explain why workers often chose to limit the length of time they were willing to labour. The explanation for this phenomenon, he argued, lay in the fact that worktime has both an intensive and a temporal dimension and that these two elements are closely interrelated. Because of this interrelationship workers often chose to reduce the length of time they spent at work, even when they had a desire for greater income, because the intensity of effort demanded during the time they did labour was so high that they were physically or mentally exhausted.

Excessive application during four days of the week is frequently the real cause of the idleness of the other three, so much and so loudly complained of. Great labour, either of mind or body, continued for several days together, is in most men naturally followed by a great desire of relaxation, which, if not restrained by force or by some strong necessity, is almost irresistible. It is the call of nature, which requires to be relieved by some indulgence, sometimes of ease only, but sometimes, too, of dissipation and diversion. (Smith 1964: Vol. 1, 73)

If employers ignored human limits, and Smith suggested they frequently did, the health of the workers would be seriously undermined and many would be worked to an early grave. Smith's recognition of the material limitations of human beings led him to point out that there was an inverse relationship between the intensive and temporal aspects of worktime and that, consequently, an optimum time schedule which balanced these two elements must exist in any given situation. He advised employers to pay heed to the existence of these optima and refrain from driving their employees at too great a pace if they wished to minimise their costs.

The factory movement

In the first years of the nineteenth century the employers' continuing attempts to compel their employees to increase their work effort gave rise to a movement demanding that the state enact legislation to limit the length of the working day. This campaign drew the bulk of its active support from the textile workers in the North of England. Over the period 1800–1860 these workers waged an ongoing struggle to attain some degree of legal protection from the demands of the employers. In their campaign the workers managed to attract support from progressive reformers within the intelligentsia. They also received assistance from Tory landowners who were hostile to the manufacturers and even received valuable aid from those factory owners who, for one reason or another, were able to curtail the worktimes of their enterprises at little cost to themselves. They did not, however, gain assistance from the economists.

In the early days of the factory movement few economic theoreticians displayed much interest in the conditions under which factory workers were compelled to labour. As the campaign for a legal maximum to the workday became more influential, however, these scholars abandoned their indifference. The worktime issue was taken up with an increasing degree of enthusiasm, becoming by the early 1830s a highly contentious theoretical question. In their initial contribution to the debate the economists did not attempt to explain why hedonistic beings should en masse choose to reduce the length of time they wished to work. Rather, they confined their discussion to the market rights of the individual. As free agents, it was insisted, individuals should be allowed to sell their labour power as they wished. If they chose to exchange this commodity in excessively large units this was their right. State regulation of worktime would clearly infringe this freedom and was thus morally wrong and had, as such, to be opposed. There was little disagreement over these propositions. What was disputed was the definition of what constituted a free agent. Children, it was generally acknowledged, were not capable of exercising sufficient independent judgement to freely enter into a contract. Was it right, therefore, for the state to regulate the sale of their labour power? Blaug (1958: 212) reports that during the 1830s there was a wide variety of opinion on this question. This diversity, however, gradually abated as it became clear that the legislation of 1833, which limited the worktimes of children, was not causing great difficulty for employers. The economists, as a consequence, generally came to agree that worktime laws for children were admissible. They insisted, though, that such legislation should be limited to that already adopted, for its extension would necessarily involve limiting the length of time adults could work. Legislation of this nature would constitute a "gross infringement" of the rights of the individual and thus could not possibly be accepted.

The economists utilised the concept of the free individual to justify their opposition to state protection of the adult working class throughout the 1830s. This was despite the fact that it was patently apparent that the individual worker had almost no bargaining power within the market place. Towards the end of the 1830s, however, the economists became increasingly reluctant to use this argument and by the 1840s they had all but totally laid it aside. They did not take this step, though, because of any newly developed humanity. Rather, the argument was abandoned because the economists were soon made aware that in the face of a demand from the great majority of workers for a legal limit to the workday, its utilisation was a serious embarrassment for the employers. In short, it came to be realised that whereas the claim that it was individual sellers of labour power who determined standard worktimes was useful as a tool to justify the extension of time schedules, the argument became double edged if a majority of the working class made it clear that they wanted to reduce the length of time they had to labour. Through the 1830s, rallies of up to 150,000 workers were held in the North of England in support of a legal 10-hour maximum to the working day.

The overwhelming nature of the working classes' endorsement of such a law caused a great deal of confusion amongst the economists. If, as they insisted, individuals should be allowed to freely determine their own arrangements, because it was only individuals who knew their own best interest, how could one justify opposition to the legislative regulation of worktime when the enactment of such a law was clearly desired by the great majority of the individuals concerned (Mill 1859: 963–965)? While initially some economists attempted to avoid this dilemma by denying there was majority support for a 10-hour law amongst the workers, most eventually were forced to concede that this was the case. Their response to this realisation, however, was not to join the workers in demanding a legal restriction on the employers' right to determine the length of the working day. Rather, they insisted that the workers did not understand the true ramifications of what they were demanding and that consequently it was necessary for more informed individuals to ensure that the unwise policies they advocated were not adopted. In 1846 *The Economist* attempted to explain this point to those who foolishly insisted that the individual-rights argument might still be relevant to the worktime debate.

It is quite contrary to our principles to restrict the factory operatives, or any other class, in the pursuit of their own interest or happiness, or for one moment to pretend that they do not understand what is good for themselves equally as well as other men; but as all classes, when they legislate, meaning only to provide for their own welfare, do affect, by multiple ramifications, of which they dream not, the whole community, and do fail even to promote their own interests . . . we may without presumption suppose it to be, at least, possible that even the factory operatives mistake their own interest, and the interest of the community, in demanding that labour in factories be limited to ten hours by Act of Parliament. If we thought that such an Act would benefit them . . . it would find no warmer advocates than ourselves. (Cited by Robson 1985: 231–232)

The growing strength and radicalism of the factory movement made the promotion of the argument that the workers did not know their own best interests extremely difficult. It was for this reason that the question of the individual's rights was quietly laid aside and the economists began justifying their support for the employers on the grounds that a 10-hour law would raise production costs. Nassau Senior opened this new line of defence in 1837, in his *Letters on the Factory Act*. Senior argued that the increasing ratio of fixed to circulating capital that tended to develop as industry mechanised made long hours of work necessary. This fact had been carefully explained to him, Senior (1837: 14) reported, by a Manchester employer. "'When a labourer', said Mr. Ashworth to me, 'lays down his spade, he renders useless, for that period, a capital worth eighteen pence. When one of our people leaves the mill, he renders useless a capital that has cost 100*l*.'" Senior insisted that, given the cost structure of modern industry, any reduction in the length of the working day would tend to raise unit costs. The openly biased nature of the argument he utilised to justify his claims, at a time when bias needed to be hidden, made it unacceptable to most of his fellow economists. His basic point that worktime reductions would raise prices and hence undermine the competitiveness of British industry, however, was generally accepted to be valid. It was, consequently, this production-based argument that the economists brought to the fore when opposing the Factory Acts during the 1840s. Regulation of worktime had to be resisted because it would have a deleterious effect on trade, and this made opposition to the 10-hour law morally just because the workers clearly stood to lose if the economy declined.

Confronted with this new strategy for countering their demands, the workers and their allies also began to emphasise the issue of production costs in their literature. Robert Owen (1815) had called for the introduction of a legal 10½-hour limit to the working day and had successfully adopted this schedule at New Lanark early in the century. When doing so he had argued that, in any well-managed enterprise, it was possible to produce as cheaply with the shorter schedule as it was with the longer because the workers were less fatigued and hence were able to labour more intensively. As those opposing the extension of the Factory Acts began to emphasise the issue of production costs, supporters of reform responded by placing increasing emphasis on this argument. This trend was accentuated by the publicity given to a number of worktime experiments that were begun in Preston in 1844. The factory inspector Leonard Horner reported on the most significant of these studies in his 1845 report to Parliament. This was a textile mill in which the workday had been reduced from 12 to 11 hours. When Horner visited the mill the experiment had been in progress for twelve months. He reported that despite the worktime curtailment and the fact that there had been no increase in capital outlay, the temporal reduction had not resulted in any decrease in output or increase in unit costs.

The declaration made is, that the same quantity of produce, and at the same cost, has been obtained by the master; and that all the workers, day hands as well as those who are paid by piece-work, earn the same amount of wages in the 11 hours as was done before by the labour of 12 hours. (Horner 1845: 449)

Horner went on to report that he had always assumed that employers would strive to ensure that they operated their plants with the greatest possible efficiency and that employees, when paid by piece work, would exert themselves to the utmost. These assumptions led him, in turn, to assume that any curtailment in the working times of a well-managed factory would necessarily result in a reduction of output. His experience at Preston convinced him that this last assumption was invalid. It also made him realise that the reason he had been in error was that he had not considered an important element, "viz., the extent to which vigilance and attention on the part of the workman can influence the amount of production" (p. 450). In short, a reduced workday could increase the efficiency of the employees' labour time by enabling them to labour more effectively.

In his report to Parliament Horner also reported that he had discussed the Preston experiments with numerous other factory owners. Some of these individuals had conceded that the results were impressive and acknowledged that it might be possible to offset worktime reductions, to some extent, by improving efficiency. Most, however, refused to even consider the idea, insisting that it was ridiculous to claim that it was possible to produce as much in a 66-hour week as could be produced in 72 hours.

The tendency for the majority of employers to dismiss the efficiency evidence out of hand was replicated by the economists. There was the rare exception, like Thornton (1971: 399), who observed that it was

not quite certain that a diminution of produce would result from shortening the duration of labour. Persons who are not obliged to work so long may work harder than before, and may get through the same quantity of work in a short time as formerly occupied them for a longer period. The business of the eleventh and twelfth hours is most likely very languidly done, and might perhaps, without great difficulty, be despatched in the preceding ten.

Thornton's hypothesis, however, was not even considered by most economists, who simply insisted that worktime and output were proportionally related. This assertion, Blaug (1958: 217) reports, "became an essential feature of the classical analysis of factory legislation."

Marx's theory of worktime

One other economist upon whom the efficiency argument did make a great impression was Marx. This scholar argued that conflict over the length of the working day was an inevitable consequence of the class relations upon which capitalism was based. He further claimed that the need for employers to strive to maximise the utility they gained from their employees' labour time would ensure that capitalism would be characterised by periodic reductions in the length of time the worker normally laboured.

Marx agreed with Senior that a shift in the ratio of capital spent on machinery and materials relative to that spent on purchasing labour power, that is, an increase in the organic composition of capital, heightens the employers' need to increase or intensify the workers' labour time. The long-term tendency for the organic composition of capital to increase and the consequent tendency for the rate of profit to decline, he argued, drives employers to forever seek out new ways to extract more surplus labour from the worker. Employees, consequently, must attempt to establish "rational limits" to the length of time they must work if they hope to live a normal life. By a normal life Marx meant normal both in terms of years and in terms of the intellectual and social norms of the society in which individuals belonged. He argued that in resisting the demand that they constantly increase the amount of labour they undertake, the workers were not only fulfilling a duty to themselves but also a duty to the human race.

Time is the room of human development. A man who has no free time to dispose of, whose whole lifetime, apart from the mere physical interruptions by sleep, meals, and so forth, is absorbed by his labour for the capitalist, is less than a beast of burden. He is a mere machine for producing Foreign Wealth, broken in body and brutalized in mind. Yet the whole history of modern industry shows that capital, if not checked, will recklessly and ruthlessly work to cast down the whole working class to this utmost state of degradation. (Marx 1969: 67–68)

If employers are not checked, in other words, the drive to attain an adequate rate of profit will compel them to extract labour from the worker at a rate that is not compatible with the latter's ability to maintain a "traditional standard of life."

Overwork, Marx argued, is particularly common where workers can be cheaply replaced once their productive capacity begins to decline. Where replacement cost becomes a significant factor, he acknowledged, employers will attempt to husband the use of the workers' labour time, to some extent, in order to minimise its overall cost. The period over which they attempt to do this, however, will not be the worker's full lifetime but rather that length of time the employer expects to retain the worker's services. From the perspective of the capitalist class as a whole, the limited nature of the individual employer's willingness to husband the use of labour power creates a problem. The workers must be able to live long enough to reproduce adequate supplies of their commodity for the market. This means that the rate at which labour power is extracted from them must be compatible with their reproductive capacities, not merely with the length of time they remain in the individual capitalist's employ. Because of the differing interests of individual capitalists and capitalists as a class, Marx insisted, it is necessary for society to establish a force that can govern the rate at which the society's supplies of labour power are consumed. In most cases this means the state. Marx's argument has been well summarised by Harvey (1982: 30):

In the absence of class organisation on the part of labour, unbridled competition among the capitalists has the potential to destroy the work force, the very source of surplus value itself. From time to time, the capitalists must in their own interest constitute themselves as a class and put limits on the extent of their own competition.

For Marx, then, the Factory Acts were a combined consequence of working-class struggle and the structural needs of
the capitalist class. He insisted, however, that the adoption of
worktime laws did not end capitalism's tendency to overcon-
sume labour power. Such laws established temporal barriers to
the rate at which the workers' commodity was consumed but
they placed few limits on what could be done within these barriers. Most important, they did not regulate how intensively
workers laboured in a given length of time. The shortening of
the workday provided employers with an immense stimulus to
raise productivity by ensuring that all the inputs into the production process were used more efficiently. In the case of labour power, Marx argued, the shorter day not only increased
the need for the employer to utilise this commodity more intensively, it also created the subjective conditions that made this
possible; that is, with the shorter schedule it was now possible
for workers to sustain a more condensed degree of effort.
Competition, moreover, would ensure that employers strove to
realise this possibility.

The compulsory shortening of the hours of labour . . . gives an immense impetus to the development of productivity and the more
economical use of the conditions of production. It imposes on the
worker an increased expenditure of labour within a time which remains constant, a heightened tension of labour-power, and a closer
filling-up of the pores of the working day, i.e. a condensation of
labour, to a degree which can only be attained within the limits of the
shortened working day. This compression of a greater mass of labour
into a given period now counts for what it really is, namely an increase
in the quantity of labour. In addition to the measure of its "extensive
magnitude", labour-time now acquires a measure of its intensity, or
degree of density. The denser hour of the 10-hour working day contains more labour, i.e. expended labour-power, than the more porous
hour of the 12-hour working day. (Marx 1976: 534)

The fact that humans are capable of raising the intensity of
their labour time if its length is shortened ensured that the
struggle between capital and labour over the quantity of labour
power normally exchanged for a given wage continued after
the passage of the Factory Acts. Employers merely shifted their
primary focus to the intensive aspect of worktime. The means
by which they attempted to raise intensity levels were diverse
and included the wide adoption of piece work, closer supervision and the reorganisation of the work process. Often these

factors alone were enough to ensure that an increase in intensity sufficient to offset the shorter day was attained. It was the employers' systematic use of machinery, however, that was the primary objective means utilised to obtain this goal. This was done by both increasing the speed and the number of machines the workers were expected to operate. Marx reports that employers also tended to increase the degree of mechanisation and significantly improved the quality of the technology utilised within their enterprises. In short, Marx argued that the Factory Acts motivated employers to overhaul the production process in a way which might well not have been done had they not had this added incentive. In support of his claims Marx was able to cite the factory inspectors:

The great improvements made in machines of every kind have raised their productive power very much. Without any doubt, the shortening of the hours of labour . . . gave the impulse to these improvements. The latter, combined with the more intense strain on the workman, have had the effect that at least as much is produced in the shortened working day . . . as was previously produced during the longer one. (Cited by Marx 1976: 540)

The introduction of the Factory Acts, then, brought about an increase in the average level of work intensity normally maintained within industry. Marx argued that given the competitive nature of capitalism such a response was inevitable. He also insisted that it was equally inevitable that this response would eventually make further worktime reductions necessary. For the employers' need for ever greater quantities of surplus labour would drive them to repeat the same mistakes that had made it necessary to pass the Factory Acts in the first place. Their freedom to intensify worktime, Marx insisted, would eventually result in the average level of work intensity rising to a point where it would come into conflict with the length of time normally worked.

The reader will clearly see that we are dealing here, not with temporary paroxysms of labour but with labour repeated day after day with unvarying uniformity. Hence a point must inevitably be reached where extension of the working day and intensification of labour become mutually exclusive so that the lengthening of the working day becomes compatible only with a lower degree of intensity, and inversely, a higher degree of intensity only with a shortening of the working day. (Marx 1976: 533)

Thus, while reduced worktimes lead to increased concentration of effort, the continuing nature of this rising intensity sooner or later makes further reductions in standard times necessary.

Capital's tendency, as soon as a prolongation of the hours of labour is once for all forbidden, is to compensate for this by systematically raising the intensity of labour, and converting every improvement in machinery into a more perfect means for soaking up labour-power. There cannot be the slightest doubt that this process must soon lead once again to a critical point at which a further reduction in the hours of labour will be inevitable. (Marx 1976: 542)

Despite the prophetic and material nature of Marx's argument, it has not attracted much attention from modern scholars. Mainstream economists have generally been uninterested in Marx's work and most radicals appear to have misunderstood the nature of the argument. With few exceptions the latter have tended to concentrate their efforts on only limited aspects of Marx's contribution to the worktime debate. A classic example of this limited perspective is that provided by Cleaver (1979). This scholar has argued that the long-term contraction of worktime is merely a consequence of the political struggle between capital and labour. As the working class grew in size and strength, Cleaver suggests, it was able to challenge capital and compel the introduction of both the modern working day and the weekend. The claims that worktime is greatly affected by the balance of class power and that it is very much a political issue are not ones with which Marx would have disagreed. He stressed the point that the establishment of a rational working day was the product of a protracted and more or less concealed "civil war" between the employers and the working class. However, while he agreed that the capitalists' ability to determine working times was limited by the "strong wills" of the workers, as Cleaver correctly suggests, he also argued that it was limited by their "weak bodies." Marx insisted that if working times are continually extended or intensified, with one or the other element being held constant, then a point must inevitably be reached where the limitations of "man, that obstinate yet elastic barrier," will be reached. It is this relationship between human capacities and human will that is the core of Marx's theory of worktime. The de-emphasis on the human-limits aspect of the argument by those such as Cleaver, however, has removed much of the materialist content from Marx's argument. What is left is clearly inadequate and has proven relatively easy for non-Marx-ists to refute. Indeed, an argument for the decrease in standard worktimes that emphasises only political power is essentially a version of the marginalist preference theory. The only real difference in the two arguments is that one stresses market forces as the primary factor that operates to transform the workers' preference for leisure over income into an actual work-time reduction while the other emphasises political struggle.

Why it is that this non-materialist approach to worktime change has managed to go largely unchallenged by modern Marxists is difficult to explain. Marx, after all, was hardly ob-scure about his conception of the relationship among human capacities, working time and work intensity. The explanation for this development lies partly in the failure of modern West-ern Marxists to follow Marx when he leaves the sphere of cir-culation and enters the workplace to study the processes of production and partly in the general overemphasis on political and cultural factors that came to dominate Western Marxism during the years of the long boom. The economic stability of capitalism during this period led Marxists to place increasing stress on noneconomic factors as they searched for new ways by which capitalism could be challenged. Unfortunately, in the process a great deal of idealist baggage was taken on board by many scholars, and in a great number of cases the economic primacy stressed by Marx was all but totally abandoned in favour of political primacy. With the analysis of worktime change this development was compounded by the emergence within the tradition of a deep suspicion of claims that in some areas of social life biology might have something useful to con-tribute. Together these factors led many Marxists to ignore, or at best to give a formal nod to, the intensive aspect of labour time. Units of labour power, hours, days and so on, came to be treated as homogeneous concepts. Developments within the workplace that were changing the qualitative content of these units were generally ignored, and all reductions in the length of time workers had to labour came to be seen as unadulterated improvements.

The Jevonian revolution

In his analysis of worktime change Marx followed and ex-tended the path pioneered by Adam Smith. In doing so, however, he chose to concentrate on that part of Smith's analysis which centred on human capacities and the production process. He paid little attention to the question of income and the subjective desires of the individual other than to comment that workers would tend to increase their worktime if their hourly wages were so low they could not attain even a "miserable average wage" with a rational schedule. The second major economic tradition to emerge in the last half of the nineteenth century, namely marginalism, on the other hand, has shown a marked tendency to play down the human-capacities and income-preference aspects of Smith's argument. The marginalists rather chose to abandon Smith's path and revert to the preclassical assumption that the major factor causing worktimes to contract was the personal preference of individuals for leisure over income.

The working classes' insistence that a legal limit be placed on the working day made it difficult for the marginalist tradition to retain a concept of the worker as an individual forever seeking to maximise the length of time spent at work in order to gain more income. What was needed was an acceptable theory that would explain why hedonistic beings might choose to reduce the length of time they were willing to labour. Jevons's utilisation of the marginal-utility concept was to partly satisfy this need. In his contribution to worktime theory W.S. Jevons (1965) abandoned most of Smith's argument. He acknowledged the validity of Smith's observation that workers sometimes laboured until they were exhausted but he insisted that, for the overwhelming mass of workers, this normally occurred only when the alternative was starvation. He cited as an example of his argument the fact that workers had been observed to increase their work effort when faced with a sudden rise in the price of the basic needs of life. For Jevons this response was proof that the workers must have been restricting their efforts prior to the price rise, and he insisted it was clear that they had done this because they preferred greater leisure rather than the greater income that could be had by working harder.

Now, a rise in the price of food is really the same as a decrease of the produce of labour, since less of the necessaries of life can be acquired in exchange for the same money wages. We may conclude, then, that English labourers enjoying little more than the necessaries of life, will work harder the less the produce; or, which comes to the same thing, will work less hard as the produce increases. (W.S. Jevons 1965: 180)

Jevons argued, in other words, that workers would limit their efforts because the marginal utility of extra income would fall as their wages rose. This was because labour was a "painful exertion" undergone either to ward off pains of greater measure or to produce pleasures which, on balance, outweighed the pain of obtaining them. Where the rewards of labouring offset the cost, he argued, humans are driven by their desires to exert themselves beyond the point where they cease obtaining pleasure from their work. The disutility experienced beyond this point will tend to increase as the length of worktime increases, while the law of diminishing marginal utility will ensure that the pleasure gained from greater income will tend to decline. It is inherent in the logic of this situation that there must be a point where the benefits gained from an extra unit of work exactly equal the pain endured to obtain them. Jevons insisted that the worker will naturally cease to labour at this point. What the workers were doing when they demanded a legal limit to the workday, then, was collectively stating that they believed that the pleasure to be had from increased leisure was greater than the disutility the attainment of extra income would necessarily involve.

Complicating this neat relationship was one factor Jevons believed was of great significance. This was the effect of a change in wage rates. When hourly wages increase, he argued, the marginal utility of an extra unit of labour is raised. This development will tend to encourage workers to increase the length of time they spend at work. At the same time, however, the fact that the worker now receives a greater reward for every hour laboured means that the marginal utility of an extra unit of income is decreased while the utility of extra leisure remains unchanged. Because of this second factor it may well be the case that an increase in hourly wages encourages workers to reduce the length of time they are willing to labour. These two influences have become known as the substitution and income effects. Which factor is stronger cannot be determined by a priori reasoning, Jevons insisted. He believed, however, that the general tendency for working times to fall during the previous quarter-century indicated that the majority of workers chose to reduce the length of time they laboured as their hourly incomes rose.

Jevons suggested that the tendency for leisure preference to intensify as income increases is inherent in human nature. Like the mercantilists, however, he argued that this tendency was particularly acute amongst the working class. He suggested that the disutility associated with the work of the professional or the manager was much less than that experienced by the lower classes because this form of work had a relatively high level of intrinsic attraction. The income of highly skilled workers, therefore, has to rise to a very high level before the declining marginal utility of extra income outweighs the disutility required to obtain this extra reward. Jevons suggested, moreover, that racial and class differences as well as differences between individuals existed which could significantly influence how workers responded to the chance to obtain greater income, no matter what form of work they undertook. He argued, for example, that the artisan class was so poor in the "habits of providence and foresight," compared with their betters, that they invariably ceased work at the earliest possible occasion. It was for this reason that he strongly opposed church charities and free medical care for the poor. Increase the income of the lower classes beyond that level necessary for them to survive, he warned, and they will never help themselves and employers will never be able to get a reasonable day's work out of them.

Jevons, then, rejected Smith's belief that workers had such a strong income preference that they often needed to be restrained from working so hard that they were burnt out in a few years. He also refused to accept the argument that the real reason workers often chose to reduce the time they spent at work was the high level of intensity they normally maintained during the time they did labour.

His rejection of the central elements in Smith's contribution to worktime theory, however, did not mean Jevons totally abandoned the whole of the classical economists' approach to this issue. He retained, for example, their preference for concentrating on the individual, rather than the production process, as the primary locus of analysis. Likewise, he adopted their policy of lauding those worktime laws already established which had not proven overly harmful to employers as examples of the benefits of capitalism while at the same time insisting that any extension of these laws should be opposed. Finally, he continued their practice of ignoring or belittling theoretical and empirical evidence which supported Smith's observation that a reduction in worktime did not necessarily have to mean a proportional decrease in the amount of labour undertaken.

To lessen the day's labour by one hour, is to lessen the supply of labour by one-ninth or one-tenth part, and to the same extent to waste the efficiency of all machinery, and of the fixed capital connected therewith. It is an economic fallacy to suppose that any adequate counter-balancing advantage can, as a general rule, arise out of this loss, except of course the recreative, sanitary, or intellectual advantages (if any) to the workman from his enjoyment of more leisure time. (W.S. Jevons 1894: 68)

Jevons's contribution to the worktime debate contains all the essential elements of the modern marginalist theory of worktime. It is individuals seeking to maximise their utility that causes working times to contract over the long term. This hypothesis has gained all but total acceptance from the economists of the marginalist tradition. The argument has been succinctly put by Reynolds (1974: 34):

Over the long run . . . changes in hours reflect worker preferences. The main reason why weekly hours have fallen from about sixty at the turn of the century to around forty at present is that most workers find the increase in leisure preferable to the higher incomes they could earn on the old schedule. If and when most workers conclude that a four-day or a thirty-hour week yields a better balance between income and leisure, management and union policies will shift in that direction.

The only really significant change that modern marginalism has made to Jevons's basic argument has been to shift analysis away from the disutility associated with work. By making this modification marginalists have been able to play down Jevons's embarrassing acknowledgement that capitalist industrialisation has failed to make labour a pleasurable experience for the overwhelming majority of workers. Jevons's recognition that the worker experiences pain and his belief that it is necessary to scientifically examine the nature of this pain and explain why it remains so prevalent in industrialised societies have thus been deleted from consideration. Indeed, even the proposition that work is the alternative the worker faces to poverty tends to become blurred in the contemporary marginalist literature. Indifference analysis depicts the individual as being confronted not with two painful alternatives, hunger and work, but rather with two goods, income and leisure. Thus it is implied that capitalism supplies the worker not only with increased income but also with increased leisure and that individuals are free to select whatever mix of these two goods maximises their personal utility.

Economic crisis and theory

The marginalists did not re-establish the mercantilist claim that worktime is primarily a function of income without great difficulty, it needs to be noted. In the years immediately after the Ten Hours Bill was enacted, the factory inspectors went to great lengths to assess the truth of the reformers' efficiency argument. As a result of their research they reported that the basic hypotheses in the argument had been validated. Thus, after the new laws had been in operation for three years, Horner (1852: 360–361) was able to come to the following general conclusion:

In all those departments of the factory in which wages are paid by piece-work (and these constitute probably not less than four-fifths of the whole, the proportion to fixed weekly wages being daily on the increase), it has been found that the quantity produced in 10½ hours falls little short of that formerly obtained from 12 hours; in some instances it is said to be equal. This is accounted for, partly by the increased stimulus given to ingenuity to make the machinery more perfect and capable of increased speed, but it arises far more from the workpeople, by improved health, by absence of that weariness and exhaustion which the long hours occasioned, and by their increased cheerfulness and activity, being enabled to work more steadily and diligently, and to economize time; intervals for rest while at their work being now less necessary.

The reports of the factory inspectors led some economists to acknowledge that they had been proven wrong by the reformers (Newmarch 1862). These concessions, however, were soon forgotten when, in the late 1860s, employers were again confronted with a major campaign for a further reduction in the length of the working day. At the 1869 Trades Union Congress a motion calling for the immediate introduction of a 9-hour day and a Saturday half-holiday was unanimously carried. The unionists defended their demand on the grounds that a shorter day would promote the "morality and the physical and intellectual power of workmen, and assist in finding employment for the unemployed" (cited by Webb and Cox 1891: 18). Since the passing of the Factory Acts, the unionists argued, factory work had so increased in intensity that hours of labour had again become excessive and dangerous to the life and health of the employee. They insisted that the only way the increased intensity could be sufficiently offset was by reducing the length of time it had to be endured. This element in their claim continued the arguments put forward in defence of the Ten Hours Bill. Their job-creation argument, on the other hand, took at face value the assertion that a reduction in the length of the working day would reduce the firm's output by a proportional amount. If this claim was valid, it was argued, then once the length of the workday was reduced employers would have to take on more workers in order to maintain production. Hence, a decrease in the supply of labour power from each employed worker would increase employer demand for more staff. It was also argued that the contraction in supply would tend to raise the price of labour power. The workers, consequently, would not only have their workday reduced but would do so at no economic cost to themselves.

The campaign for the 9-hour day generated a massive wave of strikes throughout Britain in the years 1872–1874. This offensive once again elicited a hostile response from the economists. Most of these individuals refused to allow mere historical experience or empirical evidence to influence their analysis of the worktime issue. Fawcett (1872, 1873), for example, spoke out against the 9-hours demand by reiterating the argument that adults, as free agents, should be allowed to decide the length of time they wished to labour for themselves. He also dealt with the claim that worktime reductions could increase the efficiency of workers' labour time. Here (1872: 113–15, 120) he advanced an argument that has remained to the present day a major tool in the armoury of those opposed to reductions in worktime. He admitted that there was some evidence from individual firms that could be put forward in support of the argument but insisted that these examples were unique. In general, he insisted, competition invariably ensured that employers adopted that worktime schedule which was most efficient. Any reduction in the national standard, therefore, was certain to increase the production costs of the vast majority of enterprises, and this, in turn, was certain to undermine the nation's ability to trade on the international market.

The 9-hours campaign managed to establish a 54- to 56½-hour standard workweek in Britain. This success, temporarily, caused worktime to fade as a major political and industrial issue. The debate, however, was to soon erupt once again, for in 1874 the long boom the capitalist economies had enjoyed since 1848 slumped into the Great Depression. The subsequent prolonged economic crisis was a global phenomenon brought on by the fact that those forces offsetting capitalism's long-term tendency to lower the rate of profit, which free trade and the development of transport had allowed to flower, had weakened in their intensity to such an extent that they were no longer capable of adequately fulfilling this role (Wells 1889). As profit is the primary motivating force in capitalism, this development plunged the capitalist nations into a period of decay which lasted until after the First World War. In this period of crisis profit margins were squeezed and competitive pressures greatly increased. In response observers in every nation began to question the politics and economics of laissez-faire. For the employers the result of this reappraisal was the growth of tariff barriers, cartels and interimperialist rivalry. For the workers it was a reawakening of the demand for socialism.

Besides attempting to maintain profitability by controlling market forces, employers also responded to the crisis by striving to lower wages and increase the rate at which surplus labour was extracted from their employees. In Britain this led employers to undertake a major effort to restore the 10-hour day in 1878 and 1879. They met, however, great resistance, particularly from those sections of the working class which had become highly unionised. Confronted with this resistance, employers found that it was easier to allow standard times to remain unchanged and to concentrate instead on increasing overtime and the level of work intensity. Through the rest of the century the consequent radical increase in the intensive aspect of worktime became a major source of industrial conflict (Hobson 1894; Clarke 1899; Oliver 1902).

While the economic crisis both enabled and compelled employers to demand more work from their employees, it also induced the labour movement to demand further reductions in standard times. The emergence of mass unemployment, moreover, strongly reinforced this trend, with job creation initially becoming the major issue in the revived worktime debate. The crisis also strengthened those forces who argued that if capitalism was no longer capable of improving the population's standard of living it should be replaced with a social system that could. The re-emergence of these radical forces with the onset of the crisis has been eloquently described by Hobsbawm (1977: 187).

As capitalism and bourgeois society triumphed, the prospects of alternatives to it receded, in spite of the emergence of popular politics and labour movements. These prospects could hardly have seemed less promising in, say, 1872–3. And yet within a very few years the future of the society that had triumphed so spectacularly once again seemed uncertain and obscure, and movements to replace it or to overthrow it had once again to be taken seriously.

The resurgence, in both Europe and North America, of those forces demanding radical social change provided the labour movements of these nations with new allies amongst the intelligentsia – and this even included some economists. In Britain this development led to the creation of the Fabian Society and the Social Democratic Federation, both of which immediately became actively involved in the worktime debate. The second of these two bodies called, in 1881, for the immediate introduction of an Eight Hours Bill, and this demand was taken up by an increasing number of intellectuals and trade unionists through the decade. By 1890 this demand had become so popular that a call, by the International Trade Union Congress, for a simultaneous international demonstration in favour of an Eight Hours Act brought over a quarter of a million individuals onto the streets of London (Webb and Cox 1891: 33).

As the employers became confronted, once again, with a mass demand for the introduction of legislation that would further reduce the length of the working day, some of the nation's leading economists entered the worktime debate. Initially, some of these scholars based their opposition to the workers' demand on the traditional individual-rights argument (Brentano 1894: 27–28). As it became clear that the 8-hours demand was gaining overwhelming support amongst the working class, however, those opposed to worktime reform abandoned this argument and followed the escape route their counterparts had taken in the debate over the Factory Acts; that is, they raised the issue of production costs and attempted to limit debate to that issue. Their need to de-emphasise the question of the individual's right to choose how long he or she laboured, it needs to be added, was made particularly urgent by the fact that the reformers adopted a policy of allowing individual trades to be exempted from the provisions of any legislation if a majority of those employed in the occupation voted to apply for exemption (Fabian Society 1895).

We think that it might be left to the workers in each industry, bearing in mind the risk to their own wages involved, to decide whether the normal working day in that industry should be reduced. This principle of "Trade Option" . . . appears to afford the best practicable means of combining a recognition of the desirability of an Eight Hours Day with that of the right of the workers to settle for themselves the conditions under which they will work. (Webb and Cox 1891: 11)

In the face of this demand those economists opposed to an 8-hours law were compelled to argue, once again, that the economic interests of the nation made it impossible to allow the workers to determine for themselves how long they would labour. They did not tend to come out and openly state that the individual's desires should be ignored; rather, they concentrated their resistance on attempting to convince policy makers that while this reform might be nice for the workers, in that they would gain a little more leisure, opposition to the demand was justified, for the reform could only be had at an unacceptably high economic cost. Munro, for example, entered the fray in 1890 with a paper which discussed the probable effects on wages of a general worktime reduction. He argued that a curtailment of standard times would necessarily reduce the net product available for distribution amongst the population. It was conceded that any consequent improvement in the efficiency of the labour power or technology utilised within industry would tend to limit this adverse effect. He insisted, however, that apart from those few industries in which extremely long schedules continued to be the norm the offset resulting from these factors would probably be minimal. A cotton textile worker, Munro pointed out, laboured only $56\frac{1}{2}$ hours per week and any reduction in this minimal period would be sure to produce a proportional decrease in output. As had Fawcett, then, Munro attempted to dismiss the efficiency argument by asserting that whereas it may have had some influence in the past and might even have some contemporary relevance in a small minority of instances, it no longer had any general significance. With this assumption taken as given, it was then relatively easy to show that wages, profits and international trade would all be adversely affected by a general decrease in worktime and consequently that it was doubtful there would be any positive effect on employment.

Munro presented his paper to the British Association for the Advancement of Science in the same year that the president of the economic and statistical section of this body, Alfred Marshall, chose to enter the worktime debate. Marshall accepted the validity of Jevons's assertion that the long-term tendency for worktimes to contract was explained by the fact that individuals were choosing to opt for greater leisure as their incomes rose. He also accepted Munro's claim that "a general reduction in the hours of labour would lower wages" (Marshall 1890: 732–733). Where the length or intensity of worktimes were so great they did not give the employee adequate time to recuperate, he acknowledged, a reduction in standard times could increase total output. In the Britain of 1890, however, Marshall suggested that this situation existed in only "a few trades" (1890: 733) and that in general any further reduction in standard times would necessarily have to result in a fall in output. The only concession not proffered by Munro that he was willing to make to the efficiency argument was the suggestion that some offset might also be obtained where a reduced schedule enabled the greater use of shiftwork.

The claim that a mere 56½ hours per week might be excessive was also put forward by Robertson in 1893. Following Munro, he too dismissed the efficiency argument, claiming that what evidence was available was limited in nature and tended to be confined to industries not subject to international competition. If it really was the case that the 8-hour day was more efficient, he insisted, competition would have ensured that employers adopted this schedule.

If some masters can make an Eight Hours Day profitable, so much the better: may they have many imitators. But it has never been found that employers needed much pushing to do what it would pay them to do; and it stands to reason that those who will not try an Eight Hours Day have, as a rule, no prospect of making it pay. (Robertson 1899: 65)

Robertson also refused to accept that the historical experience of the Factory Acts might give some indication of what was likely to occur if a further compulsory curtailment in standard times was forced on employers. Simply because workers had managed to maintain output when the workday was reduced from 12 hours to 10, he insisted, was in no way proof that they could do the same if times were further curtailed.

Having refused to accept the claim that an 8-hour day would increase industrial efficiency, Robertson rounded on the supporters of this reform by pointing out that their arguments were contradictory. They argued that employers should not oppose the introduction of a reduced schedule, because it would increase industrial efficiency to an extent sufficient to ensure that in most trades there would be little decrease in output, while at the same time arguing that the reduced schedule would radically expand the availability of jobs (Robertson 1899: 29–32).

The validity of Robertson's telling point that the reformers' twin arguments were contradictory caused some disarray in their ranks. He was not, however, to savour this victory for long. Between 1889 and 1893 a number of Liberal Party politicians, who also happened to be large manufacturers, introduced the 8-hour day into their enterprises as a way of attracting working-class votes. These politicians believed that the shorter schedule would necessarily reduce individual output and consequently create more jobs. They soon found, however, that there was no adverse effect on output and that no new jobs were created, because the workers were able to increase the intensity of their efforts under the new schedule (Hadfield and Gibbins 1892; Jeans 1894; Mather 1894). These experiments had a major impact on other Liberal Party politicians and, in particular, on the Secretary of War, who began introducing the 8-hour day into War Office factories and subsequently reported that the reduced schedule markedly improved the efficiency of the workers' labour time (Harris 1972: 66–73).

These experiments helped to undermine the claims of those economists who had been asserting that a general reduction in standard times would necessarily lead to a fall in output. They were reinforced, moreover, by similar studies in the United States and Germany (Schoenhof 1892; Brentano 1894). In 1894 they were used by Rae, who published a scathing criticism of both those who attempted to argue that more jobs would be created if all individuals reduced their work effort and those who refused to acknowledge that the 8-hour day would pay for itself by increasing the productivity of industry. He correctly pointed out that industrial efficiency and not some vague notion of an income–leisure trade-off was the central issue in worktime.

The question of questions therefore, in connection with any proposed further reduction of the hours of labour, is the question of the probable effect of the change on the personal efficiency of the workpeople. If short hours meant short product, they would mean short profits and short wages too; and good wages are at present as essential to the improvement of most of the working class as more leisure; but then shorter hours may not in reality mean shorter product, for they may so better the quality of labour that as much is done afterwards in the short day as was done before in the long. They have invariably had that result sooner or later hitherto; and the pith of the eight-hours question is the question how far a new reduction of the day of labour may be reasonably expected to be attended with that result again. (Rae 1894: 13)

Rae conceded that it was impossible to provide an exact estimate of the degree to which the quality of the workers' labour power would be improved by a further reduction in standard working times. Such knowledge could only be gained by experiment and could not be had merely by abstract theorising. While clearly convinced that the offset phenomenon was far from exhausted and that sufficient evidence already existed to show that the 8-hour day could pay for itself, he called for more empirical studies to be undertaken. It was only this form of research, he realised, that had any hope of overcoming the preconceptions of those who still asserted that worktime and output were proportionally related.

The general adoption of the 8-hour day, Rae argued, would be an immense benefit to the working class and to the nation generally. It would improve the workers' wellbeing, increase industrial efficiency and lengthen the effective economic life of the individual. He insisted, however, that there was one benefit it could not provide: It could not make any serious, sustainable impression on the level of unemployment. Some temporary increase in the number of jobs available might occur during the time it took employers to adjust to the new schedule, but, he insisted, except in a tiny number of instances, the inevitable consequent increase in work intensity and technical restructuring would ensure that few new jobs would be created. Nor, he argued, could an increase in employment be attained by workers restricting their work effort to less than what they were capable of. Indeed, he warned that the workers' imposition of a general restriction in the average intensity of worktime was the only serious practical danger confronting the establishment of the 8-hour day. It was generally acknowledged that the normal level of intensity maintained by British workers in the late nineteenth century was extremely high by international standards. If this high level of intensity was not kept up under the new schedule, Rae insisted, the retention of a real 8-hour day would prove impossible. This last premonition was to prove sadly true in the twentieth century, when British workers eventually managed to win a nominal 8-hour day but effectively continued to labour a much longer schedule, for no extra real pay, by institutionalising permanent overtime.

Acceptance and abandonment of the efficiency argument

Through the 1890s the leaders of the 8-hours movement gradually came to accept the validity of Rae's argument that the shorter schedule would not absorb the unemployed. Their arguments, consequently, became centred on the efficiency issue and on the positive effect the winning of their demand would have on the lives of the workers. This development was accelerated by the conversion of ever more Liberal Party politicians to the 8-hours cause and by the accumulation of an increasing mass of evidence indicating that the competitiveness of British industry would be significantly improved if the shorter schedule was adopted.

By the end of the century even mainstream economists were beginning to acknowledge that employers might indeed be better off with an 8-hour standard. The culmination of this transition was Chapman's presidential address to the British Association for the Advancement of Science in 1909. Chapman's paper dealt with why it was that worktime was a never-ending industrial and political issue. He refused to accept the claim that it was a manifestation of a disinclination on the part of the workers to maintain the degree of effort they put into their work. A mass of material existed, he insisted, that showed clearly that workers had invariably increased the intensity of their worktime wherever and whenever this had been reduced. He reported that he had not been able to find any instance in which the introduction of a reduced schedule had led output to fall by any appreciable amount. The real reason worktime was a perennial problem, he suggested, lay in the nature of the industrialisation process. Compared with rural labour, he argued, industrial work is necessarily more regular and continuous throughout the year and tends to become more intense as industry develops. The utilisation of machinery often removes much physical strain from the labour process, but this does not necessarily mean that less labour is undertaken. Mechanisation, because it demands specialisation, tends to create tasks that are monotonous and also require close supervision. Moreover, specialisation implies elimination of waste, and this includes waste worktime. The result is a partial or even total elimination of the leisure with which the work process had been traditionally interspersed. Worktimes, as a consequence, become more concentrated and more exhausting.

Humanity has no doubt been relieved of the heaviest burden of toil by inventions relating to the mechanism of production, but their application has been accompanied on the whole by the closer concentration of some kind of effort in time. The intensification of labour in a more confined sphere of activity may . . . exercise more fully the higher human faculties and thereby bring with it a deeper interest, but it will almost certainly prove more exhausting, even apart from the elimination of change, leisure, and social intercourse. And decade by decade, with the speeding up of machinery, we should expect to find more nervous strain accompanying the process of production. (Chapman 1909: 355)

Chapman's claim that it was the increasing strain of industrial labour that was the primary factor explaining the long-term tendency for worktimes to contract came to be taken as a given within the marginalist school. The explanation for why this new consensus emerged is partly to be found in the mass of evidence on the relationship between work and time that critics of the income-based argument were able to amass. The accumulation of scientific evidence, however, was far from being the most important factor explaining this development. A much more important influence was the growing disenchantment with laissez-faire economics and politics that the post-1874 period of decay induced throughout the industrialised nations. In both Europe and North America this factor gave rise to the emergence of "efficiency movements" which aimed to raise the productivity of industry. Those involved in these movements tended to reject claims that the market, if left to itself, would ensure that employers operated their enterprises with maximum efficiency. They argued that the growth of cartels gave the lie to this assertion. It was also insisted that there existed a mass of evidence to show that employers often imposed working conditions on their employees that were inefficient, from the point of view of both the individual employer and the national economy.

The inefficiency of long worktimes was one area, in particular, where these critics became especially vocal. In the United

States, for example, the reformers associated with the scientific-management movement vigorously promoted the adoption of reduced worktimes both in order to improve the condition of the working class and to increase industrial productivity. These critics insisted that employers could radically increase industrial efficiency and consequently lower prices and raise wages and profits if they adopted time schedules that were based on scientific analysis rather than on tradition or the whim of the employer. They believed the primary factor preventing the adoption of rationalised working conditions was "the unenlightened employer, who has been blind to his own larger interests and who has always seen in every attempt to protect the workers an interference with business and dividends" (Goldmark 1919: 5). As the mass of evidence these critics were able to put forward accumulated, a growing number of economists came to accept the validity of the claim that the interests of the capitalist class as a whole were being endangered by the ignorance and biases of individual employers.

This development led the British Association for the Advancement of Science to appoint, in 1913, P. Sargant Florence organising secretary of a committee charged with the task of studying the question of fatigue from the economic standpoint. A scientific investigation of this issue was needed, the committee believed, because there was an increasing mass of evidence which indicated that the systematic reorganisation of time schedules could radically increase productivity and improve the competitiveness of British industry. If more substantive data on worktime and effort could be accumulated, it was hoped, it might even be possible to construct a reliable fatigue index which would enable the scientific determination of that balance of intensity and time which would maximise the amount of effective labour the normal worker in any given occupation could undertake (Ramsbottom 1914). One result of the formation of this committee was the 1924 publication of Florence's important volume *Economics of Fatigue and Unrest*, which was a detailed overview of the scientific evidence on the economic relationship among work, industrial efficiency and human capacities. In his introduction to this work Florence asked: "Is it presumptuous to claim a place for Fatigue and Unrest in the study of economics, as well as a place for Economics in the study of Fatigue and Unrest?" (Florence 1924a: 13).

The marginalists' acceptance of Chapman's position was a

major victory for those involved in the worktime debate who based their analysis on Marx's theory of worktime. It should be noted, though, that Chapman's concessions were limited in that he placed the blame for the increasing strain of worktime on the industrialisation process as such, whereas for Marx it was capitalism rather than mechanisation that was causing the average level of work intensity to rise. Though he insisted that the increasing intensity of worktime sufficiently accounted for the ongoing contraction of standard worktimes, moreover, Chapman was clearly reluctant to abandon Jevons's income argument totally. He argued that rising income and a desire for more free time also tended to influence standard times. Ignoring Jevons's observation that an increase in wage levels induced both an income and a substitution effect, Chapman (1909: 357) argued that the utility of a unit of income was greatly influenced by the amount of free time available to the individual to enjoy the consumption of the same. He also insisted that the value of leisure is a function of the goods that can be consumed during the leisure period. It was asserted that it consequently follows that increasing income will tend to reduce the length of time spent at work.

Now you see it, now you don't

The human-capacities element in Chapman's explanation of why worktime tends to contract has remained unchallenged by those within his own tradition to the present day. Until the 1930s it appears to have been generally accepted by marginalists, who often tended merely to refer those interested in the subject to Chapman's contribution. Robbins (1929), for example, adopted this position when, with an oncoming depression reviving interest in the employment-generating capacity of worktime reductions, he attempted to determine how reduced time standards would influence wages and employment. The connection between worktime and output was not one of direct variation, Robbins acknowledged. This fact complicated his analysis without adding to what he wished to clarify. To overcome this problem he took a methodological step that was to be of major importance. He assumed a situation in which any temporal variation was away from a point of maximum productiveness. In his hypothetical world any worktime reduction would necessarily involve a fall in output. It is stressed that he did not argue that actual working times were in fact at the point where output would fall. His hypothesis was merely an abstraction undertaken to highlight an area of interest and to make analysis less complicated.

Three years later Hicks (1963) utilised a similar strategy to simplify his study of the labour supply of the individual. Like Robbins, Hicks argued that Chapman had already stated all that needed to be said on the causal determinants of changes to worktime. He recognised, however, that the fact that worktime had both a temporal and an intensive character made it difficult to utilise marginal productivity theory to determine the return on the various factors of production. The critical nature of this point has generally been missed both by those who have accepted the validity of marginal productivity theory and by those who have criticised its use because of the difficulty of measuring capital. In other words, though Hicks may not have been aware of the capital-measurement problem, he did realise that it was extremely difficult to calculate factor returns if one acknowledged that labour time could not be measured merely by its temporal dimension. To get around this problem he assumed "for the present" the existence of an optimum working day that would yield a greater supply of labour than any other (Hicks 1963: 104).

By the use of these simplifying abstractions Robbins and Hicks were able to delete consideration of the intensive aspect of worktime from their analysis. In their hypothetical world any reduction in the length of time laboured necessarily produced a fall in the individual's output. This form of abstraction was perfectly valid as a means of highlighting and clarifying those aspects of theory these scholars wished to examine. The danger with abstraction, however, is that it is possible to forget that one is abstracting from the real world. Hicks warned that when simplifying assumptions are made great care needs to be taken. "It is decidedly convenient to do this when treating some special problems; but it is a method with very considerable dangers, which can only be avoided if we think back our arguments into a more cumbrous but more realistic form as frequently as possible" (Hicks 1963: 93). If this is not done there exists a serious danger that one may come to believe that the postulated relations existing in the abstraction actually depict the real world.

Hicks gave his warning of the dangers of abstraction at the

time when unemployment caused by the 1930s depression was at its peak. Once again the working class was demanding that the state intervene to compulsorily restrict standard times in order to spread the available work amongst as many as possible. This period, therefore, was not one in which those whose sympathies primarily lay with the opponents of shorter times could afford to stress the claim that the desires of the individual worker should be the prime factor determining standard times. As rational time schedules became established within industry after the Second World War, however, the marginalist tradition found much too attractive to resist the argument that capitalism not only gave the workers more income but also a great deal more leisure. Though many within the tradition remained aware that worktime had both a temporal and an intensive dimension, this latter element was gradually dropped from worktime analysis. In postwar marginalist worktime theory Florence's call to integrate fatigue studies into economic analysis was effectively rejected and the hypothetical world postulated by Robbins and Hicks became implicitly and explicitly accepted as reality. It was presumed that a reduction in the length of time individuals laboured necessarily involves a fall in output and wages. Most marginalists went even further and again assumed that worktime has only a single dimension and that a temporal reduction will necessarily produce a proportional reduction in output. Indeed, during the years of the long boom singular concentration on the relationship between income and time laboured managed to all but completely delete the issue of human limits from the tradition's whole method of analysis.

Units of labor inputs are designated either as "workers" or as "man-hours," and variations in labor inputs affect output without reference to working hours. Just as the production function is external to economics and lies in the realm of engineering, so too the determination of the appropriate length of the working day is relegated to the physiology and psychology of labor. (Grossman 1970: 11)

And what of today?

In the early 1970s the postwar boom finally ground to a halt and unemployment re-emerged as a major social issue. This development, once again, soon revived working-class interest in the possibility of creating jobs by reducing working times. In the subsequent debate over this issue, Cuvillier (1984: 28) has reported, the workers' side has put forward arguments similar to those they advocated in the 1930s. Within those sections of the organised working class where unemployment is not high the major argument advanced in defence of further reductions in time schedules, he reports, is the workers' need for more time to recuperate from the demands of the production process. Where unemployment is high, on the other hand, workers tend to emphasise the job-creating possibilities of worktime reductions. Finally, both groups of workers also insist that further cuts to standard times should be introduced as part of their share of increased productivity.

While not disputing Cuvillier's claim that all these arguments were put forward in the 1930s, this history of the literature has shown that they have a much longer lineage. The workers, in other words, have responded to the present crisis in a manner all but identical to the way they responded to similar problems in the nineteenth century. Employers, likewise, have put forward their same old arguments, while the majority of marginalist economists who have entered the debate have behaved precisely as did their forebears in the 1840s and the 1890s. As unemployment increased, many workers' organisations around the world stated that they were ready to give preference to increased leisure as against greater income: "They appear to accept moderation as regards future rises in real wages or even to abandon this claim for the time being, if support for a reduction in working time will contribute to dealing with unemployment" (Cuvillier 1984: 20).

Numerous studies, moreover, have shown that there is an increasing demand within the working class for more time free from market work. These developments, however, have not led marginalist economists to rally to the side of the labour movement insisting that if this is what these individuals prefer then this is what they should be allowed to do. Rather, they have once again shifted the debate away from the rights and desires of the individual and raised the old argument of production cost. In other words, instead of simply accepting the workers' desire to reduce standard times, as preference theory suggests they should, contemporary marginalists have become primarily concerned with the relationship between productivity and reduced working time. They have not, however, centred their analysis of this issue on the nature of the intensive and temporal dimensions of worktime and how these interrelate and shape the nature of worktime change. They have made no real attempt to integrate the issues of fatigue and the workers' need for adequate time to recuperate from the demands of the production process into the debate, as did Smith, Marx, Chapman and Florence. Rather, the marginalists have primarily confined their efforts to proving once again that it is very unlikely that reductions in standard times would significantly reduce unemployment. Given the debates of the 1890s, however, this is hardly an original contribution, though of course its rediscovery is no less useful for undermining the enthusiasm with which the working class promotes the adoption of reduced time standards. All in all, although it is certainly true that the revived debate has produced some extremely useful empirical research, it must be concluded that it has, thus far, added little of any substance to the existing literature on worktime theory.

Marginalism and Marxism

The newfound concern of modern marginalists with the production perspective on worktime and the macro-economic implications of reduced time schedules does not mean they have abandoned the argument that the primary factor bringing about the long-term decline in working times is individual leisure preference (see, for example, the work of Bosworth and Dawkins 1981 and Blyton 1985). Like those radicals who confine their analysis of worktime change to class power, these individuals continue to assume that worktime change is essentially a function of income. Given that the dismissal of the human-limits aspect of worktime theory has never been theoretically or empirically justified, these assumptions need to be treated with some caution. Before accepting the validity of modern marginalism or of Marx's argument it would be wise to examine more closely the evidence underpinning both. It is to this issue that I shall now turn.

CHAPTER 2

Empirical evidence and worktime theory

The review of the literature presented in Chapter 1 has shown that there currently exist two major theories that purport to explain the changing nature of worktime in industrialised capitalist societies. Marginalism argues that the downward drift in standard times has occurred because the living standards of the workers and the pattern of their preferences for income and leisure have changed. Marxism, on the other hand, argues that while individual workers' desires are not necessarily irrelevant in bringing about such change, it is within the production process rather than within the consciousness of individuals that one should seek the answer to why standard times have tended to fall. In this chapter the empirical evidence underpinning both modern marginalism and Marx's argument, and hence the arguments of those radicals who limit their analysis to the political realm, will be looked at in order to determine the validity and contemporary relevance of each.

Marginalism

For modern marginalists the primary prop upon which their theory of worktime stands is the claimed existence of a negative slope in the relevant portion of the labour-supply curve. To be able to prove empirically that the majority of workers choose to reduce their worktime as their incomes rise is crucial to the theory, because even within its own parameters there is no logical reason to assume that this should be the case.

In 1930 Robbins published his classic paper "On the Elasticity of Demand for Income in Terms of Effort." In this work Robbins criticised those economists who claimed that it was possible, by a priori reasoning, to determine how a change in income will influence the labour supply of the individual. A number of marginalists had argued that if one accepted the concept of rationality in economic decision making then the worktime consequences of a change in income could be determined deductively. Pigou (1928), for example, suggested that the imposition of a tax on workers would necessarily result in extension of the length of time they were willing to work. He reasoned that since income is being taken away from the taxpayer the marginal utility of income is raised while the marginal disutility of labour remains unchanged. Consequently, he concluded, unless workers are somehow impeded, higher taxes will induce them to increase the amount of work undertaken and so of income obtained up to the point where the marginal utility of income and the marginal disutility of work are again equal.

Pigou based his conclusions on the assumption of diminishing marginal utility for income and the concept of the individual as a utility maximiser. Knight (1921) similarly argued that rational individuals will, if their wage rates increase, divide their time between work and leisure in such a way as to both increase income and decrease time worked. In his critique Robbins insisted that the arguments of these scholars were flawed because they failed to see that the price of income, as measured by effort, tended to fall as wages rose; that is, less effort needs to be undertaken to earn a given amount of income if wage rates rise. Diminishing utility could not, therefore, be assumed. How the worker responded to a reduction in worktime in such a situation depended on which factor was dominant, the income or the substitution effect. How much effort individuals were willing to undertake to earn extra income depended, therefore, solely on the elasticity of their demand for this good. If this elasticity is greater than unity a decrease in the wage rate or a tax increase will result in a reduction in the length of time spent at work. If it is less than unity the opposite will occur. After making this observation, Robbins proceeded to show that nothing in the arguments of Pigou and Knight indicated that the elasticity of demand, in terms of effort, is necessarily greater than unity. It is not valid, therefore, he concluded, for these authors to claim that they could deductively determine the slope of the labour-supply curve. Having successfully shown this to be the case, Robbins was able to re-establish Jevons's hypothesis that the determination of how a change in income will influence individual labour supply can be resolved only on empirical grounds.

If these considerations are valid we are left with the conclusion . . . that any attempt to predict the effect of a change in the terms on which income is earned must proceed by inductive investigation of elasticities. The attempt to narrow the limit of possible elasticities by *a priori* reasoning must be held to have broken down. (Robbins 1930: 129)

Since Robbins published his critique a number of marginalists have attempted to provide a logical base for the assumption of a negatively inclined labour-supply curve. These attempts have not proven fruitful and the theory remains indeterminate. Attempts at strengthening the theory by adding more variables have also been undertaken. These, however, have only tended to further cloud the income—worktime relationship by adding more indeterminate factors to an indeterminate theory and have not provided the basic argument with any greater deductive support. Mincer (1980), for example, strove to make the marginalist argument more sophisticated by shifting the primary focus of examination from the individual to the family. Since people live in households, he argued, their worktime decisions are based on household labour requirements. It is thus the labour supply of the household that needs to be examined, not the individual.

If this approach is taken, it is claimed, evidence suggests that as women increase their work outside the home husbands work less. The problem with this argument, however, is that marginalists are unable to show the causal nature of the link between the wife's increased market participation and the husband's labour-supply decision. For, as Becker (1985) has argued, the nature and rate of women's market participation are heavily influenced by the quantity of labour they need to undertake outside the marketplace. He suggests that because of the extensive amount of nonmarket work they have to undertake, many women elect to take market jobs that demand a relatively low degree of effort and hence pay a relatively low wage. Intuitively, this last part of the household argument makes a good deal of sense, though, ironically, this is because it is based on objective human capacities rather than on subjective desires. The problem is that it cuts both ways. As wives increase their rate of market participation men generally tend, after some period, to increase their nonmarket work. Given this response, it might well be the case that men decrease their worktime in the market place as their wives increase their participation for the same reason that women are claimed to restrict their market efforts, namely the need to undertake a significant degree of labour within the domestic sector.

A further difficulty with utilising the household as a basic unit of analysis is that it cannot be assumed that the family's real income necessarily rises when the wife goes out to work. In such a situation it might well be the case that the increased market income might be totally offset by any subsequent decrease in the quantity and quality of the use values formerly produced within the home. Because of the indeterminate nature of the real effect on family income of increased market participation Michael (1985: 136) has suggested that

> it would be more accurate to assume no effect on income than to assume the effect on income equals the nominal income change. Marginal changes in wage rates (especially with fixed costs of entry) can induce changes in labor supply, and the nonmarket productivity forgone may be only marginally less than the nominal income received. Almost certainly the impact on real income is a small fraction of the change in money income.

Given the indeterminate nature of these factors, the marginalists' argument is compelled to still rely on the relationship between the individual's income and his or her rate of market participation. That their theory is indeterminate is now acknowledged by orthodox marginalists. Whether the income or the substitution effect is the stronger influence at the individual or household level is not a question that can be decided upon the basis of logical deduction. As King (1972: 25) stated, it is "an empirical question, and not one which can be settled by *a priori* argument." This lack of a logical base means that the hypothesis that worktime has contracted over the long term as a consequence of rising incomes can only be assumed to be correct if it can be empirically substantiated. It is not sufficient to argue, as did Jevons, that as wages have risen and working times fallen the former must have caused the latter. This argument is clearly open to the charge of being guilty of the post hoc fallacy. If it cannot be empirically substantiated, in other words, it becomes mere assertion.

Marginalism's empirical evidence

Until the late 1960s empirical research did appear to provide support for the claim that the relevant portion of the labour-supply curve was negatively inclined. A number of marginalists estimated supply curves of aggregate working times by using time-series data or comparisons across industries, occupations or regions. This research produced results that seemed to show that the supply curve of the majority of workers was, indeed, backward leaning. Douglas (1957), for example, estimated that an increase in income of 1 per cent would induce a fall of 0.1 to 0.2 per cent in the length of time normally worked.

In 1962 Finegan undertook a cross-sectional examination of worktimes in the United States utilising 1940 and 1950 census data. He was able to establish a significant inverse correlation between income and working times, though it was necessary to include a number of new variables in order to make this possible. Despite this need to move beyond simple correlations between income and the length of time worked, Finegan concluded that the results of his research strongly supported the marginalists' position.

These results were widely accepted within the economics profession. This acceptance was undermined in the late 1960s, however, when critics began exposing theoretical and statistical weaknesses in the research. One of the most significant of the critics was Feldstein (1968), who argued that though there was impressive evidence of a negative correlation between income and worktime it was incorrect to interpret the regression lines in the earlier research as supply curves. The results of these studies, he insisted, were ambiguous because of the problem of identification resulting from the fact that more than one endogenous variable was involved. Each observation undertaken in these analyses represented the intersection of one particular supply curve and the corresponding demand curve, for example, the supply and demand in a particular location or time. "Because all of the observations in a sample do not relate to a single labour market, the least squares line which describes the association between hours and hourly earnings is not an estimated supply function" (Feldstein 1968: 75).

To overcome this problem Feldstein undertook a number of observations drawn as much as possible from single labour markets. Analysis of the results showed no clear pattern emerging. In some cases the supply curve did slope backwards; in others, however, no significant relationship could be discerned, whereas in some the supply curve was positively inclined. The ambiguity of these results led Feldstein to state that the identification problem may still have been too significant and that therefore no conclusions could be drawn from his work. He warned, however, that it would be unwise to continue basing economic policy on the assumption that the labour market is characterised by a negatively inclined supply curve.

Through the 1970s numerous studies were undertaken that attempted to overcome the weaknesses of the early research. A review of this work, undertaken by the marginalist Keeley (1981), found wide disparity in the results. Similar findings have been reported by Killingsworth (1981). Keeley argued that it is difficult to compare directly the findings of these studies because of the varying estimates and parameters utilised by the researchers. Labour-supply estimates, he pointed out, are very sensitive to the researcher's choice of assumptions. Even allowing for difficulty of comparability, however, he conceded that technique alone cannot explain the wide variation in the results. Some researchers have produced results that clearly accord with marginalist theory. Others, however, have found precisely the opposite, and some have not been able to come up with any statistically significant evidence whatsoever. This assessment holds whether one considers "first" or "second" generation research. As Killingsworth (1983) has conceded, a "cynic" would be justified in concluding that the marginalists have not produced much in the way of evidence to support their theoretical base despite repeated attempts to refine their work. In short, collectively they have reproduced Feldstein's results, which showed that there is no clear relationship between income and worktime. There is, therefore, no substantive proof for the claim that the labour-supply curve is negatively inclined.

Taxation evidence

The undermining of the marginalists' argument caused by their failure to provide empirical support for their primary assumption has been compounded by the research findings of those who have sought to determine the shape of the supply curve by examining the effects of taxation on the supply of labour power. As a change in the tax rate amounts to a change in the amount of income the individual receives, how workers respond to marginal changes in taxation should provide evidence of the relationship between income and worktime. Again theory does not predict how individuals will respond to any given change in the tax level, because of the dual influences of the substitution and income effects. Belief in a negatively inclined supply curve, however, induced until the 1970s a widespread assumption that high marginal rates of taxation would tend to reduce the supply of labour power. Consequently, it was assumed that individuals moving into high tax brackets would display a marked tendency to substitute leisure for income. Three principal methods were utilised to determine whether this was the case: observed behaviour, experimental evidence and surveys of attitudes. None of these techniques produced the results expected.

Studies of market behaviour have not been able to provide support for the claim that high marginal rates of taxation reduce incentives to work. Indeed, some research suggests that high taxes may well act as an inducement to many workers, causing them to work harder or longer or both in order to maintain living standards. The only safe conclusion one can draw, given the present state of research, is that the influence of the income and substitution effects on male family heads is small, with the corresponding effects on working wives being somewhat greater. An O.E.C.D. survey of the empirical work undertaken in this field concluded that "the net effect of taxation on labour supply is not large enough to be of great economic or sociological importance" (1975: 126).

The experimental research has produced similar results. Most of the evidence for this conclusion was obtained from the studies of negative income tax undertaken in the United States in the late 1960s and the early 1970s. In these studies families were randomly selected and assigned to one of several experimental groups or to a control group. Experimental families were given economic assistance from cash-transfer programmes on the condition that any income obtained beyond this minimum would be taxed at a rate varying from 50 per cent upwards. The control families received no extra income but continued to receive whatever benefits they were legally entitled to under existing welfare programmes.

At the outset the researchers expected to find that the payment of substantial amounts of unearned income would reduce the amount of labour power workers would be willing to sell in the market place. The experiments were conducted over a number of years and cost approximately $100 million. It was found that the effect of taxes on the supply of labour power was very small. A negative income tax did appear to reduce the workers' willingness to labour, but the reduction was only substantial for supplementary earners. Even the little support these results give to the marginalists' theory, moreover, has since been questioned, for there is a problem in determining to what degree the results reflected under-reporting of worktime by experimental families. Such under-reporting was possible because the data as to actual time worked was obtained from household interviews. Very little was done to determine the validity of this information while the experiments were continuing. This was despite the fact that experimental families had a vested interest in under-reporting both the length of time they spent at work and their income, for the size of the transfer payment they received was inversely related to their income, which was, in most cases, directly related to the length of time spent at work.

A number of studies have since attempted to determine the degree to which under-reporting may have invalidated the significance of the results obtained. Most of these have found significant degrees of under-reporting by experimental families. Consequently, estimates of the degree to which people chose to spend less time at work would appear to have been severely overstated. "Indeed, if the responses are reestimated with data that have been corrected for underreporting, adverse effects for wives and female family heads tend to disappear and those for husbands become less severe" (Greenberg, Moffitt and Friedmann 1981: 587).

Finally, Lewis (1982: 200) reports that findings of a similar nature have been obtained from studies utilising interview and survey techniques. The majority of respondents interviewed invariably state that taxation levels have no effect on the length of time they are willing to work, and among the rest the replies tend to cancel each other out. Summing up the collective contribution of the taxation research, Brown (1983: 167) concluded: "There are *no* studies of labour supply that are not open to serious objection on at least one important ground. Therefore the most intellectually-defensible position is that after a decade and a half of effort we can say very little about labour supply elasticities."

The validity of the marginalist argument

The failure of the marginalists to substantiate their assumptions empirically either can be used to justify a rejection of their theory or it can be simply taken as an indication of continuing econometric problems. Most marginalists have chosen the latter alternative. They can do this because of the empirical nature of their theory. The fact that a negatively inclined labour-supply curve cannot be shown to characterise the labour market does not prove that it does not. It is not possible to confirm or deny the theory purely on the basis of empirical research. It is always possible that further work will produce supporting empirical evidence for the hypothesis. The lack of an empirical foundation for the marginalists' theory does not invalidate it, but rather, given its lack of any logical deductive base, it turns its claims into unsubstantiated assertion. Belief in the theory becomes a matter of faith.

The empirical evidence for Marx's argument

Marx argued that within certain limits it was possible for capitalists to offset reductions in the length of time workers laboured by raising hourly output levels. He also suggested that capitalism would be characterised by a tendency to raise the average level of work intensity and that this higher intensity, because it would come into conflict with human limitations, would make necessary periodic reductions in the length of time workers were compelled to labour. These claims are the primary, empirically testable hypotheses underpinning Marx's explanation of how and why the struggle between the capitalist class and the working class over standard working times has taken the form it has. The validity of these claims will now be looked at and an attempt will be made to assess their contemporary relevance.

Marx based his theory of worktime change on his belief that the efficiency of labour power is in inverse ratio to the duration of its expenditure. Since he first put forward this hypothesis a vast mass of research has been undertaken into how the relationship among effort, efficiency and time manifests itself within the production process. In many of these studies the researchers examined situations where production methods and conditions could be held constant, with the only variable being the length of time laboured. A fixed group of workers would then be studied and their physical output recorded both before and after the worktime change. This was the methodology followed, for example, by those 1890s Liberal Party politicians and factory owners, such as William Mather, whose results were so significant in shifting the worktime debate from job creation to defence of the worker's health and the efficient utilisation of labour power.

The extent to which studies of this nature were undertaken was given a massive impetus by the First World War. In Britain the need for the maximisation of output that the conflict engendered led the Government to establish the Health of Munitions Workers Committee in 1915. This body was asked "to consider and advise on questions of industrial fatigue, hours of labour, and other matters affecting the personal health and physical efficiency of workers in munitions factories and workshops" (Florence 1924b: 730).

A summary of the committee's results was published by Vernon (1921). From 1915 to 1918 this scholar attempted to determine the "maximum achievement" of which the worker is capable in times of prolonged stress such as may occur during a period of war or in times of industrial pressure. He was particularly interested in determining the time schedule which would maximise production. The war provided Vernon with an unrivalled opportunity for obtaining the type of information he needed. Under normal industrial conditions it is difficult to undertake extended observations of a wide range of work situations where nothing else changes but the length of time laboured. In the first eighteen months of the conflict, however, the British War Office imposed extremely long schedules on the workers in the munitions industry. The Government refused to heed the fatigue researchers' warnings that intensity levels in industry had risen to such an extent that time schedules considered normal during the nineteenth century were no longer efficient. The evidence that an extension of working time did not necessarily produce more output, accumulated over the preceding forty years, was in effect ignored. The dramatic increase in worktimes, however, established excellent conditions for testing this hypothesis. The workers in the munitions industry were highly motivated by patriotism. Despite this high level of motivation when working times were extended to 12 hours a day, 6 days a week, total output fell from what it had been in the shorter time period. The Government, as a result, acknowledged that there did appear to be an inverse relationship between effort and time and consequently reduced standard schedules in order to increase the level of output. To

Table 2.1. *Comparative output from longer and shorter hours of work 1915–17*

	Average weekly hours		Relative output	
	Nominal	Actual	Hourly	Weekly
80–95 women turning fuse bodies on				
capstan lathes				
First period (Aug. 15–Jan. 16)	74.5	66	100	100
Second period (Jan. 16–July 30)	63.5	54.4	121	100
Third period (July 30–May 5)	55.3	47.5	156	113
56 men sizing fuse bodies				
First period (Nov. 14–Dec. 19)	66.7	58.2	100	100
Second period (Feb. 27–Apr. 16)	62.8	50.5	122	106
Third period (Nov. 11–Dec. 23)	56.5	51.2	139	122

Source: Florence 1950: 53.

discover the schedule that would maximise productivity, gradual curtailments in standard times were introduced through the period of the war. These staggered reductions made it possible for Vernon to study the output of groups of workers under varying schedules. As it was found that workers often took several months to fully respond to a reduction in the length of time worked, each new schedule was maintained for an extended period. A representative example of the results Vernon obtained is provided in Table 2.1.

In the United States the war also made worktimes and productivity a problem of "national scope and concern." In order to determine standard times that would maximise output, the federal Public Health Service in 1917 authorised Florence to begin a study of the output, accident, labour-turnover and lost-time records of two plants working different schedules (Goldmark and Hopkins 1920). The two factories were both large establishments. One operated 22 hours in the 24 under a two-shift system of 10 hours by day and 12 by night. The other operated three shifts of 8 hours each. The factories used similar technology and both were metal manufacturers, though their products were not identical. The 10-hour plant produced munitions, the 8-hour plant motor vehicles. Management was considered equal in quality. The study found that as production proceeded through the day, hourly output at first rose but eventually began to fall. The outstanding feature distinguishing the two schedules was the level of output maintenance. This was markedly higher in the 8-hour plant. It was also found that there was an increase in spoilt work with the longer schedule and a very considerable increase in accidents. The last hour of the day, in general, had the lowest output and the highest accident ratio. A correlation between nominal worktimes and actual times was also found by the fatigue researchers. As nominal schedules were reduced, absenteeism and poor time keeping decreased at an even more rapid rate. The men sizing in Table 2.1, for example, lost only 5.3 hours a week when on a 56.5-hour schedule as against 12.3 hours when nominally working 62.8 hours.

A summary of the primary reasons why there is not a proportional reduction in output when worktimes are reduced has been provided by Evans (1975).

1. The majority of people are capable of working more intensely during a relatively short period than they are over a relatively prolonged period.
2. Where working times are particularly long, their reduction often has a favourable impact on absenteeism and sick leave.
3. The "shock effect" of an enforced worktime change often stimulates management to re-examine methods of production, thus generating increased productivity.
4. Higher hourly labour costs stimulate increased capital intensive production methods.
5. It may be possible, as a result of the time cut, to introduce shiftwork, thus facilitating greater use of capital equipment.
6. The reduction may elicit a more congenial climate of industrial relations. This may in turn facilitate the introduction of productivity-increasing modifications to the production process.

The pattern of worktime

The general conclusions made by the worktime researchers as regards the working day, have been summarised by Friedmann (1955: 89):

1. A reduction in the working day from twelve hours to ten increases both hourly and daily output.

2. A reduction from ten to eight hours has a similar effect except for certain tasks that are machine paced.
3. Below eight hours hourly output continues to rise but not sufficiently to outweigh the decrease in time worked.

It was realised that this pattern is a generalisation. Though having wide applicability, it is influenced by numerous factors including age, sex, climate and so on. This point was stressed by Florence, who observed that the nature of the specific task could radically influence the length of worktime that would maximise output. In order to determine the significance of this factor, Florence subdivided work tasks into five basic categories:

1. Semi-automatic machine work.
2. Muscular body work.
3. Fully automatic machine work.
4. Dexterous hand work.
5. Sense and brain work.

By studying these five groups he was able to compare their performance during common work periods. He found that fully automatic machine work was least elastic in relation to output, followed by semi-automatic work. In general, it was found the greater the degree of independence from the machine the worker enjoyed, the greater was the potential capacity to vary work intensity. Florence pointed out that within the firm the existence of a range of optimal time schedules needs to be balanced with the need for a common denominator. It is often extremely difficult to differentiate within any one workplace or even industry the worktimes of different employees. Some common rule generally needs to be implemented that best suits the average type of operation and the capacities of the average individual. From his experiments Florence concluded that an 8-hour day was generally the optimum schedule in industry.

The diminishing capacity of workers to increase their hourly intensity as the working day is reduced limits the degree to which this work period can be shortened if output is to be maintained. It does not follow from this, though, that the curtailment of standard times ceases to be an effective means of offsetting rising work pressures when an 8-hour day is established. Once this occurs, the fatigue researchers found, alternative forms of modifying schedules can have a very positive effect on overall productivity. This point has been stressed by Collier (1943: 136):

It must not be forgotten . . . that the daily and weekly *distribution* of hours of work may be as important as the actual number of hours worked during the week. Thus, to reduce hours of work from 48 hours to 44 hours might have relatively little or no effect upon health or well-being if the shorter hours were still distributed over the six days of the week. If, however, the reduction of hours enabled a 5-day week to be worked, the resultant effects upon health might prove to be beneficial.

Besides attempting to determine the optimum length of the working day, therefore, the fatigue researchers also examined numerous other work periods. They found that varying amounts of rest are necessary to offset the diverse influences that cause fatigue. A night's rest is sufficient to offset most of the deterioration in work capacity normally accumulated over a day. A residue of chronic fatigue, however, tends to accumulate in the individual as the work period is extended. This form of fatigue requires longer periods of rest to dissipate. The weekly and annual rests necessary to restore long-term work capacity also have a positive effect on the intensity level that can be sustained during an 8-hour day. Daily worktimes, in other words, can be maintained at 8 hours, even though the work becomes greatly intensified, if longer periods of rest are provided in place of reductions to the daily schedule. It is the existence of this phenomenon that largely explains why in every industrialised nation once an 8-hour day has been established the downward movement in the length of the working day invariably ceases. When it becomes necessary to further reduce standard times after this daily standard has been reached, it is generally more efficient to maintain 8 hours as the daily norm and make alternative temporal adjustments. At this stage short breaks during the day and reductions in the length of the working week have generally proven more effective modifications for attaining a high degree of offset. It was primarily for this reason that the 7-hour day, 6-day week was abandoned in the U.S.S.R. in the 1960s (Bronson 1968; Grossman 1970).

The advantage to be gained from the shorter week lies in the tendency for worker efficiency to fall as the workweek progresses (Alluisi and Morgan 1982: 171). As early as 1915 the

Health of Munitions Workers Committee advised that if maximum output was to be attained, a day's weekly rest was imperative. The committee concluded that Sunday work gave "six days output for seven days work on eight days pay." Florence (1950) argued that the introduction of a 5-day week could be particularly beneficial when the Saturday was normally worked as a half-day. This is because of the lower output per hour and the high levels of absenteeism generally found on half-days. The abolition of half-days also has a number of other advantages. It reduces some overhead costs such as heating and provides more time for maintenance.

A similar relationship to that existing between the working day and working week appears to exist with the working year. Once the 5-day week is established, greater degrees of offset can usually be obtained by increasing holiday entitlements rather than by introducing a 4-day week. The fatigue researchers found that annual output records were characterised by features similar to the daily and weekly pattern. Over a period of several months an accumulation of residual fatigue manifests itself in the need for prolonged periods of rest; in other words, in a need for vacations. Vernon found that when the worker returned from holiday there tended at first to be a diminution of weekly output. This is soon overcome, however, as the individual settles to the work. Average weekly output then tends to rise above the pre-holiday period so that total output rises overall.

The need for human beings to take periodic vacations has been discussed by Grinstein (1955). During holidays, he suggests, even if arduous physical effort is undergone, energy normally consumed by the ego in meeting the daily demands of reality is freed and can be utilised in what is a healing or recuperative process for the mind and body. In those countries where a 5-day week 8-hour day is now the standard, employers tend to regard the extension of annual holidays as one of the least objectionable forms of reducing worktime. At a 1982 O.E.C.D. meeting of management experts on the adjustment of working time, for example, the participants emphasised that long vacations had the least disruptive effects on production.

Indeed, the interesting point was made that where shorter time work reductions were effected, such as reductions in the length of the work week by an hour or so, then it was preferable to aggregate the extra leisure hours and grant them as extensions to holidays rather than as minimal, though potentially disruptive, changes to the working day. (Hart 1982: 27)

At the close of the First World War studies of the relationship between worktime and output were continued in both Europe and the U.S.A. Most of this research, however, was limited in scope, and it was not until the Second World War again made maximisation of national output a matter of urgency that large-scale worktime studies were undertaken. During the crisis that followed the fall of France in 1940, the workweek in most British munitions factories was extended from 56 to 69.5 hours. An initial outburst of energy and patriotism enabled workers to maintain this schedule for a number of weeks without any corresponding decrease in the average level of intensity. Output was consequently increased by 10 per cent. Within six weeks, however, there was a sharp increase in injuries and lost time. Average times actually laboured fell to 51 hours per week where they had been 53 when the nominal workweek was 56 hours. The corresponding mass of output was 12 per cent less than at the 56-hour level. Workers throughout the country were fatigued and strained as a result of the excessive length of time they were compelled to work (Industrial Health Research Board 1942: 3). The Government was consequently forced to recognise its mistake and shorten the workweek, and a month later it introduced a system of authorised holidays. To justify these reductions, the experiments conducted during the First World War were repeated in 1941. The I.H.R.B. concluded from this study that even in wartime the workweek should not exceed 60–65 hours for men and 55–60 hours for women. Thus a 10-hour day, which during the nineteenth century had been the norm in British industry, was by 1941 an absolute maximum even in time of war, where economic cost was of greatly reduced significance.

The war also stimulated the United States Government to again undertake a large-scale worktime study. This was conducted between 1944 and 1947 by the Department of Labor. The purpose of this research was "to measure objectively the effects of working hours on the performance of workers and to determine how the schedules compared in obtaining the goal of increased output" (Department of Labor 1947: 8). In this examination seventy-one case studies were undertaken covering

2,445 men and 1,060 women workers in thirty-four plants across a wide range of industries. The conclusion drawn by the researchers was that there was no such thing as a single optimum workweek for all individuals. Workers performed differently when working the same time schedule because of a variety of factors: incentive to work, demands of the task, control over pace, nature of shift, working conditions and relations with management. In other words, optimum times were influenced by social, technological and historical factors.

Recognition of these influences, however, did not lead the researchers to conclude that there were no absolute human limits relevant to the determination of optimum worktimes. Rather, they argued that, while variability existed, there were norms shaped by workers' social and innate needs which had wide applicability within industry. With few exceptions, they reported, a marginal extension of the time worked increased the mass of goods produced. As a rule, however, the increase in output fell considerably short of the temporal increase when the workweek was longer than 48 hours. For hours above 8 per day and 48 per week it usually took 3 hours to produce 2 additional hours of output if the work was light. When the work was heavy, it took 2 hours to produce 1 hour of additional output. Working 7 days of the week, moreover, produced no greater output than working 6 days.

The objective of the wartime research was to discover that schedule which would produce the greatest volume of goods. The criterion of effectiveness, accordingly, was the schedule's capacity to produce use values. Cost minimisation and profitability were not considered major criteria. If the cost factor is taken into consideration, as is necessary under normal peacetime conditions, the researchers concluded, then, all other things being equal, "the eight hour day and the forty hour week are best in terms of efficiency and absenteeism and the higher levels of hours are less satisfactory" (Department of Labor 1947: 1).

In the period since the end of the war the general conclusions of the wartime researchers have gained a great deal of further empirical support. A study undertaken by the Norwegian Government in 1959, for example, found that hourly output rose sufficiently to offset most of a reduction from 48 to 45 hours per week. Similarly, a study commissioned by the West German Ministry for Economic Affairs in 1962 concluded that a reduction in worktime below 45 hours per week would have "*no* significant adverse effect upon output per man – that is, that the productivity offset would be complete" (Denison 1967: 61). The German study also concluded that the effect on unemployment would be minimal and that reductions in worktime boosted productivity growth and gave a significant impetus to structural adjustments within the economy. Finally, Tsujimura (1980) has reported that reductions in worktime in Japan during the 1960s produced no adverse effects upon output. Rather, even after allowing for changes in the nature and utilisation of capital equipment, for every 1 per cent reduction in time laboured there was a corresponding 2 per cent increase in labour productivity.

The governments of numerous other countries have undertaken studies similar to those listed. All of these have produced results showing that worktime and output are not proportionally related even where weekly hours are below 48. These studies, it should be noted, are of a macro nature. They consequently blur the degree of offset that has been achieved at the level of the individual firm. The experience of specific enterprises has tended to vary considerably. Some firms have enjoyed significant increases in total output as a consequence of a reduction in worktime while experiencing no increase in costs. Others, however, have found that decreased standard times have increased production costs and that in some cases these increases have been quite significant. A French study undertaken in 1968–1969, for example, found that offset was lowest in small firms. While total loss of production resulting from a worktime change at this time was estimated to be 0.35 per cent for every 1 per cent reduction in the length of time worked for all enterprises, in those firms with over 500 employees it was only 0.14 per cent (Evans 1975: 71–72).

The evidence that reductions in worktime do not necessarily reduce the amount of labour undertaken is overwhelming. Indeed, Denison (1967) has argued that the intensification process was so significant during the period 1929–1957 that it was the third most important source of increase in national income per worker hour. As working times contract, however, marginal reductions in the length of time worked increase in proportional significance. If all else remained constant, this would make it increasingly difficult to obtain a high degree of offset. Indeed, through the 1950–1970 period it was widely accepted that the offset phenomenon was largely exhausted when standard times approached 40 hours per week. This belief broke down in the 1970s, however, as it became increasingly clear that there was no theoretical or empirical evidence that could substantiate this claim. Consequently, numerous macro-econometric studies were undertaken to get data. The main objective of most of this research was to determine to what extent reduced time standards would ease unemployment. It was soon realised that the offset phenomenon was far from exhausted, though there was wide disparity in the results produced by the various studies. This is not surprising, given the wide variety in the basic assumptions and underlying hypotheses of the various econometric models utilised. Consequently, if one were forced to rely solely on these studies it would not be possible to predict with any certainty what would happen to output if working times were further reduced. Fortunately, there is a growing quantity of empirical research that has produced more definite indications of what may be expected.

The most comprehensive of the empirical studies undertaken to determine the exact nature of the offset phenomenon with a workweek of under 40 hours was that carried out during the years 1979–1984 by the Policy Studies Institute in the United Kingdom. What this research found was that significant increases in hourly productivity invariably followed the introduction of reduced time standards below 40 hours per week. Many of the firms studied, indeed, had been able to reduce the length of time normally laboured without any reduction in the level of production and without any increase in the number of employees or any change in the level of overtime. In other words, offsets of 100 per cent and greater were obtained under the reduced schedule.

What the survey showed, then, was a considerable increase in productivity over the years 1981–82, sufficient to compensate for the effects of the reduction in working time. . . . It was shown that, for each industry, the number of establishments which had increased their labour productivity between 1981 and 1982 was much greater than the number in which productivity had declined over the period. (White and Ghobadian 1984: 179)

The British researchers found that initially employers attained the increase in hourly output by the relatively straightforward process of further closing up the pores of the working day and by speeding up the pace of work. Subsequently the intensification process was reinforced by more complex types of improvement of a kind not at all dissimilar to those described by Marx in the nineteenth century.

As a result of these studies the British Ministry of Labour advised employers that it was possible to reduce working times below 40 hours per week without necessarily reducing output or raising unit costs. The ministry insisted, however, that this did not mean all firms would be able to achieve this objective.

What the results do show is that it is possible to reduce working time at little or no cost provided the management and workers are willing to cooperate in devising and implementing measures which improve productivity and avoid the other costs stemming from reduced working time. But whether firms in general will develop such cost offsets is an open question. (Ministry of Labour 1981: 426)

Results similar to those found in Britain have been obtained in Belgium and France in the 1980s. Much to the surprise of many marginalist economists, it has been made clear, once again, that worktime has both an intensive *and* a temporal dimension and that Marx's claim that working times can be reduced without necessarily reducing output would appear to have as much relevance for modern time schedules as it did for those of 1867.

The level of intensity

As a result of their studies the fatigue researchers endorsed Marx's argument that capitalism was characterised by a tendency to increase the intensity of labour time. In 1970 Poper produced the results of an empirical examination of the validity of this belief. In his study he examined the results of 1,677 separate worktime studies that had been conducted over the preceding eighty years. His specific purpose was to assess the validity of the fatigue researchers' claim that "fewer hours imply better rested and more energetic workers who, as a consequence, will increase the intensity and speed of their work. Reduced hours will thus lead to increased labor productivity and part or all of the decline in hours will be offset" (Poper 1970: 118). The mass of evidence compiled by the fatigue researchers, Poper concluded, gives overwhelming support to their claims. Workers can and have offset the fall in the length of time they normally labour by raising the average level of intensity they apply to their work. Denison, likewise, examined the evidence of the fatigue researchers and came to a similar conclusion.

The quantity and quality of work done in an hour is affected by the length of the workweek or work year. As hours are shortened . . . the product turned out in an hour typically increases as a direct consequence of the change in hours, so that the loss of output is less than proportional to the reduction in hours. (Denison 1967: 59)

That average intensity levels in industry have risen significantly over the last century has been generally accepted by scholars familiar with the work of the fatigue researchers. Even such an ardent advocate of unqualified marginalism as Becker (1985) has not denied the validity of this evidence when compelled to consider the intensity issue. Individuals less conversant with the fatigue research, on the other hand, often find it difficult to accept that there has been any general increase in the level of work intensity. It is asserted or implied by these critics that the production process no longer demands any significant degree of effort from the working class. Such a conclusion necessarily follows if it is insisted that work intensity has not risen during a period when worktime has been reduced by 40 per cent. Indeed some go so far as to argue that through the twentieth century "it has become less and less necessary to do a great deal of work of any sort in order to maintain a high level of economic productivity" (Tanner 1969). This claim, however, is merely an unsubstantiated assertion which can be sustained only if one ignores the evidence of heightened physiological and psychological work intensity accumulated by the fatigue researchers.

Indeed, the evidence of these scholars suggests that even the claim that the physical demands of the labour process have declined needs to be treated with a great deal of caution. In his presidential lecture to the Ergonomics Research Society, for example, Edholm (1970) confronted this claim. Concentrating on changes to the physical demands of the production process, he attempted to determine whether "the average energy expenditure of the present population is higher or lower, or the same, as it was 20, 40, 60, etc. years ago." To answer this question he examined the available British data on (1) food intake; (2) numbers engaged in different occupations and how these have changed over time; (3) demographic changes; (4) direct studies of energy expenditure of workers in different occupations. He conceded that it was true that mechanisation had reduced radically the number of workers it took to undertake many tasks. It did not follow from this, however, that the workers who continue working at the task necessarily have a lower energy expenditure than those replaced by machines. The evidence on the food intake and effort demands of the coal industry, for example, show that British coal miners of 1924 could not have undertaken as much physical work as miners in 1952. This was, in short, because the quantity of food consumed by miners in 1924 was so low it could not possibly have provided the energy output demanded of the miner in 1952. In terms of society as a whole Edholm concluded there was insufficient evidence to provide a conclusive answer as to whether overall physical activity had declined. The most important data upon which such a decision could be based is food intake, which has increased significantly since 1939. Prior to this period, he estimates, approximately one-third of the British population had a calorie intake less than necessary to undertake the physical demands of the present day. It follows from this that if, as he shows, the physical demands of nonwork activities have not increased, then the average level of intensity within industry must have risen.

Since energy expenditure cannot, over a long period of time, exceed energy intake I would argue that in spite of long hours of work and the early age at which a working career began, the average energy expenditure of the population in, e.g., 1910 would be less than it is today. (Edholm 1970: 641)

Their awareness of the long-term trend of rising work intensity led most fatigue researchers to support periodic reductions in standard worktimes. Florence, for example, while supporting a standard 48-hour week, in 1924 insisted that this schedule was not an abstract optimum that existed independently of specific times and locations, for it was clearly related to duration and intensity of activity. The reduction in the length of time workers need to labour to earn their wages, he argued, leads capitalists to concentrate their attention on increasing the intensity of the labour process. Their success in attaining this objective, over time, tends to gradually increase the pace of work considered normal for the society. He concluded that the decrease in standard worktimes that had been introduced in

Britain through the nineteenth and twentieth centuries had been largely offset by this process. "There is little doubt that what was gained by decrease in hours was largely offset by an increase in the intensity of work, and the worker is more and more becoming concerned with questions of speeding up as hours are gradually reduced" (Florence 1924a: 71). Writing twenty-four years later, he again considered the question of industry's general optimum. He argued in 1948 that the case for a reduced working week had been greatly enhanced since 1924 by the increase in the average level of intensity experienced in industry. If a 48-hour week had been the optimum for Britain in 1924, he concluded, a 44-hour week was the more likely optimum in 1948 (Florence 1950).

Human limits and the production process

The reasons why contemporary marginalists became prone to underestimate the significance of work intensification as a factor influencing worktime change are many. One of the most important would appear to be their general assumption that human capacities no longer conflict with the needs of the production process. Twentieth-century reductions in working time have occurred concomitantly with improvements in the workers' food intake, housing and general living standards. Given these changes, many scholars have assumed that the capitalist production process, rather than being characterised by a tendency to constantly come into conflict with human limits, tends to impinge less on the workers' capacities while concomitantly raising these capacities by improving the workers' health and general wellbeing.

If this assumption is valid, then the aspect of Marx's argument which suggests that the "weak bodies" of human beings are a major factor tending to lower standard times would no longer have much relevance. Its validity, however, is open to serious challenge. As Doyal (1979: 23) has noted:

While the development of capitalism may have facilitated an improvement in the general health of the population (as measured, for example, in life-expectancy rates), the health needs of the mass of the population continue to come into frequent conflict with the requirements of continued capital accumulation. This produces contradictions which are ultimately reflected in historical changes in patterns of morbidity and mortality.

An examination of the data relating to health and work would certainly appear to endorse Doyal's proposition. In the United States, for example, official figures indicate that about 14,000 workers are killed each year and 2.2 million suffer disabling injuries as a result of their employment. American research, moreover, indicates that there is an "iceberg" character to work-related afflictions in terms of their incidence. The ratio of official to real figures has been estimated at 1 : 10 in the case of nonfatal on-the-job accidents and as high as 1 : 100 for occupational diseases. Other studies have indicated that as many as 40 per cent of medically diagnosed health problems are work-related.

In considering the conflict between the demands of the capitalist production process and human limitations it also needs to be remembered that the adverse effects of work are not necessarily directly physical. Effort involves energy but it also involves many other things and the two terms should not be equated or confused. Many tasks may require a low energy output and yet necessitate a high level of effort. If the energy content of a task is diminished so that it is well within an individual's muscular capacities while at the same time the wearying or boring aspects of the job are increased, it is not valid to claim that the level of effort required has necessarily fallen. Different human capacities are now being placed under strain. Marx (1976: 548) made a similar observation when discussing factory workers.

Factory work exhausts the nervous system to the uttermost; at the same time, it does away with the many-sided play of the muscles, and confiscates every atom of freedom, both in bodily and intellectual activity. Even the lightening of the labour becomes an instrument of torture, since the machine does not free the worker from the work, but rather deprives the work itself of all content.

Margolis and Kroes (1974: 136) have argued that there are basically three sets of needs that are common to human beings, even though their specific manifestations may vary among cultures.

"Maintenance needs." The need for food, shelter, and activity is derived from man's physiology. Work provides the means to obtain physical objects which permit satisfaction of these needs. . . . "Social needs." The need for companionship, recognition, and a feeling of belonging is derived from society. Work can often be a major source of satisfaction of these needs. . . . "Growth needs." The need for self-actualization and the development of competence and mastery over one's environment is derived from man's psychology. Satisfaction of this need is often characterized as attainment of positive mental health.

Most marginalists, on the other hand, appear to conceive of human capacities as a relevant factor in their theories of labour supply solely in terms of maintenance needs. They consequently fail to recognise that conflict between human limits and the demands of the production process can still occur even where workers are well fed and do not have to undertake hard physical labour. Certainly the prevalence of forms of effort more closely associated with the social and psychological capacities of workers have increased. Though such society-wide change across time is not easily measured, the consequences are becoming increasingly clear. Through the twentieth century there has been a significant decrease in infectious diseases in the industrialised nations. The benefits of this change in terms of longevity, however, have been increasingly offset by the growth of coronary and rheumatic disorders and by the incidence of carcinomas. Such stress-related illnesses have been on a steady upward trend throughout the postwar years. In England and Wales, for example, the death rate in men between thirty-five and forty-four nearly doubled between 1950 and 1973 and has increased much more rapidly than that of other ranges. Of these young deaths 41 per cent were due to cardiovascular disease formerly considered an affliction of the aged. The rate of growth of such chronic and degenerative diseases is such, Naschold (1979) argues, that it can no longer be believed that they are primarily symptoms of the ageing process. He suggests that it is the nature of work in contemporary capitalist society that is a major factor bringing about this change. His conclusion that work is central to this problem is supported by a major study of ageing. This research found that the strongest predictor of longevity was work satisfaction, the second predictor being overall "happiness." "These two socio-psychological measures predicted longevity better than a rating by an examining physician of physical functioning, or a measure of the use of tobacco, or genetic inheritance. Controlling these other variables statistically did not alter the dominant role of work satisfaction" (O'Toole 1973: 77).

For two decades after the late 1940s the fatigue and health

aspects of work failed to attract the attention of industrial psychologists in the way they had in the first half of the century. Baldamus (1961: 51) has argued that the abandonment of fatigue research occurred because it was eventually realised that fatigue was such a complex phenomenon that it could not be adequately quantified and thus controlled. What this meant for worktime research was that it was realised that it was impossible to determine abstract working times and patterns that would ensure maximal extraction of labour from the worker. It was only when stress-related afflictions clearly connected with work began to reach epidemic proportions during the late 1960s that interest in studying the effects of work on the worker was re-stimulated. This newfound interest has, thus far, produced little new data on the temporal aspects of work and human deprivation. What research has been undertaken in this area has been of a peripheral nature and has concentrated primarily on "abnormal" work patterns with particular emphasis on shift-work, overtime and, more recently, flexitime.

A rare exception to this dearth of data is a report on work-time-induced stress and strain prepared by Naschold (1979) for the International Institute for Comparative Social Research. In their work Naschold and his colleagues have attempted to determine whether the time element, in all its dimensions, is so important in overall strain and stress that a strategy to curtail worktime constitutes a meaningful attack on the real source of the problem. Their conclusions, based on research primarily undertaken in West Germany, are that changes in the production process have led to changed requirements as regards skill and work capacity. These, in turn, reflect changes in the form of physical and mental strain and stress emanating from work, and these changes are increasingly undermining the health of the working population. These researchers have castigated those scholars who presumed, without any evidence, that working times and human capacities are no longer in conflict. "The abstract and moralistic argument often heard during the fifties and again today, that a forty-hour week (five times eight hours) is an optimal duration overlooks and underestimates a historical change in the risk structure" (Naschold 1979: 36). By this is meant the danger to the worker brought about by an increased level of work intensity in a time period that has remained unchanged. Those who argue that the 5-day, 40-hour week is an abstract optimum, Naschold suggests, neglect this point just as they fail to consider the non-work-related strain and stress problems of many groups within society.

The point that the 40-hour week is not necessarily an optimum for present industrialised societies (even if it may have been at some time in the past) because of changes in the life, work and play of individuals has also been made by Alluisi and Morgan (1982: 180). Likewise, Schultz (1978) in attempting to answer the question "What, then, is the optimal period of time for work?" has endorsed this proposition. He argues that the answer keeps changing. What is most productive at one time may be exceedingly long and unproductive at a later date. He concedes that research in the past has indicated that the 40-hour week was the most efficient. He suggests, however, that this research was primarily undertaken at a time when the workweek ranged from 48 to 60 hours per week. "The same studies conducted today would be in a totally different context. The 40-hour week is now expected – not 50 or 60 hours – and it seems likely that current research would show a workweek shorter than 40 (nominal) hours to be the most effective" (p. 340).

A drastic quantitative reduction in working time is needed, Naschold has argued, if workers' health is to be protected from the heightened level of work intensity. He suggests that any quantitative reduction can, per se, be considered synonymous with a reduction in strain and stress. He warns, however, that this is not enough. The traditional trade union policy of countering increased intensification by curtailing the length of time the workers labour fails to consider the consequences in terms of intensity that will follow a contraction of this nature. The very fact that workers achieve a reduced worktime, he suggests, makes it possible to raise the average level of intensity. He insists that this must be prevented. For this reason it is imperative that the unions develop policies that consciously strive to both limit the time spent at work and control the level of intensity maintained in the new time period.

Human limits and the pattern of change

There is then strong empirical support for Marx's argument that there would be a recurring conflict between human capacities and the demands of the capitalist production process. His claim that changes in intensity levels would be both a cause and a consequence of the downward movement can also be substantiated. The significance of human capacities in this changing situation, what is more, is further evidenced by the pattern the downward movement has followed. Such change has not been totally random. Although there is great variation among nations as to the schedule that is actually worked at any one time, there is a distinct pattern to the way in which change tends to occur. In virtually every society, when working times first begin to contract it is the hours of the day that are initially curtailed. This daily movement tends to flatten out as it approaches 8 hours. The few countries that have shortened the working day below 8 hours, such as the Soviet Union, have invariably reverted to the longer daily schedule, choosing instead to reduce the number of days in the week. In the capitalist nations as the 5-day week has become established this flattening out and stabilisation can be widely observed. As this schedule is established the length of the workweek ceases to contract and the growth of holidays becomes the main means of introducing further cuts in time schedules.

The similarity between this all but universal pattern and the nature of human capacities in relation to worktime and the maximisation of output in industrialised societies is not difficult to perceive. What appears to have happened is that as worktimes have shortened the least efficient marginal times have been invariably disposed of first. Because human capacities are such an important factor in the determination of efficient worktimes and because the capitalist industrialisation process has tended to follow a similar path within these diverse societies, there is a close correlation between the pattern of the downward movement and human capacities. It can be seen then that Marx's argument that the "weak bodies" of human beings play a central role in the determination of standard times has a great deal of empirical support. Consequently, Marxists who wish to contribute to the worktime debate must include this aspect of his theory in their work if they wish to be taken seriously. As was made clear in Chapter 1, this does not mean Marxists should not continue to emphasise the ability of human agents to shape their history, but it does suggest that they must be aware both that human beings make circumstances what they are *and* that circumstances limit and shape what humans are capable of achieving.

Theory choice

This chapter has examined the empirical support underpinning the primary postulates of the marginalist and Marxist theories of worktime. Marginalism, it has been shown, is particularly dependent on the empirical evidence because its adherents have proven incapable of providing a logical explanation for why worktimes should fall when incomes rise. Their failure to supply this empirical support constitutes a major problem for marginalist theory. Without empirical substantiation the argument degenerates into assertion. This does not mean it is disproved or that the vast majority of marginalists need soon abandon it. The theory has no substantive proof but this does not mean it is wrong. There is always the possibility that further, more refined empirical research will provide the necessary evidence. Given this possibility, the majority of marginalists will probably continue endorsing the theory for the foreseeable future. Belief, after all, does not always require scientific evidence; faith is often enough.

The primary, empirically verifiable elements in Marx's theory, on the other hand, have been shown to have a solid foundation. The fall in standard working times has been greatly offset by a heightening of the average level of intensity. The argument that human limitations would be a central factor in the worktime movement has also proven correct. Marx's argument, then, has much stronger empirical support than that enjoyed by marginalist theory and, it may be added, by arguments which are limited merely to the political realm. It has a stronger deductive character than both of these theories, moreover, and is able to explain all that they can and much more besides. Not only can it explain the downward movement of worktimes without the need for a negative slope in the relevant portion of the labour-supply curve or the existence of strong unions, but it can also explain why this change does not result in falls in output, why the change tends to be unidirectional and why the change has followed the pattern it has.

Critical discussion, Popper has suggested, can never establish sufficient reason to enable one to claim that a theory is true. But, he suggests, it is possible for rational analysis to provide sufficient reason to enable the following to be claimed (1972: 82). "This theory seems at present, in the light of a thorough critical discussion and of severe and ingenious testing, by far the *best* (the strongest, the best tested); and so it seems the one nearest to truth among the competing theories." In other words, it is possible, in the light of the evidence available at any one time, to justify the claim that one theory better approximates the truth than any other thus far produced. If this hypothesis is accepted as valid, then it is suggested that the greater deductive strength, empirical support and explanatory power of Marx's argument should leave one with little doubt that this theory is a better approximation of the truth than that put forward by any other. In the rest of this volume this is the position that will be accepted.

CHAPTER 3

Worktime and the effort bargain

Thus far this work has validated Marx's claim that the temporal and intensive aspects of worktime are inversely related. It has also been shown that human needs and limitations have been a major factor restricting the length of time workers labour, that changes in the level of work intensity are both a cause and a consequence of the downward movement of working times and that time schedules considered normal during the nineteenth century are now too long to be considered efficient. What will now be examined is the way the intensive and extensive worktime dimensions together influence and shape the struggle between the classes over the mass of labour that workers normally undertake.

A fair day's work

Central to the worktime issue is the concept of a fair day's work. Significant differences generally exist between employer and worker as to what this consists. This reflects the fact that the former is a buyer and the latter a seller of labour power. The differing perspective is not resolved by the forging of an employment contract. Such an arrangement normally consists of two elements: first, an agreement on the wage per unit of time or piece; second, an agreement on the amount of work to be undertaken, that is, an effort bargain. It is normal for the wage rate to be precisely defined in the employment contract. The effort bargain, on the other hand, is generally implicit and indistinct. Little is said about efficiency or about "how much effort is expected for a given wage. . . . The details of the arrangement are left to be worked out through the direct interaction between the partners of the contract" (Baldamus 1961: 35). At most there are vague references to an implied level of effort considered acceptable which rests on intuitive norms of what constitutes a fair day's work. The wage–effort contract, then, is incomplete in a very fundamental sense. What the em-

67

ployer pays is predetermined while what is received for this payment is open-ended. The precise mass of work the employee will undertake is determined in the workplace, not at the point of purchase. Maximising the size of this mass is, for the employer, a central objective of industrial organisation.

Control of production

Within the workplace how much labour workers will undertake for what they are paid is greatly affected by the degree of control over the production process enjoyed by employer and employee. Participants in the wage–effort bargain who can enhance their control over the labour process can shift the ratio of effort to pay in their favour. Both workers and capitalists utilise various techniques and strategies to attempt to gain at the expense of the other. Workers use both individual and collective methods of struggle to maintain or lower established effort norms. In this endeavour they have enjoyed a degree of success in developing institutional controls that have enabled them to retain a degree of influence over the production process. These controls are wide-ranging: "They apply not only to standards of effort and output restriction, but also to the practices that govern job demarcations, work routines and the whole web of social relations that surrounds the individual workman" (Flanders 1964: 234).

The means by which workers attempt to adjust effort norms take many forms. The activity may be undertaken on either a collective or individual basis. Collective action can involve highly organised and institutionalised forms of action or may be "spontaneous." Besides the application of peer pressure on potential "rate busters" or "gold brickers," collective action may take the form of peaceful negotiations with management, output limitations, political action and strikes. Unorganised, individualistic pressure includes absenteeism, poor time keeping and effort restriction. Unorganised methods of struggle are at least as important in the determination of effort norms as are those that are organised. Hyman (1975) has argued that though unorganised forms of worker opposition are not normally considered industrial resistance, they can represent a conscious or unconscious response to adverse working conditions. Research, he reports, has found that organised and unorganised forms of opposition are to some extent interchangeable. Both constitute a "withdrawal from work," the primary difference being that organised pressure involves a deliberate attempt to change a given situation. Unorganised action, by contrast, is not normally part of a deliberate strategy and may not even be recognised by the participants as an attempt to remedy an uncongenial situation.

Employers also utilise a wide range of tactics when attempting to shift effort norms in their favour. These tactics have changed and expanded through the long history of capitalism. The changes reflect developments in the size, operation and environment of the firm. They also reflect the fact that workers have been successful in countering many of the employers' policies. The specific means by which effort norms are changed are diverse. This is necessarily so because of the varying degrees of bargaining power enjoyed by different sectors of the working class, because of the differing technical, legal and organisational structure of the various parts of the economy, and because of the nature of the historical evolution of many jobs. The employers' greatest asset in the struggle over effort norms is the control they enjoy over the production methods utilised in industry. The capacity of humans to indirectly control the design of technology and the ability to change its form have been seized upon by employers as the "prime means whereby production may be controlled not by the direct producer but by the owners and representatives of capital" (Braverman 1974: 193).

Factors external to the workplace

The precise amount of work employees will undertake during a normal work period is also influenced by factors outside the place of work. Changes in the workers' social needs and general pace of life can influence the time schedule that maximises efficiency and the amount of labour the workers are able to undertake. In nonindustrialised societies the direct producers, whether by choice or not, experience a "time surplus." The whole pace of life in these societies is of a slower nature than it is in the industrialised states. In these latter nations, Linder has argued, all slack in the use of time has been eliminated so far as is humanly possible. Punctuality, he suggests, has become a virtue that we demand of those around us, and consequently we tend to experience a constant "time famine."

People are dominated by their awareness of the clock. They are haunted by their knowledge that the shining moments are passing without things having been done. The clock in Times Square shows what second it is to those hurrying by. . . . We live under the tyranny of the clock. This tyranny has developed, step by step, with our successful revolution against the dictatorship of material poverty. (Linder 1970: 23)

Linder further argues that the increased tempo both within and outside the workplace often entails an actual decline in the efficient use of time. Time, he suggests, is a dimension into which only so much activity can be compressed. To ignore this fact is to invite inefficiency and personal cost.

At the personal level, this means a risk of stress. A fully packed schedule can lead to our jumping from one task to another and actually performing less than would otherwise be possible. In the worst case – and this is no uncommon thing in a time famine – people die an early death from overstrain and insufficient time instead of, as previously, from a shortage of goods. Deaths are now caused by high productivity, not low productivity. (p. 25)

The faster tempo of life outside the workplace invariably influences the performance of workers at the point of production. Likewise the great mass of unpaid work that individuals must undertake outside the workplace, because it acts as a tax on human capacities, lessens the potential reserves of mental and physical resources that workers can sell on the market. This last fact has been stressed by many of those who have contributed to the debate on the relationship between paid and unpaid labour. It has been correctly argued that the workers' capacity to engage in paid work is very much influenced by the mass of labour normally undertaken within the home. Feminist literature in particular has emphasised the positive role played by women in this regard. It has been realised that, because women have traditionally been the primary suppliers of labour power to the domestic sector, the quantity of this commodity men have been able to sell in the marketplace has been greatly enhanced. Were men compelled to undertake an equal share of domestic labour, it is likely that their capacity to undertake paid labour would be seriously taxed. The extent of the influence the demands of the domestic sector can have on time schedules, it needs to be added, can be observed in the disproportionate number of women who undertake part-time jobs in order to allow themselves time and effort to fulfil their domestic roles.

The state

The connection between paid and unpaid work has attracted the attention of the governments of all industrialised capitalist nations. A primary reason for this interest has been a desire to aid the accumulation process by raising the quality of the workers' labour power. State intervention in this area can radically modify the working class's willingness and ability to sustain a given time schedule or a given level of work intensity. Policies designed to achieve this objective include:

1. The inculcation of an appropriate ideology, in particular the maintenance of the work ethic and the teaching, via institutions such as the education system, of socially accepted effort norms.
2. Expansion of working capacities. The health services, welfare payments and the provision of social goods to the extent that they enhance workers' productive capacities are among examples of these activities.
3. Socialisation of the cost of work. Maintaining and repairing those workers psychologically and physiologically damaged by the production process may be considered examples of this activity. The payment of state pensions in order to facilitate the intensification of the labour process by enabling those workers unable to maintain the heightened effort norms to retire, for example, has become a common phenomenon in many industrialised nations.
4. The provision of legal and infrastructural facilities. Examples here include legislative regulation of shopping and working times and the provision of facilities that diminish household labour and commuting time.

To the extent that the state expands the workers' capacities and absorbs the costs of damage they experience, intensity levels can rise without undermining capitalist efficiency. That the state plays a major role in the reproduction and modification of labour power has long been recognised. As was shown in Chapter 1, it has also played an important role in the establishment of standard worktimes from the earliest days of capitalism. During its embryonic stage, when the force of economic relations alone was not sufficient to compel an adequate supply of labour power, it was towards the state that the purchasers of

this commodity turned. As the relative power of the bourgeoisie grew, its need for the state to ensure that the workers
were willing to work lessened. Though capitalists were to continue periodically requiring the state's direct assistance, they
were increasingly able to rely on the market to take the place of
law. Within the marketplace, however, the interests of individual capitalists are not necessarily compatible with the interests of
the accumulation process taken as a whole. The existence of
this anarchic situation necessitates the existence of a force
standing apart from and over individual capitalists that can
restrict the rate at which the society's supply of labour power is
consumed. Where institutional and market pressures permit,
this external force may take the form of collective agreements
between trade union and employer bodies. Such agreements,
however, normally require some form of assistance from the
state to make them enforceable. This support will necessarily be
of greater significance where the participants to the collective
bargain do not have the capacity to ensure that the agreement
is respected by all employers and workers. Then it may be
necessary for the state to compel adherence to a limit on the
length of time workers may labour by the force of law.

Marx argued that the interventionist policy followed by the
English state in the determination of working times had historically displayed two distinct tendencies.

Compare, for example, the English factory legislation of our time
with the English Labour Statutes from the fourteenth century to well
into the middle of the eighteenth. While the modern Factory Acts
compulsorily shorten the working day, the earlier statutes tried forci-
bly to lengthen it. (1976: 382)

These apparently contradictory policies had, in fact, the same
objective: the regulation of the rate at which surplus labour was
extracted from the direct producers. With its enactment of the
Labour Statutes the English state intervened in the labour market because the high mortality caused by the Black Death had
driven up the bargaining power of the direct producers. This
enabled them to demand higher wages and reduced worktimes
without any corresponding increase in the degree of intensity
they put into their work. The desire of the rulers to make the
workers labour harder and longer had, however, to be tempered by the need to ensure that their actions did not prove a
danger to the system as such. There were strict limits to how far

labourers who retained a significant degree of bargaining power could be compelled to labour more than they wished. It was several centuries before the direct producers could be driven to a level of subjugation where the length of time they were forced to labour became, in itself, a danger to the accumulation process, both by threatening to destroy the supply of labour power by crippling the workers and by engendering in them an overt and increasingly active hostility to capitalism.

It should be noted that the state is not free to resolve worktime crises by intervening whenever and wherever those who control its institutions wish. Its power to do this is limited because it is subject to structural constraints and to the pressures generated by numerous class forces. This is not to deny that the state does have a degree of power that is independent of other power centres in society. This independence, indeed, is crucial given that the majority of capitalists appear to have so much difficulty accepting that worktimes can be reduced without necessarily reducing output. The state is often able, precisely because it is somewhat distant, to take a more objective view of the needs of the class as a whole. It was only when the working times forced upon the workers reached a point where they clearly endangered the long-term viability of the accumulation process that the state, under pressure from the workers and some sections of the ruling class, was both willing and able to intervene by introducing regulatory legislation.

The balancing act that those who administer the state must undertake in their attempt to aid the formation and consolidation of efficient worktimes is compounded by the existence of serious divisions amongst the employers as to what constitutes the most appropriate industry-wide schedule. At the same time the state needs to ensure that the time schedules maintained by industry do not develop in a manner which endangers its legitimacy or the class dominance of capital. The difficulties involved in achieving this last objective are great under any type of regime but are probably most difficult in liberal democracies where not only the demands of the various fractions of capital must be considered but also those of organised labour. To maintain the balancing act involved in formulating worktime policies in the face of what are often conflicting demands, some form of compromise must invariably be forged among the demands of the workers, the needs of the various sectors of industry and the interests of the bourgeoisie as a class. The nature of this compromise cannot be stated a priori for it is an empirical problem. It will depend on the balance of forces involved in the struggle, on the historical background, the specific form of the state and the specific nature of the government within any given society.

The market and industrial efficiency

It can be seen, then, that many factors mày influence the efficiency of worktime schedules. Consequently, the possibility always exists that if the length of time normally laboured is held constant, while these other factors remain free to change, the efficiency of a schedule may be undermined and unit costs raised more than they need be. To suggest the existence of this possibility raises the question of just how effective is the capitalist market at ensuring that employers adopt the most efficient schedule potentially available to them.

The 1931 International Labour Office study *The Social Aspects of Rationalisation* attempted to determine the effect of changes in standard worktimes on the methods of production utilised in the workplace. A central problem this study attempted to resolve was whether a reduction in standard times motivated employers to adopt productivity-inducing measures which they might not otherwise have undertaken. The report noted that many observers had argued that reductions in working time did have this effect. Goldmark had observed, for example:

An interesting point brought out by the commission is the incentive to invention and greater economy on the part of the employees under the short-hour system. When working hours are diminished, the loss in time tends to be at least in part compensated, almost automatically, by time and labour-saving methods of production, as well as by increased energy on the part of the workers. . . . While a particular machine will not go faster in eight hours than in ten hours, the substitute for that machine, which the eight-hour day presses upon the employer to adopt, will go faster. Less hours in this way have an indirect as well as a direct compensating effect. Not only do they make it possible for the workman to keep up his intensity of personal exertion during each hour of the day and to work more days at a high rate of speed, but they cause the employer to economise his labour at every point and to improve its quality by better selection. (Cited by I.L.O. 1931: 94)

What such observations suggest is that a "normal" level of competition is often not a sufficiently effective mechanism for ensuring that capitalists utilise the resources available to them in the most efficient manner. As had Marx, Rae (1894) stressed this point in his contribution to worktime theory. He argued that often firms had "reserves of personal efficiency" of which they were not aware and which tended to be discovered and tapped wherever and whenever reductions in standard times were introduced. The introduction of reduced time standards invariably increased the efficient utilisation of the firm's resources, Rae argued, first by enabling both machine and worker to labour more intensively. This factor was particularly important at raising productivity where the established schedule was so long workers were compelled to labour at a relatively slow pace in order to conserve their energy. He recognised that there was a long-term danger that the increased pace might eventually cause problems for the new schedule, but he insisted that initially the general experience with employers who introduced the 8-hour day tended to be that they removed more strain from the worker by the diminution of normal times than they added by the consequent increase in intensity.

Besides allowing the workers to labour more intensively, Rae argued, the introduction of shorter times also enabled the employer to tap the potential of workers to labour more intelligently when they were less fatigued. Where employees are given more time to recuperate from the demands of the production process, in other words, they are more likely to improve the quality of their input irrespective of whether or not they labour at a higher rate of speed. He stressed the relevance of this point for those who insisted that in machine-paced jobs shorter times must reduce output. It might be true, he conceded, that a lathe will not work in 8 hours as much as it will in 9, "if it is properly worked on both occasions." The point is that with the shorter schedule the worker will tend to work the machine in a more efficient manner, and where fatigue is a significant factor the enhanced productivity may be significant. "Men need leisure, and if they are not granted it, nature will evidently take her revenge by wasting in the end more genuine working time than the length of the relaxation she is denied" (Rae 1894: 121).

A third reserve of personal efficiency that was capable of being tapped when worktime reductions were introduced, Rae observed, lay in the poor management practices that long time schedules enabled employers to maintain. Where employers were compelled to adopt reduced schedules, he argued, they invariably responded by overhauling "dilatory or indolent habits of management." In other words, they put more effort into ensuring that labour time was utilised as efficiently as possible. They became, moreover, more willing to put greater capital and effort into ensuring that modern production methods were utilised, and they became more insistent on punctuality and made greater efforts to ensure that breaks in production and the waste of time were kept to a minimum.

The fact that Rae's research and that undertaken by many other scholars has shown that in many cases reductions in worktime that have been forced on employers by the state or the labour movement have actually increased total output shows in turn that the market is not capable of ensuring that inefficient time schedules are not worked. If normal market pressures were fully effective we would expect to see a significant number of voluntary worktime reductions introduced by capitalists as intensity levels came into conflict with the time schedule maintained by industry. Such voluntary action, however, is rare, though it is true it is not totally unknown. Rae (1894: 13–14) has provided an accurate description of what normally occurs.

The first experience of a reduction of hours has always been very various. Some enterprising manufacturers have generally made the experiment before the restrictive law came into force and found it advantageous; then, after the introduction of the law, while some reported favourably from the very beginning, the majority reported a decrease of product for the first few months, or the first year or two; but eventually the favourable experience became general, either because the shorter hours had time to tell on the vital and mental energies of the workmen, or because employers had one after another discovered the secret, which some of them discovered at the outset, of making up for the diminution of work-hours by improved arrangements of the work.

White's (1981) evidence has shown that this situation still exists. The national worktime research he undertook in 1978–1979 found a significant number of nonunionised workplaces where employers had voluntarily chosen to introduce reductions in standard times below the national standard. These voluntary curtailments represented a disproportionate percentage of the enterprises operating on lower schedules. While nonunionised establishments constituted fewer than 10 per cent of the 401 firms examined, 30 per cent of those working below 40 hours per week had no union. Such voluntary reductions are, however, the exception. The vast majority of employers normally reduce standard schedules only as a result of national or industry-wide collective bargains which they have to obey, or as a result of the enactment of a new legal standard by the state. The need of most employers for ever greater quantities of surplus labour time, combined with their general lack of knowledge of the intensive–temporal relationship involved in worktime, makes them fervent opponents of voluntary reductions in worktime and in some cases even induces them to make adjustments to time schedules that have the opposite effect to that desired. Thus, North and Buckingham (1969: 2) report that some productivity agreements signed in Britain in the 1960s "took the form of the 'buying out' of tea breaks – though it should be noted that, apart from machine- or process-controlled operations, all the research evidence suggests that tea breaks improved productivity."

How it can be that the market fails to ensure that employers adopt the most efficient schedule available to them has been discussed by a number of scholars. Pigou (1962), for example, argued that this apparent paradox is explained by lack of knowledge and foresight on the part of both employer and worker as to the efficiency-promoting capacities often inherent in the reduction of time schedules. Hicks (1963: 106) likewise argued that the vast majority of employers were not aware that as a consequence of the tendency for the level of work intensity to rise within industry "the output optimum length of day probably falls." The idea that worktimes can be shortened without necessarily undermining output, Hicks suggested, probably never enters the head of most employers. Consequently, they simply assume that reduced time schedules must invariably increase unit costs and lower profits.

Hicks was aware, however, that this explanation was not adequate to explain all employer unwillingness to experiment with reduced time schedules. He noted that history provided many examples of situations where employers did have adequate knowledge of the possible beneficial long-term consequences of worktime curtailments but had still refused to allow any reductions in existing schedules. Why employers behaved in this manner, he argued, was explained by the fact that worktime curtailments often produced significant short-term increases in unit costs. If the temporal reduction increased the quality of the workers' labour time to a sufficient extent, these costs, in the long term, might be more than offset. Even so, unless the worktime curtailment is accompanied by a sufficiently large wage reduction, the increased short-term costs have to be borne by the employer. The consequent profits thus forgone, Hicks suggested, might be considered as a form of investment. He pointed out, however, that most employers would consider such an investment to be extremely risky, for they could not know for sure to what extent, if any, the increased free time available to the workers would increase the quality of the time they continued to labour. It might be added that the risk is compounded by the tendency for industrial reforms to have a ratchet effect; that is, it is easier to introduce a reform than it is to take it away. If the hoped-for increase in efficiency does not materialise, the employer might find that the effort bargain has shifted to a significant extent to the workers' advantage. Hicks also advised that there was a further problem making the voluntary introduction of reduced time schedules extremely risky for the employer. When the transitional period during which any consequent increase in the quality of the workers' labour time takes place is over, employers may find that their employees fail to remain in their employ. Hicks's argument has been succinctly put by Rothschild (1960: 55):

The beneficial effects of more leisure and "better nerves" will need some time to make themselves felt. In so far, then, as employers tend to take a rather short view of their actions, they will quite logically resist any reduction of working hours unless it is accompanied by a corresponding reduction in total wages. And finally, even if an entrepreneur is advanced enough to take a long view, he will hesitate to reduce hours in his establishment, if his competitors continue to work beyond the optimum level. For while his reduction in hours will result at any rate in an immediate reduction of output, the long-term beneficial effects may be lost if some of his workers leave him at the time when their output goes up, and he has to replace them by some of the overworked employees from other firms.

Rothschild argued that, because of the high level of risk aversion generally displayed by employers, it was unlikely that rational time schedules could be established by sheer force of competition. He suggested that employers normally need to be subjected to an external shock before they will introduce changes to standard times even when the new schedule is more productive than the old. A similar conclusion has been put forward by Leibenstein (1966: 402–403) in his work on the concept of X-efficiency.

Economists frequently assume that for a given capital stock and quality of work force, output will be proportional to number of hours worked. Experiments during World War I and later showed that not only was the proportionality law untrue, but that frequently *absolute* output actually increased with reductions in hours – say from a ten-hour day to an eight-hour day. It was also found that with longer hours a disproportionate amount of time was lost from increased absenteeism, industrial accidents, and so on. In many cases it would obviously have been to a firm's interest to reduce hours below that of the rest of the industry. Firms could have investigated these relations and taken advantage of the findings. For the most part, governments sponsored the necessary research on the economics of fatigue and unrest under the stimulus of the war effort, when productivity in some sectors of the economy was believed to be crucial. The actual reduction of hours that took place was a consequence of the pressure of labor unions and national legislation.

The sources of the external pressure needed to ensure that time schedules are reduced as average intensity levels rise are diverse. There would appear, though, to be three that are most significant: changes in the level of competition, changes in the degree and nature of state intervention and changes in the package of working conditions acceptable to the workers. In point of fact, actual worktime change invariably involves all three factors. In the following discussion they will, however, be handled somewhat separately because in some instances, only one or two are involved to any significant extent.

Competition

The shock effect of major changes in the level of competition within the economy has already, to some extent, been dealt with in the discussion of the period of global decay at the end of the nineteenth century. A heightening of competition sufficient to strongly influence time schedules, however, need not develop in quite so dramatic a fashion as it did in this period. A general, rapid and prolonged rise in business activity which absorbs virtually all surplus labour power available on the market may have a similar effect. In such a situation, even if workers do not

use their enhanced bargaining power to enforce worktime
changes, employers may find they need to shorten standard
times in order to be able to buy sufficient of this commodity.
Competition between employers may thus cause standard
working times to fall even if the workers take no collective
action to compel such a change.

Competition between employers for available labour power
lies at the centre of the contemporary marginalist theory of
worktime. It is argued by the more narrow of those within this
tradition that employers who perceive a change in the preferred distribution of income and leisure amongst the workers
and adjust the package of wages, conditions and working times
to accord with this shift will attract employees from their competitors. This process will, in turn, compel other firms to make
similar changes, and thus a general downward movement in
standard times may occur. (The reason why these times do not
move back up when the market for labour power eases is generally not considered by these theorists.) There are many problems with the marginalist tradition, as has already been argued.
To reject the theory as a whole, however, it is not necessary to
deny that some aspects of the argument may have some validity. It certainly is the case that capitalists adjust the package of
rewards and demands they offer the workers to accord with
shifts in the availability of labour power. These changes in the
nature of the package offered may or may not reflect changes
in the preferences of the workers. The crucial point where
these narrow marginalists fall down badly, however, is in their
failure to consider what steps employers will take to adjust the
intensity of work to accord with the new schedule that competition has forced them to introduce.

A clear economy-wide example of how competition between
employers can contribute to major adjustments to time schedules has been provided by postwar Japanese industry. Working
times in Japan, as in Europe, began to fall in the postwar years
as soon as the surplus of labour power engendered by the wartime destruction of industry had been absorbed and a shortage
of this commodity began to emerge on the market. Tsujimura
Kotaro (1980: 78) reports that the ratio of demand to supply
for middle-school graduates rose from 1.2 : 1 in 1959 to 2.7 : 1
in 1963. The ratio of high-school graduates rose from 1.1 : 1 in
1959 to 2.7 : 1 in 1962. Japanese firms for the first time, he
reports, began to experience a serious shortage of labour

power during the 1960s. As this shortage intensified, competition amongst firms to secure the workers' commodity also grew more intense.

Despite the consequent dramatic increase in their bargaining power and the relatively long standard worktimes in Japan, the Japanese trade unions "continued to take a rather ambivalent stance on shorter hours of work" (Yamaguchi 1980). Tsujimura reports that the unions failed to launch any significant campaign for shorter worktimes during the 1960s. A consensus existed, he suggests, between employers and labour leaders that curtailment of time schedules would hinder Japanese international competitiveness and should therefore be avoided. Despite this aversion to shorter time standards by both employers and union leaders, a dramatic fall in both standard and actual worktimes took place during the fifteen years after 1960. What happened during this period, Tsujimura suggests, was that employers were forced by the tight labour market to compete for labour power by offering both higher wages and better working times.

The data presented in Tables 3.1 and 3.2 suggests that Tsujimura's argument has a good deal of validity. Competition for scarce high-quality labour power was a major factor inducing employers to offer shorter standard times during this period. In granting that the argument has some validity, however, it should be noted that factors associated with the quality of labour power and productivity were at least as important.

The pace at which Japanese worktimes contracted slowed markedly with the onset of the 1970s depression. The reduction in demand for labour power that the crisis induced raised the quantity of this commodity available on the market. With Japanese unions still unwilling to campaign seriously for shorter worktimes, employers were subjected to significantly less external pressure to introduce worktime changes. This lack of external compulsion appears to have worried the Japanese Government, and it is almost certainly the reason the Japanese state has intervened to encourage both capitalists and workers to strive for further cuts in standard times. The Japanese Ministry of Labor, which undertakes ongoing econometric studies of the degree of offset that is likely to be gained from further curtailing worktimes, has since 1978 practised what it terms "administrative guidance" of working times. By 1979, Yamaguchi (1980) reports, the Government was eager to see shorter

Table 3.1. *Reasons for introducing the two-day weekend (in percentages)*

Size of firm (no. of employees)	Total no. of firms with some form of two-day weekend (actual no. in parentheses)	Reason for introducing the two-day weekend							
		To bolster attendance	To improve productivity	One way to compensate workers for improved productivity	To attract new employees	For the health of employees	Because of problems in commuting	Other reasons	Not clear
Total	100.0 (1,449)	19.6	44.2	13.7	28.8	67.9	2.3	7.9	6.7
1000+	100.0 (535)	17.2	49.2	15.3	29.2	77.2	3.6	7.9	5.2
300–999	100.0 (418)	18.2	43.5	14.8	31.3	70.6	3.1	6.9	5.0
–299	100.0 (496)	23.4	39.5	10.9	26.2	55.6	0.4	8.7	9.7

Note: In some cases several answers were supplied. Therefore the breakdowns total more than 100%.
Source: Tsujimura 1980: 80.

Table 3.2. *The effects of introducing the two-day weekend (in percentages)*

Size of firm (no. of employees)	Total no. of firms with some form of two-day weekend (actual no. in parentheses)	Effects									
		Positive effects							No change	Ill effects	Not clear or no answer
		Subtotal	Improvement in attendance	Improvement in productivity	Decrease in industrial trial accidents	More competitive in the recruitment of new employees	A decrease in attention due to retirement or changing jobs	Other beneficial effects			
Total	100.0 (1,449)	72.7	35.2	36.1	8.6	44.6	12.5	7.2	20.2	0.5	6.6
1000+	100.0 (535)	73.6	32.7	40.2	8.2	47.5	12.0	12.0	17.6	0.7	8.0
300–999	100.0 (418)	72.3	32.5	37.1	10.5	46.4	14.1	5.0	20.6	0.2	6.9
–299	100.0 (496)	72.0	40.1	30.8	7.3	42.9	11.7	4.8	22.8	0.4	4.8

Note: In some cases several answers were supplied. Therefore the breakdowns total more than 100%.
Source: Tsujimura 1980: 81.

workdays and the 5-day week more widely practised in Japan. Workers and employers have also been urged by the Government to abandon the working of excessive amounts of overtime and the tradition of not taking annual holidays even where they are allowed for in collective agreements. State bodies have been actively promoting this policy in industry. It has been suggested, moreover, that the administration may even be willing to introduce legislation into the Diet that will compel employers to introduce a 5-day week if they do not take action themselves.

State intervention

The attempt of the Japanese Government to stimulate innovation and efficient resource utilisation by promoting reductions in standard working times has been a technique adopted by many governments. In many instances such intervention has gone as far as legislative control of standard times. In other cases the state's activities have been limited to stimulating competitive pressures within the economy. The specific nature of this activity varies widely, reflecting the different combination of political, economic and institutional forces operating at different times and places. In some nations, for example, the state intervenes merely by providing conciliation and arbitration facilities which assist the formation of collective agreements. Such agreements, even though they may result in a strengthening of the monopoly sectors of the economy, can increase the competitive pressure on the less efficient firms in industry, especially if the new standard is one better suited to the more efficient enterprise. In other situations the state may stimulate worktime changes simply by attempting to enlighten employers and unions as to the potential degree of offset that could be achieved with a given curtailment of standard times or by agreeing to absorb some of the costs experienced by less efficient firms in their attempts to improve productivity.

In West Germany, for example, the state did not implement any new legislation to control standard times between 1938 and 1981. Postwar governments instead retained the Fascist legislation on worktime maxima. Both Conservative and Social Democratic West German governments, however, have continued playing a significant role in the determination of standard times. Rather than legislating for shorter times, they have chosen to aid the establishment of collective agreements which have given the workers the shorter schedules they demanded and which stimulated economic growth. This policy has been based on the extensive research that has been carried out in the Republic on the economics and politics of worktime. West German state officials, with varying degrees of enthusiasm, have promoted the idea that worktime curtailments do not necessarily mean reduced wages or profits. Thus the Government funded and gave wide publicity to the investigations into worktime and efficiency undertaken when the workweek was reduced from 48 to 45 hours in 1955–1956. The "static" loss in working time, the report of this research stressed, contrasted poorly with the "dynamic" gain resulting from the changed attitude of employers to technical development.

There is no doubt that in the future also, thanks to the dynamism released thereby, a growth policy can be followed with the help of a reduction in hours of work and many of the tasks of an economic and social nature which lie ahead of us can be solved more easily with a reduction of hours of work than without it. The authorities responsible for the economic policy of the Federal Republic should regard the reduction of hours of work not so much – as hitherto – as a necessary evil, but rather as a new tool in the set of instruments available to them for the conduct of economic policy. (Cited by Evans 1975: 74)

More recently the Government's Council of Economic Advisers has recommended shorter working times as a means of combating unemployment. If the unions would agree to wage cuts, the council has stated, even the 35-hour week might be acceptable.

Besides aiding the accumulation process by encouraging worktime curtailments that will increase the efficiency of industry, the state may also intervene to oppose a reduction in working times that it sees as being harmful to accumulation. The most common example of this phenomenon is state intervention to aid employers who are resisting a demand from the labour movement for cuts to standard times. In opposing trade union or popular demands for cuts in working times politicians and state functionaries, however, must remain aware of the need to promote legitimation as well as accumulation. Where these two needs conflict, some pathway that concedes a little to each may need to be found. The dramatic increase in unemployment that has taken place since 1974 has created such a situation. As with earlier economic crises, this depression has motivated the trade union movement to agitate for cuts to worktimes as a means of creating jobs. The political and economic power of the labour movement and the electoral repercussions and costs of high unemployment make demands of this nature difficult to ignore totally no matter what the complexion of the government. On the other hand, the accumulation process must be protected. The existence of these dual and to some extent contradictory needs has been reflected in the policies advocated by a number of governments in the post-1974 decade. In this period most administrations within the O.E.C.D., for example, experimented with or at least discussed policies designed to create jobs by manipulating working times. These policies have included the promotion of part-time work, the introduction of shorter worktimes in return for higher productivity and/or lower wages and the subsidisation of employers who agreed to cut standard times and hire extra workers.

Despite this apparent concern for the unemployed, it would seem thus far that accumulation rather than legitimation remains the primary factor influencing the worktime policies of most of these governments. At a 1982 ministerial meeting of the Manpower and Social Affairs Committee of the O.E.C.D., for example, great emphasis was placed on the need to investigate a wide range of possible worktime changes that might reduce unemployment.

However, as with all major political initiatives, it was realised that such desirable goals could only be approached subject to somewhat severe constraints. Thus, the ministers went on to emphasise that working time reductions should not be such as to damage industrial production costs or affect general inflationary conditions. (Hart 1982: 55–56)

What about the workers?

As important as is pressure from competitors and the state in compelling employers to institute worktime changes, the most important stimulant is usually the labour movement. In the liberal democracies in particular the unions are probably the major primary source of pressure that is commonly placed on employers to remove worktime-based inefficiencies from the production process. Within the mainstream literature, trade unions have traditionally been treated as a force tending to increase rather than reduce inefficiency. Those who support

this perspective argue that unions are monopolistic organisations that create inefficiency in resource allocation. These
bodies, it is argued, raise costs first, by compelling firms to hire
more workers, use more capital per worker and utilise higher-
quality workers than is economically necessary. Second, by expanding the social factor in effort norms, unions reduce the
output that could potentially be created with a given quantity of
labour power and capital. Third, by utilising their collective
pressure, unions reduce management flexibility, and when this
pressure takes the form of strikes or bans, output is significantly reduced.

During the 1970s this traditional approach was subjected to
serious criticism. It has been argued that, on the contrary,
"unions produce X-efficiencies through the expression of a
'collective voice' and that these efficiencies more than offset any
union induced inefficiencies. In short, unions produce *net*
X-efficiencies" (Addison and Barnett 1982: 146). Supporters of
this perspective suggest that unions aid the removal of inefficiencies from the production process first by inducing employers to abandon inefficient methods of production and adopt
more efficient methods; second, by providing a collective voice
for the workers that enables employers to determine their preferences and thus choose a better package of wage and nonwage
rewards; third, by improving morale amongst the workers and
thus reducing labour turnover; and fourth, by improving com-
munication between capitalist and worker. Slichter, Healy and
Livernash (1960), for example, have argued that unionisation,
viewed broadly, has in general created superior and better-
balanced management and that employers under the pressure
of unions extract more output from a given quantity of inputs
than do those employers whose firms are not unionised. Duncan and Stafford (1977), moreover, "report that while union
workers spend more time on formal breaks they spend a comparable amount *less* time on informal ones and report working
harder than non-union workers."

What the net effect of trade unionism is on efficiency is very
much an unresolved problem around which an extremely important debate is being conducted. Whatever the outcome of
this debate, it has already established two major points. While
unionism does create some inefficiencies, it also assists in the
removal of many others, and the market, under normal conditions, needs the assistance of these bodies if efficiency is to be

maximised. The removal of worktime-based inefficiencies is not the least of the ways by which the labour movement assists this process.

Collective bargaining and worktime

Reductions in standard working times characteristically occur at irregular intervals. They are, moreover, normally of a significant magnitude, with their introduction usually being followed by a prolonged stable period. It is not, in other words, common for worktimes to fall five minutes per week this year and ten minutes next. The reductions also tend to be industry-wide. Exceptions to these sweeping statements do exist. White's 1979 study of the British engineering industry, for example, found that 10 per cent of firms surveyed had instituted a standard workweek of less than the industry norm of 40 hours. Those employers who were willing to utilise a standard below the norm were then very much in the minority. Yet by 1982 a workweek of less than 40 hours was standard throughout the whole of this industry. What had happened in the interim was the contracting of a national agreement between the trade union movement and the employers that made the 39-hour week the new industry norm. The vast majority of employers, in other words, despite the fact that this worktime reduction was to cost them little, if anything at all, had not been willing to reduce working times voluntarily. Because of the herd instinct that employers normally adopt when bargaining over worktime, this aspect of the employment contract is conducted, in virtually all nations, at the industry or national level.

A demand for a downward change to time schedules in one form or another is normally included in a list of claims trade unions periodically submit to employers. This is often, however, little more than a formality. The 1957 Australian Council of Trade Unions, for example, resolved that the introduction of the 35-hour week was a matter of major priority. "Congress now places in the forefront of its fighting platform the demand for the reduction of the working week from 40 hours to 35 hours per week without loss of pay and initiates a nation wide campaign to compel employers and governments to bring about the necessary reform" (cited by Hardie 1978: 97). Despite the assertiveness of this declaration, the resolution was not promoted with any great vigour until the late 1970s. While the shorter week was to become a major industrial issue in some isolated industries during the intervening twenty years, in general it was treated more as an objective to be desired than one to be fought for.

The reasons why trade unions fail to promote demands for reduced worktime with the constant vigour they apply to wage demands have been discussed by a number of scholars. Marginalists generally argue that the explanation is that leisure preferrers will not oppose an increase in income, gained at the cost of greater leisure, to the same extent that income preferrers will oppose a decrease in worktime that involves a loss in earnings. This results, it is suggested, in the preferences of income preferrers generally being dominant. As a consequence, employers can usually buy off most demands for reduced schedules by offering higher wages.

Income preference probably is a factor influencing the extent to which unions promote reductions in worktime. One would expect, however, that in labour organisations, where unity, solidarity and the need to maintain internal cohesion are extremely important, conflict between income and leisure preferrers would normally manifest itself in compromise rather than in an outright decision one way or the other. The normal outcome to be expected from the preference argument surely is regular small reductions in worktime with moderated wage rises.

A more substantial explanation for the labour movement's normal lack of vigour on the worktime issue may lie in the degree to which the unions believe that shorter standards can be won. In collective bargaining, unions generally submit a list of claims that are open to negotiation. These claims will have varying degrees of priority. The exact nature of this priority will be determined by numerous factors. Of these, one of the most influential will be the extent to which the unions believe a claim can be won. Labour movements normally only struggle seriously for those gains which they believe they can hope to win. This belief will be largely determined by the response of employers to the total claim. Capitalists will wish to grant that package of wages and conditions that they believe will minimise unit costs. The unions' individual claims, as a result, will meet varying degrees of resistance depending on how much it is believed each will affect profitability.

If the temporal–intensive relationship widely adopted in industry reaches a point where a decrease in standard times can be largely offset by the removal of inefficiencies and a further heightening of work intensity, there exists a high probability that unions and employers will be able to negotiate an industry-wide worktime reduction. This is because little is in fact being conceded by the employer, and the smaller the prize the easier the victory. Individual employers, moreover, who recognise that a general agreement of this nature is likely to be concluded in the foreseeable future may find that they can even gain by initiating the worktime change of their own accord. By so doing they will not only gain greater control over the precise timing of the change, but they will also be in a good position to negotiate significant concessions from their employees. If they are adroit in negotiating the change they may even find that the worktime reduction shifts the effort bargain significantly in their favour.

Because neither employer nor union may be aware that in the existing situation a high degree of offset is potentially attainable, a heightening of union pressure for a worktime curtailment may be needed to make both aware of the existence of this situation. As employers do become aware that they can reduce worktimes with little cost, this will influence the extent to which they will resist a demand of this nature. The perception by the unions of this relative weakening will influence the degree of priority with which they will view the issue. This is because the claim comes to be seen as being of greater viability. A shift in emphasis will, in turn, manifest itself in an increase in the degree of pressure unions will place on employers to grant this particular concession. There is thus a dynamic interaction between capitalists and workers that strongly influences the extent to which unions promote worktime change. The insistence by the vast majority of employers that curtailments to standard times must be undertaken on an industry- or nation-wide basis explains why, when such change is introduced, it tends to be sweeping. The spasmodic nature of these changes, moreover, is explained by the prolonged period normally required for the growth of noteworthy inefficiencies of both an internal and external nature to develop once again across a wide sector of industry following their partial removal by a temporal reduction.

Intra-class conflict

The existence of inter-class conflict between employer and employee, it has been argued in this volume, is a crucial factor explaining how and why working times in capitalist societies tend to fall. Intra-class divisions amongst employers are also of major importance in bringing about these changes. Such divisions were, for Marx, a crucial factor in explaining the British workers' victory in gaining the 10-hour day, and this aspect of Marx's argument remains valid for modern capitalism. The vast majority of employers normally display a rare degree of unity when confronted by a demand for a reduction in worktimes. This unity, however, will begin to break down if individual capitalists become aware that to concede a demand for a cut to standard times would cost little. Those firms in which it is recognised that a worktime change would not raise unit costs to any significant degree may be expected to put up the least resistance to a downward adjustment of schedules.

Those capitalists who introduce a reduced schedule ahead of the rest of their industry, whether by choice or as a result of worker militancy, have an interest in ensuring that their competitors do likewise. Where the firm has been compelled to introduce a schedule below the industry's norm as a result of successful pressure from the workers, then its short-term competitive position will be undermined unless it can find some means of offsetting the reduced schedule. If the workers have the capacity to enforce a worktime reduction against the employer's wishes, the latter may not be in a position to demand wage cuts or make the workers labour more intensively. Capitalists in this position stand to gain if other employers in their industry are compelled to adopt the same schedule. Employers who voluntarily reduce worktimes because the existing schedule is inefficient may also stand to gain if a compulsory, universal reduction in standard times is introduced. If the competitors of these capitalists are compelled to work the same schedule and consequently experience significant increases in costs, then the relative competitive position of the former employers will be enhanced. The tenor of the demands of those employers with a lower than average time schedule for universal standards may even take on a moral element. Yamaguchi (1980), for example, reports that U.S. automobile manufacturers have denounced the morality of their Japanese competitors, who, they insist, are not abiding by "fair labour standards" because they maintain longer time schedules than those worked in the U.S.A. This moral indignation is not mere facade, it needs to be noted, for as Marx (1976: 405) suggested, in capitalist society exploitation of this nature is immoral because "the most fundamental right under the law of capital is the equal exploitation of labour power by all capitalists."

The 1979 engineering strike in Britain

Where there are serious divisions amongst employers over the most efficient standard schedule for an industry, a demand for a universal worktime reduction can seriously undermine their solidarity. The recognition and exploiting of such divisions by the unions can significantly enhance their capacity to win worktime claims. As it was the British experience that Marx used to formulate his worktime argument, it is appropriate that the most recent major worktime change in Britain be used as a contemporary example of how divisions amongst employers and union militancy can assist the introduction of a new standard schedule.

In 1979 the British engineering industry experienced the longest-running strike in its history. Indeed, in terms of days lost on strike, this dispute was the most significant to occur in the United Kingdom since the General Strike of 1926. The agreement that ended the dispute included the introduction of a 39-hour standard week. The worktime aspect of the conflict's outcome is particularly interesting, as the initial priority given to the shorter workweek by the unions does not appear to have been very great. In their initial ambit claim, submitted formally in February 1979, the unions asked for a planned reduction in the working week from 40 hours to 35 over an agreed period, without any loss of wages, and a minimum 5 weeks' holiday. These items were effectively rejected by the employers at an early stage in the negotiations. It was suggested by the latter that the discussion of the worktime issues should be separated from the claim and referred to a "harmonisation meeting" which would examine the whole question of basic conditions within the industry. The unions, evidencing the low priority with which these items were considered, initially suggested that they had no objections to this suggestion providing the employers were willing to increase the national minimum wage for skilled workers to somewhere near 80 pounds per week with pro rata increases for other grades. The employers, in turn, replied in early June that they were willing to pay 68 pounds per week for skilled workers and 49 pounds for unskilled with

9 per cent extra on this basic rate for the semi-skilled. They insisted, however, that these rates must be implemented on domestic anniversary dates rather than on a common date for the whole industry. It was this issue that was to prove the initial major obstacle to an early settlement. Abolishing a common implementation date was an important objective for the employers, as it would considerably decrease the cost of introducing national increases in the minimum earnings level. At the June meeting the union representatives intimated that if the employers were willing to add an extra 2 pounds to their offer then the only issue separating the two sides would be the question of implementation dates (Rice 1980: 64).

By mid June, then, the negotiations over what was to prove a historic change to standard worktimes in this industry was all but resolved, the apparent outcome appearing to differ little from most other years. At this stage, however, a shift within the union leadership temporarily gave the left on the national committee of the Confederation of Shipbuilding and Engineering Unions (C.S.E.U.) majority control. Using this majority, the left was able to successfully move an amendment which rejected the agreement, which was close to being finalised. It was moved by the left that the Executive Council immediately seek a meeting with the Engineering Employers' Federation (E.E.F.) to:

(a) Achieve in full the claim in respect of M.T.R.'s.
(b) Secure a reduction in the working week of one hour this year, with further staged reductions towards achievement of the 35 hour week in 1982.
(c) Secure two days extra holidays this year.
(d) Secure the common operative date of April 1979 for the implementation of the agreement.

(Cited by Rice 1980: 85)

The subsequent rejection of these demands by the employers elicited a response from the workers that completely changed the whole tenor of the negotiations. In the months that followed, the employers were to be overwhelmed and were forced to make significant concessions. The defeat of the E.E.F. was brought about by two central factors. First, the degree of militancy displayed by the workers, the positive response of those on the factory floor to their leaders' call for industrial action in the form of overtime bans and weekly short-term strikes, appears to have surprised not only employers but union officials as well. Second, major divisions emerged amongst the employers over the degree to which they would sustain a major campaign to prevent a cut in the length of the working week.

The left within the C.S.E.U. had been encouraged to promote their amendment by the fact that a number of employers had contracted agreements with their own employees that reduced working time. Other employers, moreover, had informed the unions that they were willing to contract an agreement with their own workers that would grant the minimum conditions insisted upon. Despite the fact that these capitalists were not affiliated with the E.E.F., the union leadership exploited these intra-class divisions by offering all firms, federated or not, exemption from the industrial action if they were willing to individually sign contracts that granted the unions' demands. This strategy proved very effective.

Whilst there were very few of these firms, it did allow the C.S.E.U. an early propaganda advantage, for they were able to point to settlements fulfilling their claim before the action commenced. Other non-federated employers whose domestic agreements were near to the Unions' claim were also under pressure to ensure conformity with the Unions' criteria and seek speedy dispensation. (Rice 1980: 88)

The granting of exemptions had the added advantage of bringing pressure to bear on individual employers. The possibility of gaining a dispensation meant that each had a means of withdrawing from the dispute. It was not possible, therefore, for them to claim that they could not prevent the conflict from escalating within their enterprises. By this tactic, Rice reports, the unions were able to turn a national dispute into a vast number of domestic disputes. The individual employer, rather than the E.E.F., thus became the immediate protagonist.

To exploit fully the divisions amongst the employers and to boost the morale of union members, the C.S.E.U. published regular bulletins reporting the number of employers who had broken with their peers and agreed to the unions' demands. The longer the dispute progressed, the greater the number of these deserters became, with their ranks eventually including many federation members. The philosophy of those capitalists who abandoned their peers was well summed up by a company spokesman for British Timken when announcing an independent settlement for this firm's 2,500 employees. "We can admire employer solidarity but our business and customers must come first" (cited by Rice 1980: 147).

By early October the combined effect of the workers' continuing offensive and the growing disunity in the ranks of the employers compelled the latter to capitulate on the issue of working time. It is interesting, when examining this dispute, to compare Rice's report of what was won and what the unions conceded in the settlement that was finally agreed upon.

Claim	Settlement
Hours.	
39 hours immediately	39 hours by 1981
35 hours by 1982.	
Holidays.	
2 extra days immediately	2 extra days immediately plus 1 for each succeeding year up to 1983.
Rates.	
£80 skilled and pro rata.	£73 for skilled with wider pro rata relationship.
Implementation date.	
Common date of April 1979.	November 1st 1979 for premia purposes. Domestic anniversary dates for other provisions plus commitment to domestic anniversary dates in all future settlements.

(Rice 1980: 181)

The unions also committed their members to giving maximum co-operation to ensure that sufficient productivity was generated to offset completely any increase in unit costs that might arise from the reduction in worktimes. The employers, moreover, were given a virtual free hand in determining how this offset would be achieved.

As the employers had let it be known before the series of strikes and bans had begun that they were willing to pay skilled workers 70 pounds per week, the campaign would appear to have won an extra 3 pounds per week. The workers had also gained a significant reduction in working time. Offsetting these advances, however, was the fact that the employers had been victorious on the issue of implementation dates and the widening of differentials. Given the priority with which the former issue was viewed by both employers and unions, this concession was a significant defeat for the workers. At the time, however, there was little doubt by all concerned that the campaign had been successful in significantly shifting the effort bargain in the workers' favour.

Although this conclusion has a good deal of validity, developments since 1979 must seriously bring into question just how great the victory was. A number of studies undertaken during the intervening period have examined both how employers responded to the worktime curtailment and what was the effect of the shorter schedule. Two regional studies, undertaken prior to the common implementation date for the new times, found that employers were taking very seriously the issue of productivity offsets. The vast majority of employers were found to be convinced that an offset of a magnitude that would prevent any increase in costs would be achieved. Indeed, most employers suggested that it was essential for their firm's survival that an offset of at least 100 per cent be gained (Bastin 1981; Fahey 1981).

A survey conducted by White (1982) during November–December 1981 concurred with these findings. White suggested that the "great majority" of engineering employers had introduced or were intending to introduce changes to the production process that they hoped would offset the shorter times. As reported earlier in this volume, subsequent studies were able to report that the employers were successful in achieving their objective. The shorter times cost them little, if anything at all.

Despite the fact that the apparent improvement in the effort bargain gained by the workers in their 1979 campaign was largely, if not totally, eroded by increased intensification, British trade union officials remained generally pleased with the outcome. At a time when they were losing members and were probably in their weakest state since the depression of the 1930s, they managed to wage a successful campaign to reduce the length of the basic workweek and to increase holidays to an extent originally not even asked for. Because of their refusal to consider employer responses to enforced worktime curtailments and indeed to the whole question of the relationship between working time and work intensity, they were able to delude themselves that the winning of the shorter week was an unadulterated victory. Ron Edwards, a research worker with the Trades Union Congress, in a rare exception to this general rule, reports that the T.U.C. literature gives the impression that employers play a totally passive role in this area. In an excellent study that sought to explain why employers would remain obstinate on wage increases yet grant significant improvements in working times during a period of mass unemployment, he concluded that a victory of this nature was possible because the unions were willing to make concessions on existing levels of control within the production process which, in the long term, were certain to rebound against the workers' interests (Ron Edwards 1982: 37).

The trade union campaign was based on the creation of employment and in this it has so far failed. What is evident from a brief survey of productivity and work practices is that the reduction in hours achieved so far have probably not resulted from purely trade union pressure, but have often come about as a result of management strategy and decision-making. It would also appear that management have tightened their control over the production process generally and over the activities of workers in particular. Sometimes of course this may have been the result of the necessity to keep costs down once shorter hours had been conceded, but it seems that on as many occasions the shorter working week was on offer as part of a management package to increase productivity.

Edwards's argument that the 1979 reductions in worktimes did not result purely from trade union pressure, while insightful to a rare degree, has a conspiratorial tone that is not justified. There can be little doubt that the vast majority of British engineering employers were opposed to any reduction in standard worktimes prior to the 1979 campaign. There is no evidence to suggest that changes of this nature would have been voluntarily put forward by employers on a wide basis if the unions had not included such a demand in their ambit claim. It was the dispute itself which forced these manufacturers to consider seriously the likely costs involved in the curtailing of schedules. Left to themselves, in other words, the vast majority of employers would have refused to make such modifications to the conditions of work because they believed changes of this nature would necessarily involve serious increases in costs. When faced by the need to settle what was proving a very effective campaign, however, such a belief would be examined in some detail as employers attempted to quantify the likely costs involved in conceding the various items in the claim.

The post-settlement evidence that the temporal reductions in fact cost the employers little and that they may even have gained, given the concessions they were able to wrest from the workers, does not justify any suggestion of conspiracy on their part or even awareness that the costs of conceding these particular claims would be negligible. When the representatives of the E.E.F. decided to grant the shorter times they were undoubtedly in possession of estimates of the likely effect on unit costs of granting each of the claims. One can presume, therefore, that they believed the temporal changes would cost them less than would the granting of some of the other demands. This, though, does not justify any suggestion that the E.E.F. was aware of how little the changes would cost. Given their members' hostility to reductions in standard times and their persistent overestimation of the cost of introducing changes of this nature, their estimates would almost certainly have been overly pessimistic. It is more likely, therefore, that when granting these claims they were simply making those concessions they had estimated would cost them least. This is not conspiracy, it is rather part of the normal collective-bargaining process. As suggested earlier, in this type of bargaining both participants invariably first concede those claims they believe will cost them least. In the case of the 1979 dispute, the cost simply proved to be less than both the unions and the employers had expected.

In conclusion, it needs to be added that proof of the negligible cost of the temporal changes would not necessarily convince employers that their introduction was a favourable development. The majority of capitalists, with their firm belief in the profitability of long worktimes, would invariably respond with the assertion that if the workers could intensify their efforts under the shorter schedule, they could also have done so under the longer one, and thus even more output could be produced. Given this approach to the question of worktime, British engineering employers might well be pleased to see the standard returned to 40 hours or, if possible, even longer.

CHAPTER 4

The rationalisation of worktime

To show that the accelerated rate at which working times have fallen during the twentieth century has been accompanied by higher levels of work intensity and that much of the gain workers have attained by the temporal reduction has been offset by the greater intensity of modern working times raises the question of how such rapid intensification was brought about. This issue will now be looked at, and it will be argued that the crucial factor inducing this development has been the rationalisation of the production process that has occurred this century. The term "rationalisation" originated in Germany and was defined by the Committee on Industry of the World Economic Conference held in Geneva in 1927 as

the methods of technique and of organisation designed to secure the minimum waste of either effort or material. It includes the scientific organisation of labour, standardisation both of material and of products, simplification of processes and improvements in the system of transport and marketing. (League of Nations 1927: 41)

In the United States the essence of this movement was known as scientific management or Taylorism. It is the contention of this work that Taylorism was a phenomenon that has been greatly misunderstood and its significance underrated by modern scholars. The extent to which the rationalisation process proved to be a powerful force rejuvenating a decaying capitalism has not been sufficiently appreciated. This failure, it needs to be added, was not shared by the labour and socialist movements of the 1920s, the period during which scientific management became established as an international phenomenon. It is common knowledge that Lenin gave a qualified endorsement to Taylorism in 1918. It is not generally recognised, however, that Lenin's action was replicated by working-class leaders throughout the world during the 1920s. During this period both reformists and revolutionaries such as Gramsci became firm advocates of the widest possible development of the positive elements within scientific management. In part, this chapter and the next will attempt to explain why this was so.

The need for system

As argued earlier, the period of economic decay that followed the end of the long boom of 1850–1873 stimulated the development of the monopoly sector, imperialism, mechanisation and strong labour and socialist movements in a number of nations. With the exception of the last, these developments were particularly significant in the United States. The greatly expanded size of U.S. corporations enabled them to exercise a significant degree of control over the market. This control was used to restrict the degree of competition experienced by these firms, which saw in collusion and the restriction of production a more attractive means of obtaining an acceptable rate of profit than the traditional method of increasing efficiency (Veblen 1921). The enhanced size of the firm, however, created major problems for this strategy. Large-scale production required a dramatic expansion in the volume of overheads. Growth of these fixed costs meant it was necessary for the corporations to operate at a high level of capacity if an adequate rate of profit was to be attained.

The growth in the size of the firm also created difficulties with labour control, a problem which tended to be compounded by the growth of the union movement, which not only expanded in size and strength but also, as Hobsbawm (1964) has put it, came to understand the rules of the game . In particular the workers became aware that, given the existing wage system, there was little to be gained by working harder. This was because capitalists believed that the buying and selling of labour power was a "zero-sum game" in which a gain to the employee was necessarily a loss to the employer. A fair day's wage was normally taken by the latter as being given by the customary time wages paid in the locality. The fixing of piece rates was also based on the area norm, as was the amount of labour required to earn this wage. Piece rates, moreover, were frequently cut if wages rose much above those paid on time rates. Employers considered that rate cutting was essential if their firms were to remain competitive. Workers, however, responded with hostility to this policy, vehemently resisted the introduction of incentive-based wage systems and invariably concealed the degree of effort they were capable of sustaining. The employers responded, in turn, by demanding that piece work be accepted and used repression to "drive" the workers. This approach to the wage—effort bargain meant that the workers had no interest in raising productivity. Indeed, given that higher individual output probably meant a cut in rates, harder work and possibly layoffs, they had every interest in restricting its growth. Over the long term the end result of these developments was a decline in the rate of productivity growth, an increase in the organic composition of capital and a decline in the rate of profit (Gillman 1957).

In the United States it was these problems that gave rise to the systematic-management movement during the 1880s. The "systemisers" were a diverse group of engineers, accountants and works managers who argued that U.S. firms had grown to a size where the internal functioning of the enterprise was becoming increasingly chaotic and wasteful. Traditional management methods with their crude approach to the problems of organising, controlling, developing and administering the firm's resources, it was insisted, were not suitable for highly mechanised and concentrated forms of production."Method" and system, these theorists argued, had to replace the improvisation associated with traditional management practices (Litterer 1963; Haber 1964). The growth of the systemisation movement was closely associated with the rise of accountants and industrial engineers to positions of prominence within industry. In the last half of the nineteenth century accountancy ceased being a mere record of past events and developed into an applied science designed to provide management with an increasing degree of control over production and distribution. Likewise engineers, who had come to replace their traditional rule-of-thumb methods with an increasing emphasis on exact calculation and measurement, expanded their horizons during this period to the organisation of production. As the decline in the rate of profit continued, the influence of these technicians expanded. Large firms found that to an increasing extent they needed the technicians' services if they were to survive. With most employers, though, the wider arguments of the systemisers were largely ignored, price fixing and established management methods being considered more attractive. In only a small number of firms were the technicians given sufficient scope to show what they could achieve.

Scientific management

Of those technicians who took up the quest of systemising the production process the greatest and most influential was without doubt Frederick Winslow Taylor. As the "father of scientific management," Taylor pulled together the diverse influences attempting to induce the greater use of scientific method in industry. In the process he radically accelerated the development of the systematic-management movement along lines that changed not only the workplace but the whole nature of modern industrialised society. When asked to define what he meant by scientific management Taylor used to reply that it involved a mental revolution. He meant by this that it could not be defined by method alone but also involved a new attitude of mind.

It meant that the methods developed over a century of industrial life by rule of thumb and tradition could not, for that reason, be accepted without question. The whole situation in any undertaking, in any trade, must be re-examined, with the detachment from preconceptions, the intellectual technique, and the integrity to truth of a worker in the exact sciences. (Urwick 1930: 26)

Taylor believed that his systematic approach to the problems of management provided a means by which productivity, wages and profits could be boosted radically. He also believed it was able to provide something of even greater importance. This was a means of easing the intensity of the struggle between the classes. What workers wanted from their employer above all, he argued, was high wages, and what the employer wanted from the worker was labour power at a price that would lower the cost of production. These two conditions, he insisted, were not diametrically opposed. On the contrary, they could be made to go together with all forms of work if both employer and worker turned their attention from the division of the spoils of production and concentrated instead on applying science to increasing the magnitude of the output and surplus. The increase in productivity this would make possible would be so large that all major sources of friction between employer and worker could be overcome. There were, he suggested, two primary obstacles preventing this goal from being attained.

The chief causes which produce this loss to both parties are: First, and by far the most important: The profound ignorance of employers and their foremen as to the time in which various kinds of work should be done (and this ignorance is shared largely by the workmen). . . . Second: Their indifference and ignorance as to the proper system to adopt and the method of applying it, and as to the individual character, worth, and welfare, of their men. . . . On the part of the men the greatest obstacle to the attainment of this standard is the slow pace which they adopt, or the loafing, soldiering or marking time, as it is called. (Taylor 1903: 1348–1349)

Taylor and the workers

To overcome these obstacles, Taylor argued, employers needed to take steps to increase their knowledge, of exactly what was the most effective means of undertaking any task and to determine precisely how much work their employees were capable of sustaining. Because employers did not have such knowledge they had no accurate way of knowing whether they were receiving a fair return for the wages they paid. Consequently, when subjected to pressure from competitors, they were invariably tempted, by the possibility of lower wage costs, to cut rates. They thus undermined their own incentive schemes. It was not possible to rely on the workers' goodwill to ensure they provided a fair day's work, Taylor insisted, because workers were both naturally indolent and subject to the pressure of social-effort norms which they had to maintain if their wages were not to be reduced. Given their circumstances, Taylor believed that the actions of both the employers and the workers were perfectly rational. He was convinced, however, that if profits and real wages were to be improved it was imperative that these practices be eliminated. As intensity levels could not be left to the workers to determine, employers had to be given greater control over these norms. The key to attaining this greater control was accurate knowledge of all aspects of the production process including the limits to human capacities.

At an abstract level Taylor's means of providing the employers with the knowledge he believed they needed was, as Kelly has put it, "striking in its simplicity." He proposed that employers utilise the methods of science to carefully measure what workers actually did and utilise the information thus obtained to develop the "one best way" of working (Kelly 1982: 8). Taylor's method for attaining the knowledge he required involved first the detailed study and recording of all aspects of the production process; second, the systemisation of this data into a form which would make it possible for the design of jobs to be undertaken by technicians away from the shop floor; third, the accurate determination of optimum standards of performance for worker and machine; fourth, the redesign of all jobs to a form which maximised the employer's control over all aspects of the production process.

Both to make the introduction of significant increases in the pace of work possible and because he believed it was morally correct that workers be given a share of the rewards generated by increased productivity, Taylor also urged employers to adopt a more positive approach to the payment of high wages.

If . . . you expect your workmen to work very much harder than they do on Day Work (and my experience is that the greatest gain is to be made by increasing the pace of all your men) then you must recognize the fact that workmen will not double their rate of speed for the same wages for which they will work by the day. My experience is that it is necessary to pay them on Piece Work from 25 to 50 per cent more than they get on Day Work in order to stimulate them to their maximum. (Copley 1969: 13)

If employers used his methods, Taylor argued, they would be able to ascertain just how much labour workers were capable of undertaking. This knowledge would permit the establishment of incentive systems that would induce workers to increase the intensity of their labour time but would not raise wages so high that employers would be encourged to cut piece rates.

After his death Taylor was to come in for a great deal of criticism for his concentration on financial reward as the worker's primary motivator. He was accused of ignoring human relations and the fact that the worker was a social being who was capable of responding to factors other than money. The search for these other motivators which would satisfy human needs and make the worker happier and more productive was to become a major element in industrial psychology. Indeed, the overwhelming bulk of incentive studies have, since the 1930s, downgraded money as a motivator and have had as their primary objective the discovery of nonfinancial ways to increase worker productivity. This is despite the fact that money can be shown to be a very effective motivator and that "no generalizable, functional, replicable relationship between workers' satisfactions and their productivity has yet been found" (Macarov 1982: 119). The search for other motivators is simply based on the assumption, unproved, that a happier worker will be willing to work harder. The "satisfier equals motivator" assumption, Macarov has argued, is almost incredibly naive. Yet despite this, and despite their continued failure, employers and industrial psychologists continue to pour money and effort into research based on this assumption. This is primarily because capitalists have never been happy with having to accept that those such as Taylor who insisted that a high-intensity work process necessitated high wages were correct; that if the workers are to be motivated to increase the amount of effort they put into their work they have to be paid for it. Employers consequently have continued to finance those human-relations schools which have attempted to find new ways by which the amount of labour taken from the worker can be increased without its having to be paid for. As part of this process these "scientists" have attempted to denigrate Taylor by de-emphasising his belief in the moral and technical necessity of paying high wages. Instead, they have stressed his high-handed and often insensitive attitude to workers. That Taylor was often authoritarian and even repressive is not to be denied, but at least he was willing, unlike these individuals, to pay the workers for what he took from them.

Scientific management has also been accused of being an instrument for the systematic deskilling of the working class and of being a tool for strengthening the power of employers. Braverman (1974), for example, argued that the widespread application of Taylorism through the twentieth century has enabled employers to all but totally degrade the nature of work. His argument, however, has been challenged by numerous scholars. It has been pointed out that although the utilisation of scientific methods in the design of jobs certainly did increase capital's ability to deskill many tasks, this was not a unilateral tendency. In many cases the skill content of jobs, both old and new, has tended to expand through the century (Elger 1979). Often this enrichment has been a direct consequence of the rationalisation process.

Kelly (1982) has gone even further and challenged the claim that scientific management was a cause of deskilling. The fact that the methods pioneered by Taylor were often used by capitalists for this purpose, he has pointed out, does not mean deskilling was necessarily an inherent element of Taylorism. Likewise, the fact that employers and indeed Taylor himself saw his techniques as tools which could be utilised to undermine the power of workers to determine shop-floor standards and methods of work does not mean they necessarily had to be used for this purpose. How the results of the scientific study of the labour process were utilised was a question of struggle between capital and labour. There is no reason to presume that only employers stood to gain from this research. In other words, if guided in certain directions, the power of workers to advance their demands could possibly also gain sustenance from the rigorous application of scientific method within industry.

Because Taylor and many of the practitioners of his methods utilised their skills to enhance the control enjoyed by employers, many observers have argued that scientific management's claim that it has a scientific base has no substance. Braverman, for example, argued that scientific management lacked the characteristics of a true science because its assumptions reflected nothing more than the outlook of the employer as regards the conditions of production. "It enters the workplace not as the representative of science, but as the representative of management masquerading in the trappings of science" (Braverman 1974: 86). Assertions of this nature, however, constitute a mirror image of Taylor's unjustified claim that his use of scientific method in industry was always value free and neutral in its implications for the different classes of society. In short, it confuses essence with execution. Paraphrasing Marx, it assumes that any utilisation of the techniques of scientific management other than the capitalist one is impossible (Marx 1976: 569). This is all but equivalent to suggesting that because physics has repeatedly been utilised in forms opposed to the interests of the working class it is inherently exploitative. Braverman's perspective should be contrasted with that of Lenin, who recognised that Taylorism could be utilised by employers to enhance their control over labour but also realised that scientific management did have a scientific core which, if developed correctly, could advance the interests of the working class (Lenin 1947: 327).

Taylor and technical knowledge

Another misconception that is common in the modern literature is that scientific management was not particularly concerned with advancing technical knowledge. Braverman, for example, argued that Taylorism's contribution to the development of technology was minor. He has difficulty sustaining this position, however, for his honesty compels him to acknowledge that Taylor alone made a number of significant contributions to the technical knowledge of machine-shop practice. To maintain his position Braverman (1974: 85) is forced to claim that Taylor's innovations were merely "by-products" of his efforts to expand the employer's control over labour.

Burawoy (1985), in his attempt to define Taylorism as narrowly as possible so that he can then justify dismissing its significance, goes even further than did Braverman. A primary objective in Burawoy's work has been to expand the subjective factors in Braverman's *Labour and Monopoly Capital*, which he correctly observes were not given sufficient emphasis. In his eagerness to stress the importance of these subjective elements, particularly the role played by ideology and class conflict, however, he fails to adequately consider those material and technical aspects of Taylorism which, as will be shown, were central to its nature. As a consequence, in many ways his work obscures more than it reveals of the real nature of scientific management.

Burawoy's singular concentration on subjective factors leads him, for example, to criticise Braverman for conceding that Taylor did make some significant technical contributions to the production process. Taylor's work in this area, he asserts, was not fundamental, because "the intervention of scientific management perfected tasks already defined rather than reorganising the division of labour" (Burawoy 1985: 40). Burawoy does not bother to explain or attempt to sustain this assessment but quickly refocuses his attention on the issues of labour control and ideology.

Fortunately, this blindness to the importance of Taylorism's technical contribution has not afflicted all those who have contributed to the revived debate on the labour process. Kelly (1982: 6), for example, has argued that the tendency of many scholars to concentrate only on the issue of labour control has detracted from and obscured the important role Taylor's technical work played in the raising of labour and machine output. He notes that this narrow perspective has led many observers to see in Taylorism little more than a combination of time study and wage incentives. Such an assessment ignores the detailed nature of the Taylorists' research and the breadth of their approach to the problems of production. Taylor, for example, made significant contributions to the systemisation of the production process in the areas of accounting, stores management, purchase, standardisation and plant design and layout. He also developed a number of important new products the most significant of which was high-speed steel. Outside the workplace he was involved in the development of government administration, city planning and the restructuring of institutions of higher education. In his study of the engineering profession Layton (1971: 135) has concluded that so extensive were Taylor's technical contributions that, even had he not pioneered the development of management science, his joint discovery of high-speed steel, his research with metal cutting and his many other engineering innovations would have been sufficient to make him famous.

Kelly has also pointed out that the *systematic* nature of scientific management has tended to be overlooked: that as his research advanced Taylor came to place increasing emphasis on organisation as the key element determining the efficiency of the production process. This point has been endorsed by Meiksins (1984), who has observed that Taylor's ideal programme of systemisation involved much more than just the regulation of the workers' labour time. It involved the application of the scientific method to the realms of organisation, administration, distribution and indeed all areas in which a systematic approach to problem solving was beneficial. The first step in his plan for organising a workshop was always the improvement and standardisation of tools, machinery and equipment together with the systemisation and planning of the workplace. This last step invariably involved the introduction of more efficient storage systems, cost-accounting procedures and the establishment of a system of routine maintenance and repair. Once these "preliminary" steps had been undertaken – and he suggested this could be expected to take about a year – the scientific manager was then to turn to the task of reorganising the management of workplace activities. Central to this process was the establishment of a Planning Department which was responsible for organising and controlling the flow of production throughout the workplace. As Meiksins correctly observes:

The Taylor system, then, while it did involve time study and incentive wages, was really a program for the overall reorganization of the shop. In general terms, it placed control over virtually all shop activities in the hands of a centralised planning department directed by engineers. (Meiksins 1984: 181)

In Taylor's early works the planning department had been known as the rate-fixing department. It is crucial that the exact nature of this change of name be noted, for it signifies the dramatic maturation in Taylor's conception of what was required in the production process that was to give his work so much significance. The planning of production within the firm was, of course, not a totally new idea in industry. Managers had always, to some extent, planned and supervised the production process. Indeed, many of Taylor's planning and control mechanisms were taken from established shops. What made his contribution unique was the degree to which his commitment to the systemisation of management increased industry's capacity to effectively plan the production process. As Person (1929: 81) has observed:

[Taylor] integrated mechanisms into an interlocking whole, and the degree to which planning and precise control were developed by him was so great in quantity as to create a new qualitative situation. Planning generally had not been effective because it was based on so many chance factors. Now, with the aid of standardization, calculations could be made with a fair degree of certainty. This made possible the planning-room procedures of routing, scheduling and complete and economical utilization of facilities. It was this precise control through planning and preparation which secured most of the results of increased productivity by eliminating idle times and misapplied efforts, which are the result of many different causes under uncontrolled conditions.

The centrality of planning in Taylor's work was stressed by Alfred Marshall (1927) in his analysis of the nature of scientific management. The point has also been eloquently expressed by Tugwell and Banfield (1951: 133).

In the early eighties of the last century Frederick Winslow Taylor was a young man working in the shops of Midvale Steel. Through a series of accidental changes in a life which might normally have followed a more routine middle-class course, he had become a foreman. He was, however, a new species of that all-important animal. For he did not believe in foremanship, at least of the old-fashioned kind, and almost at once he set out to displace the foreman's rule of thumb with a scientifically arrived at "one-best-way." He intended to reduce the functions of the shop to clearly and precisely stated locations, quantities of materials, forces applied, motions to be gone through, and output to be expected. These would then be the terms in which a planning office would set out the job to be done. The directions would be precise. And foremen – in the old sense – would be eliminated. He called it, later on, scientific management. Actually it was planning.

The argument that what made Taylor's work so significant was his contribution to the development of systematic and rational methods for planning the efficient utilisation of resources was made by Tugwell throughout his life. This scholar was an institutional political economist who was convinced that the domination of production and the state by business condemned the human race to scarcity. In Taylorism he recognised the existence of tools that had the potential to overcome this situation. For this reason he argued that "the greatest economic event of the nineteenth century occurred when Frederick W. Taylor first held a stop watch on the movements of a group of shovellers in the plant of the Midvale Steel Company" (Tugwell 1932: 86). What made Taylor's activities at Midvale so important, Tugwell realised, was not his use of scientific method to give capitalists greater control over their employees. Rather, it was the fact that in order to do so, Taylor developed planning techniques which could enable the anarchic conditions that existed within the production process to be brought under greater *human* control. What was done with this control was of course an extremely important question. Singular concentration on this issue, however, has led many scholars to miss the point that tremendous possibilities were created by the development of these techniques. In short, in his technical contribution to the systemisation of production Taylor provided basic planning tools which, if developed, could enable human beings to gain much greater influence over market forces and thus enhance their capacity to direct and control their own history.

While generally lauding Taylor's use of scientific method in the management of resources Tugwell made two important criticisms of his work. First, he advised that it was necessary to be careful not to push too far the analogy between scientific management and science. Management, he observed, was an "industrial art" rather than an "industrial science." Taylor had consistently stressed this point. His attempt to establish rigid management principles consequently had been misguided. What was central in scientific management was not any set of fixed rules but rather the notion that "intelligence in contrivance, accuracy in measurement and willingness in adaptation can make for greater productivity" (Tugwell 1927: 128). The development of science in the management of resources, Tugwell noted, had soon outgrown the principles that Taylor had initially attempted to establish. This development, however, did not detract from the value of his original contribution, which showed the way the development of systematic planning could advance.

Taylorism served its purpose, however, in the same sense that Darwinism did. Study of the evolution of life soon outgrew any of Darwin's accounts of the means by which it took place; and intelligent management similarly outgrew Taylor's theories. We no longer call it "scientific management" usually. That term can now be seen to have been something of a misnomer. What was needed most, and what industrialists accepted after a normal period of hesitation, was the idea Taylor had that intelligence could always modify existing practice and improve upon it. By genuinely careful study, such as a laboratory scientist would employ, by exact measurement, analysis, and comparison, in a field where rule-of-thumb had been the accepted guide, and what men had traditionally done was considered to be the best, or, at least, the only possible thing, much could be done, as has been proved again and again. The idea that it could was genuinely revolutionary. (Tugwell 1927: 124)

Tugwell's second criticism of Taylor was that he had largely confined his use of scientific management to the workplace when what was needed was its extension to the entire economy in the form of a national development plan. In an address to the American Economics Association in 1932 he observed that Taylor had provided the basic technical tools that could make the construction of such a plan possible. It was only in the Soviet Union, however, that the necessary conditions thus far existed for fully realising the potential in these tools. Though a liberal who was critical of Soviet socialism because of its lack of political democracy, Tugwell was convinced that in a technical sense the future was becoming visible in the U.S.S.R. (Tugwell 1928). His interest in Soviet attempts to apply Taylorism on a national scale through the 1920s was accentuated by the onset of the depression in 1929. As the crisis deepened, this interest was shared by increasing numbers within the United States. Many of these individuals saw in the practices of the Soviet planning institutions policies which could be adapted to save capitalism from its tendency to experience periodic crises. In his 1932 address Tugwell lambasted both those who adopted this position without thinking through the difficulties involved in grafting planning onto a market economy, and those who failed to see how limited the planning mechanism would necessarily be in an economy dominated by the market. Most of these individuals, he noted, had no idea of how extensive and fundamental were the changes required to give the planning mechanism sufficient power to ensure permanent growth and stability.

Most of those who say so easily that this is our way out do not, I am convinced, understand that fundamental changes of attitude, new disciplines, revised legal structures, unaccustomed limitations on activity, are all necessary if we are to plan. This amounts, in fact, to the abandonment, finally, of laissez faire. It amounts, practically, to the abolition of "business." (Tugwell 1932: 76)

The fact that Tugwell criticised those who naively called for the introduction of economic planning without thinking through the implications of their demand did not mean he rejected the possibility of introducing some degree of planning in market economies. Rather, he insisted that a certain degree of planning was not only possible in these societies but that very important advances could be had if this was done. The gains thus obtained, however, would be of a limited nature compared with what could be attained under a system of comprehensive planning. He likened the benefits possible with limited planning to those accruing to an industry which systemised and mechanised certain elements in the production process. The benefits attained by this procedure, while impressive, were limited compared with those which could be had when all the elements had been rationalised and, more important, when they had been linked together to make a total process. Similarly, important gains could be had by rationalising separate sectors of an economy, but this process must eventually end in the return of economic crisis unless the final step of linking these various sectors into a single system was taken. What was required to bring about this linking is a national plan.

Tugwell was convinced, however, that the conditions that would be necessary to attain this final goal had not yet been established in the United States. He therefore supported the introduction of limited planning wherever this was possible on the pragmatic grounds that such steps could provide some immediate improvement in living standards and economic security. He also advocated this policy because he believed that the introduction of a limited form of planning would establish the conditions that would eventually make possible the attainment of a planned economy. The primary obstacle to the attainment of this latter goal, he believed, was political rather than technical. It was the employers' control of the means of production and their vested interest in ensuring the continuance of a market economy and the dominance of the profit motive. In the drive for profit, however, he recognised a contradiction. National planning of production, he argued, was the deadliest and most subtle enemy of the profit motive. Nevertheless, employer bodies were being compelled by their need to maintain profitability to agree to its limited introduction. Thus the Chamber of Commerce of the United States had come to accept, however grudgingly, the formation of a National Economic Council. Tugwell realised that the employers had taken this step because they could see that they stood to gain from the existence of such a body and because they believed it would have no real power and certainly that it would not be able to plan effectively.

He also realised that this assessment was correct; however, he insisted that the establishment of such organisations was crucial for creating the conditions that would make the introduction of a planned economy possible. In their daily activities such bodies would demonstrate what could be attained with order and rationality; moreover, the existence of such bodies would "be a constant reminder that once business was sick to death and that it will be again" (Tugwell 1932: 84). For although limited planning could achieve significant improvements, the essential problems, caused by allowing the pursuit of profit to be the primary motivating force in the economy, would remain unresolved. Eventually, as the limits of piecemeal planning were reached, the profit motive would again lead society into crisis. This crisis, however, would occur in a different environment. It would be one in which people had experienced the benefits to be had from planning, even of a partial nature. In such an environment the position of those who supported the continued existence of a market system would be seriously undermined. For this reason, Tugwell was convinced, the acceptance of partial planning by the owners of the means of production had ensured the eventual demise of capitalism, a fate which would be long and lingering but which would be inevitable. When this inevitability was realised, the potential within Taylorism to provide human beings with the capacity to guide their own history towards consciously foreseen ends would at last be able to be realised. Hence:

The setting up of even an emasculated and ineffective central co-ordinating body in Washington will form a focus about which recognition may gradually gather. It will be an action as significant as the first observations of Taylor; and it can lead eventually to the completion and crowning of that genius' work. (Tugwell 1932: 88)

Taylor and the employers

One final aspect of the contemporary literature on Taylor's work deserves comment before we move on to discuss the rationalisation of working time. This is the failure of most observers to consider adequately his criticisms of what he considered the primary obstacle to greater industrial efficiency: poor management. Taylor was very much aware that the market was not always a sufficiently effective mechanism for ensuring that employers invested sufficient effort and capital to ensure they were utilising the most efficient methods of production (Taylor 1903: 1340–1343). Any doubt he may have had on this score would certainly have been dispelled by the reception employers gave to his ideas. In general, he met either lack of interest or active hostility. The correct use of Taylor's programme necessitated extensive research by highly trained and experienced technicians. For the average firm this research and its subsequent implementation normally took two to four years. The adoption of his system also necessitated the commitment of a significant amount of capital and the introduction of major changes to the traditional pattern of authority within the firm. The existing linear hierarchy utilised by most enterprises, he suggested, had to be replaced by a system of functional management based on specific expertise. Within this system each foreman or manager would control only that aspect of the production process for which the individual had special training and expert knowledge. This specialisation was to be combined with an "exception" principle in which, at each level of management, the responsible person would receive information about exceptions to routine but not about everyday performance. Executives were not to be omitted from this specialisation. They were expected to cease involving themselves in those aspects of the daily running of the firm for which they had not been specifically trained and confine themselves to those areas in which they did have a high degree of expertise (Filipetti 1946: 42).

The reorganisation of management practices, Taylor insisted, would enable a much higher degree of efficiency to be attained. It necessarily involved, however, a significant shift in power from the traditional manager to the technician. This attempt to limit the scope of the individual manager's authority alienated many employers and was strongly resisted even by those who did make some attempt to reorganise their production methods by utilising Taylor's techniques.

Taylor's conclusion was that this was the greatest problem in organization. These men have been given or have acquired power, they have obtained their positions because of unusual force of character, they are accustomed to directing rather than in being directed, and their managerial methods, as far as they can see, have been successful, so they can see no reason for changing them. (Filipetti 1946: 35)

Indeed, Taylor and his supporters found that initially employers in general had little interest in the wider aspects of their plans for raising industrial efficiency. Their ignorance and indifference to the introduction of more efficient management methods led them to refuse to consider the level of personnel and economic investment Taylor's strategy necessitated. They invariably demanded, moreover, immediate results and refused to countenance the undermining of their traditional prerogatives. As Filipetti put it:

The . . . points, that time and money needed to be spent to realize the ends sought, were essentials that were not accepted by many of those who started shop reorganization. Too many were impatient for results; too many wanted something for nothing, the very thing that they, themselves, denied anyone had a right to expect. (1946: 34)

Employers, rather, tended to regard scientific management as merely a technique making the utilisation of incentive wage systems more effective. In short, they equated Taylorism merely with time study and payment by results. Indeed, they even attempted to achieve this aspect of the total system on the cheap. As time study and work study became popular, many untrained "efficiency experts" offered their services on the market. Most of these individuals sold cut-price wage systems that were nothing more than crude attempts to speed up the pace of work while offering the worker little, if anything, in return. The employers' wide use of these bargain-priced experts was to make the labour movement even more hostile and resistant to any form of wage system that involved incentives (Louden and Deegan 1959: 3–13).

Scientific management and worktime

The elimination of effort restriction should be supported by the workers, Taylor insisted, not only because they would receive higher wages but also because they would be able to enjoy improved home and working conditions and because they would gain more free time (Taylor 1917: 15). Taylor was convinced that there were laws governing the relationship between work and fatigue. Though he was unsuccessful in specifying the nature of these laws, being forced consequently to introduce arbitrary percentages for rest periods into his standard times, he spent many years undertaking research into the relationship among work, time and effort (Layton 1974: 378). One aspect of worktime that Taylor did recognise correctly was that workers were often forced to labour for excessively long periods and that as a result much of the workers' capacity to undertake productive work was wasted, for it was consumed simply by their having to be at work. Taylor and his associates were aware of the fatigue studies undertaken in Europe towards the end of the nineteenth century which showed that it was possible to reduce standard times without necessarily reducing output. Taylor believed that where such a situation existed the length of time the workers were compelled to labour should be reduced. This curtailment was to be part of a complete reorganisation of all aspects of production. If this was done, and if intensity levels were raised as the temporal reduction was introduced, it would be possible to thereby discover the balance of time and intensity which was most efficient.

An example of Taylor's approach to the determination and implementation of optimum worktimes was his experience at raising the output of women employed to inspect ball bearings at the Simonds Rolling Machine Company. Taylor reports that in this firm 120 women were employed for 10.5 hours per day inspecting bearings for defects. After conducting a study of this task, he concluded that the working day was too long because of the high degree of concentration and attention that had to be sustained. He suggested that although there was little physical effort involved in the work, the "nervous tension" required was too high for a workday of this length. The work, his assistant Sandford E. Thompson reported, was hard on the workers, for it was "very confining, and it was difficult to maintain order . . . because they very naturally became tired before the day was done" (Nelson 1980: 73–74). Taylor concluded that because of the fatigue induced by the long hours much of the workers' labour time was wasted. Therefore, he suggested to the women that they should have their workday shortened without a cut in pay. Taylor allowed the workers to vote on this proposition. They did not respond in the way he expected. The women were unanimous that not only did they not want any reduction in the length of time they worked, they wanted none of Taylor's innovations. He responded to this decision by compulsorily shortening the workday while holding wages constant (Taylor 1917: 86–88). The first reduction shortened the workday to 9.5 hours, and a five-minute break was introduced in the morning and afternoon. A month later he further reduced the workday to 8.5 hours and extended the breaks to ten minutes (Nelson 1980: 73–74). With each reduction, Taylor reports, output increased. Indeed, the curtailment in worktime and the heightened supervision, improved organisation, layout, selection and incentives eventually enabled 35 women to do the work previously done by 120 (Taylor 1917: 95).

When reducing the worktime of the women Taylor retained the half-day Saturday so that the workers continued to labour 5.5 days per week. He recommended, moreover, that the women – indeed he suggested all young women workers – should be given two consecutive days of rest per month (with pay) to be taken whenever they chose (Taylor 1917: 96). These worktime aspects of Taylor's research during the 1890s enabled Taylorists to argue justifiably that their mentor was a pioneer in this area. "Mr. Taylor was one of the first to recognize and to prove the fact that overlong working hours are not conducive to high output, and that in very many cases hours of work may be sharply decreased to a certain point and output increased simultaneously" (Farquar 1924: 40).

Taylor's interest in rational worktime schedules, however, was actively shared by few of the engineers who took up scientific management prior to the First World War. Apart from Taylor's own contributions, the literature of the scientific managers before this time contains few examples of scientific investigations of worktimes or, indeed, studies of physical or social working conditions in general. In practice the engineers had little interest in the role of the "human factor" in industry. By this term was meant "the degree of *capacity* and *willingness* to produce exhibited by any set of human workers" (Florence 1924a: 97). Rather, they tended to stress those aspects of Taylor's work which they believed employers would find most attractive. As far as the worker was concerned, they generally assumed that additional income and the enmeshing of workers in a system of tighter management control by the use of a more intense division of labour and greater discipline and regimentation would solve the "labour problem." Apart from the development of time study and wage incentives, in other words, the engineers were much more interested in the technical than in the human problems of production. Most of these individuals, initially at least, displayed an almost total lack of concern for the effect the introduction of their techniques had on the worker and had little interest in those aspects of their research pertaining to social justice. These aspects of Taylorism were taken up by few of the engineers active in the scientific-management movement until the cost of ignoring them was forced to their attention by the labour movement, progressive employers and social reformers.

In making the claim that the engineers generally failed to take up the worktime aspects of Taylor's research prior to the war, it is not being suggested that his work in this area had no influence before this period. His research greatly influenced those activists within the "Progressive Movement" who were attempting to reform many aspects of society (Haber 1964). Taylor and other scientific managers, for example, actively collaborated with those progressives such as Brandeis and Goldmark who campaigned for the enactment of laws which would place limits on the length of the working day. Indeed, it was Brandeis who coined the term "scientific management." In the U.S.A. worktime laws had traditionally been considered unconstitutional, as they supposedly breached the right to freedom of contract. During the nineteenth century the only major exception the Supreme Court had allowed to its ban on such laws was where the nature of the work to be regulated was particularly dangerous. In 1908 Brandeis achieved a breakthrough which partly overcame this legal barrier. He was approached by his sister-in-law Josephine Goldmark, on behalf of the National Consumers' League, and asked to defend, in the Supreme Court, an Oregon law which sought to establish a 10-hour working day for women. Brandeis accepted the brief on the condition that he represent the State Government and that the league provide him with scientific data on the effects of worktime on females. These conditions were agreed to and Goldmark contracted to work with Brandeis on preparing the brief.

In presenting his case Brandeis chose largely to ignore abstract constitutional and political arguments as to whether a legal limit to the workday constituted an infringement on the individual's life, liberty or property. Rather, he chose to base his argument on the fact that there were many international precedents for such laws and on the scientific evidence showing the relationship between human psycho-physiological capacities, worktime and the rising intensity of work (Brandeis and Goldmark 1908). As Haber (1964: 81) has put it, like Taylor "Brandeis, based his law on facts." Faced with the mass of data compiled by the Consumers' League the Court upheld the constitutional validity of Oregon's legislation.

Following his victory Brandeis argued a similar brief in a number of state courts. These cases were fought out over a number of years. In 1915, however, he was named to the Supreme Court. At the time he and Goldmark were preparing a brief, again for Oregon, in support of a 10-hour law for men. The Consumers' League then approached Felix Frankfurter, who agreed to take on this work without fee. Frankfurter also continued Brandeis's collaboration with Goldmark and with Frederick Taylor. The brief that was subsequently produced in support of the Oregon law was based on the work of the Taylorists and on European and American fatigue researchers. It was over one thousand pages long and it gathered together a vast mass of information on every aspect of worktime (Frankfurter and Goldmark 1915). It contained comprehensive tables on worktime legislation in both the United States and other nations and it presented virtually all the known data on the psycho-physiological, social and economic factors the rationalisers insisted made necessary a legal limit to the length of the workday. In its determination the Court conceded the validity of this evidence and ruled that worktime laws for men were not at variance with the constitution.

Taylor's worktime research was also of importance prior to the war in that it greatly influenced the work of those physiologists, psychologists and economists undertaking research into the relationship between fatigue and industrial efficiency. As reported in Chapter 1 of this volume, for example, the spread of scientific management through industry had been a significant factor influencing the British Association for the Advancement of Science to establish a select committee to study the economics of fatigue. In general, the fatigue researchers found Taylor's work fascinating. The efforts of Schmidt, the Pennsylvania iron worker, were even more widely publicised in the psychology literature than they were in that of the engineers. Taylor's attempts to determine scientific laws that would enable him to calculate the balance of work and rest that would maximise production were seen by these individuals to be similar, in a number of respects, to their own research. Also, his insistence that all of a worker's movements not strictly necessary for the completion of a given task be eliminated appealed to those wishing to avoid "useless wasted effort" (Myers 1920: 3–35). It was their attempt to establish conditions of work which were based on scientific analysis, Muscio (1917) observed, that differentiated the scientific managers' means of increasing the intensity of worktime from simple speed-up.

The fatigue researchers' enthusiasm for Taylor's ideas, however, was severely tempered by the engineers' general failure to adequately emphasise and apply sufficient scientific rigour to the study of the human factor in industry. If scientific management was to achieve its potential in this area, they insisted, it was essential that this situation be remedied. It was argued that two central factors were required. First was a more rigorous application of the scientific method to the study of the human factor. This necessarily had to involve the close alliance and collaboration of the industrial psychologists and the engineers. The latter, it was insisted, needed the knowledge only trained psychologists and physiologists could provide. The scientific managers did not have this knowledge and so their work with the human factor lacked any strong scientific base. Muensterberg (1913: 56), for example, accused Taylor of being guilty of "helpless psychological dilettantism" and insisted that it was the psychologists' duty to come to the aid of the engineer. If this were not done, the engineers, precisely because they were engineers, who by training were conditioned to work with machinery, would treat the workers as machines.

The second factor necessary for the complete realisation of scientific management's potential, it was argued, was acceptance of the need for integrating the unions and collective bargaining into the rationalisation movement. Trade unions, it was argued, could play an important role in convincing workers that they stood to gain by the introduction of scientific method into the management of the production process. Trade unions were also necessary, it was suggested, to prevent employers from misusing the techniques of scientific management. That employers would need to be pressured, either by the unions or the state, if they and the workers were to gain the full benefits of Taylorism was, for example, argued by Goldmark (1919: 209–210). She insisted that if this did not occur scientific management would be "perverted," the human factor would be largely ignored and the higher wages and reduced worktimes she believed were so necessary would not be introduced. A similar position was put forward by British critics. These latter individuals welcomed the technical contribution of the Taylorists but warned that scientific management had the potential to inflict acute distress upon the working class. For this reason they insisted that its development had to be accompanied by the growth of a strong, independent labour movement able to influence effectively the way in which Taylor's tools were utilised. As Cole (1928: 77) put it:

Time-study, motion-study, and the other expedients of Scientific Management may have some beneficent results, especially in such spheres as the study of industrial fatigue and the relation of output to hours of labour. But here again science must not be the monopoly of the management or of the employer. The Trade Unions must equip themselves with the knowledge that is required, and "science" must become the handmaid of collective bargaining.

Prior to the First World War the Taylorists, with few exceptions, were hostile and extremely critical of trade unions, believing them to be self-seeking bodies opposed to the public good. As Taylor believed he had found the natural laws governing work and production, he considered trade union demands that they be given a say as to how the production process should be managed to be "interference" with these laws and with science. This animosity was soon reciprocated and, during the five years after 1910, the American unions fought bitterly the employers' narrow use of scientific management in the workplace (McKelvey 1952; Nadworny 1955). The basis of labour's opposition, even where employers were willing to pay higher wages for greater work intensity, was, first, the Taylorists' common practice of "diluting" craft workers' jobs so that some of their work could be given to less skilled employees and women, and, second, the fear that wage incentives would lead to such an increase in the intensity of labour time that workers would be crippled. Extra wages in the short term were not very attractive, it was argued, if the long-term consequence was an early death. As Samuel Gompers (1911: 117) put it, "science would thus get the most out of you before you are sent to the junk-pile." The opposition of the unions was sufficient to induce Congress in 1915 to forbid the use of stop watches in army workshops. Criticism of Taylorism by the skilled unionists, indeed, was so violent "that even the employers who were the most favourable to it dared only experiment in secret for fear of disturbances or strikes" (Devinat 1926: 466).

The war and scientific management

In the immediate pre-1917 period the labour movement's resistance to Taylorism led a number of the more liberal scientific managers to begin reappraising their attitude towards the trade unions (Nadworny 1955: 97–121). This reappraisal was made easier by the death of Taylor in 1915. It was also aided by the beginnings of a tentative re-examination by some unions of what scientific management had to offer. The benefits that systematic management of the production process could bring to the worker in the form of higher wages, improved working conditions and shorter working times appeared very tempting to some union leaders and to many workers. What the unions wanted in return for their co-operation in introducing the new techniques, however, was a say as to how and where they were to be utilised and how the benefits were to be distributed (McKelvey 1952: 21). What they wanted if they were to have scientific management, in other words, was collective bargaining and the right to retain some control over the production process.

Prior to the First World War, then, there was within the United States a slow, even if weak, convergence of the attitudes of some of the scientific managers and some of the leaders of the trade union movement. This convergence coincided with, indeed was partly induced by, a growing awareness on the part of the scientific managers of the validity of many of the criticisms made against them by the industrial psychologists. This was to induce some of the leading Taylorists, most notably Frank and Lillian Gilbreth, to begin taking a much more rigorous approach to the human factor and particularly to the study of fatigue (Gilbreth and Gilbreth 1916).

The war acted as a tremendous stimulant to the expansion of scientific management. It made it necessary for U.S. industry to maximise production while at the same time it generated an acute labour shortage which strengthened the labour movement. The dilemma caused by these combined factors motivated both the state and an increasing number of private employers to turn to the Taylorists. Most of the leaders of the movement became involved in the planning and development of war production, and this enabled them to gain a rare opportunity to test and display their techniques on a large scale. The need for maximum production also acted as a dramatic catalyst accelerating the growth of a more harmonious relationship among the trade unions, the scientific managers and the fatigue researchers. The war compelled the leaders of these three groups to work together on an unprecedented scale. The success of this experience convinced many of the leading Taylorists that an essential condition for the successful introduction of scientific management into the workplace was the co-operation of the trade unions, and it made the unions aware of the tactical advantages greater scientific knowledge could provide them.

The central figure promoting this shift amongst the scientific managers was Morris Cooke, an engineer who had worked closely with Taylor and who, indeed, has been described as Taylor's "favoured disciple" (Jacoby 1983: 21). Cooke was highly critical of the pro-employer bias shown by the majority of engineers and actively attempted to promote a wider understanding within the engineering profession of the need for unions and of the need to adopt a more sympathetic attitude towards the human factor. During the war he worked for the Ordnance Department and was largely responsible for its issuance of General Order number 13, which recommended that government contractors accept collective bargaining, minimum wages, various health and safety conditions, and the 8-hour day. These activities were to gain him the approval of the American Federation of Labor and bring him into intimate contact with its president, Samuel Gompers. It was in order to capitalise on the goodwill generated within the labour movement by such activities that the Taylor Society, in the immediate postwar period, began actively prompting a policy of conciliation with the unions and began paying much greater attention to the human factor.

The eight hours campaign

At the end of the war the American unions, emboldened by vastly increased numbers, a newfound militancy and low unemployment, unleashed a major campaign to secure what they believed they were due. Through 1919 a massive wave of strikes swept across the United States. A major demand of this offensive was the standardisation of the 8-hour day, which, it was insisted, should be granted to the workers not only because of what they had contributed during the war but also because the scientific managers and the fatigue researchers had shown that this reform could be had at little or no cost to employer or worker. Why, therefore, the unions demanded to know, should it not be had by all?

Prior to the war the 8-hour day had been enjoyed by comparatively few American workers outside the building and printing trades and government employ. From 1914, however, the adoption of this schedule spread widely through industry. The percentage of employees working 48 hours or less per week in manufacturing, for example, increased from 11.9 per cent in 1914 to 48.6 per cent in 1919 (Bowen 1923: 1306). In the unions' wartime campaign to spread the adoption of the 8-hour schedule, they gained valuable assistance from the state, which was anxious to maintain war production. Besides Cooke a central figure providing this assistance was Frankfurter, who was appointed advisor to the Secretary of War on matters dealing with worktime and who was also made official arbitrator on all worktime disputes involving workers employed by the Federal Government or its contractors. Frankfurter utilised this position to actively promote both the wider adoption of the 8-hour day and knowledge of the productivity-inducing possibilities of rationalised time schedules (National War Labor Board 1918; Goldmark and Hopkins 1920).

In the 8-hour campaign that the labour movement launched after the war, great use was made of the scientific research into worktime and fatigue that had been undertaken by the rationalisers. The information gained was used both as a stimulant to activate the militancy of the workers and as an argument to undermine the opposition of the employers. For example, at the first International Labor Conference, held in Washington in 1919, Gompers utilised Maurice Cooke as his advisor on the shift system. At this conference Gompers lambasted the employers for their refusal to acknowledge the greater efficiency of the 8-hour day. In his attack he abandoned the A.F.L.'s traditional arguments for reduced worktimes, the rights of the citizen and the spreading of the available work, and stressed the efficiency of the 8-hour standard. "Everything being equal, without improved machinery, without any additional driving force or power, a man, working in a factory or any other establishment 8 hours a day will produce more than in another establishment under the same conditions, if the workmen in that establishment work 10 or 12 hours a day." (International Labor Conference 1920: 45).

Production, Gompers argued, would be enhanced if the shorter day was introduced, because employers would be compelled to rationalise the use of their resources so as to eliminate many of the inefficiencies in the production process. He noted that it was in those industries that had the longest time schedules that the least improvement in technology was to be found and it was those with the shortest times that had the most efficient methods and equipment. Employers had to be made to realise, he insisted, that the longest workday did not necessarily produce the greatest output. They must also be made to realise that the managers as well as the workers needed to have their practices rationalised. In this regard, he said, he endorsed the arguments of the French workers' delegate to the conference, who stated:

We wish that at the beginning of its work the conference state explicitly that it has done with that human slavery which binds the laborer to his factory; and that it is no longer the human machine alone which determines production, but also the development of machinery and the rational organization of labor. (International Labor Conference 1920: 42)

The labour delegates to the conference argued that the war had shown that employers, left to themselves, were not competent to ensure that the nation's resources were used in the most efficient manner. The state, it was pointed out, had been forced to intervene to plan and control production in every nation involved in the war as capitalists had proven inadequate to the task. Now that the conflict was over it was necessary for all concerned to ensure that the old practices were not reverted to. In particular, employers should not be allowed merely to concentrate their efforts on driving the workers as the main means of raising output while allowing gross inefficiencies to continue to exist within and among enterprises. Gompers in the following year used this argument as a defence of both the trade union movement and the 8-hour day. The promotion of the 8-hour-day standard, he insisted, was a demand that should be supported by all, for its introduction would be beneficial to the whole society. This included employers: The shorter schedule would compel them to raise the efficiency of their firms, and thus their profits would be enhanced.

That the movement of labor to reduce the hours of labor has much to do with the acceleration, with the development of industry that is taking place, no keen observer will dispute. Necessity is said to be the mother of invention. Each successful effort to reduce the hours of labor makes the laborers larger consumers of their product. It brings into the ranks of the employed thousands previously unemployed, makes of them consumers as well as producers. . . . Each such stage and step brings forth the necessity for still further improvement in the means of production – improved machinery. This process is either quickened or lessened in each and every industry in the same ratio as the movements of the workers to reduce the hours of labor is successful or otherwise. (Gompers n.d.: 7–8)

Employers, however, responded with scepticism and hostility to the arguments of the unions and the rationalisers. They vigorously opposed the introduction of the 8-hour day in many areas and challenged the scientific validity of the worktime experiments (National Industrial Conference Board 1920). As the unions' combined use of industrial power and scientific knowledge won a growing number of successes, employers became increasingly hostile towards unionism and increasingly vocal in their criticism of the independent role being played by the more progressive of the engineers and psychologists. In September 1919, for example, workers in the steel industry struck in support of the 8-hour day. This strike was bitterly opposed by the employers and by January 1920 it was effectively crushed.

Their victory was not to be savoured for long, however, for at a meeting of management engineers held in December 1920 Horace Drury of the Taylor Society, which had supported the striking workers, read a paper on the 12-hour system which argued that the experience of those firms which had already abandoned this schedule indicated that the 8-hour day could be had at little cost to worker or employer (Drury 1921). The main question Drury was concerned with was to what extent the increased hourly wage rate that the 8-hour day necessarily involved could be offset by greater efficiency. He argued that the experience of firms that shifted from 12 to 8 hours indicated that initially there was some increase in unit costs. Before long, however, increased intensity of work and technical restructuring tended to minimise these costs. Where the amount of work undertaken depended on the degree of effort the employee put into the time laboured, Drury concluded, experience suggested that workers in the 8-hour plants undertook as much work as did those in 12-hour firms. This increased intensity combined with improvements in management had been found to increase efficiency by some 20 per cent.

As a consequence of his paper the Federated American Engineering Societies (F.A.E.S.) commissioned Drury to undertake a larger study of the shift system. The subsequent report, which was submitted in September 1922, argued that the change from the 12-hour to the 8-hour day in continuous industries was not only practical but advantageous to all concerned. It argued that in those firms that had made the change increased costs had been negligible and great improvements had been attained in the morale of the workers and in the quality of both their work and that of management (Committee on Work Periods 1922). The compiling of this report was a major factor helping to further improve relations between the Taylorists and the trade unions, who used it extensively. Layton (1971: 205–206) reports, however, that it was considered by the employers a "stab in the back," and it eventually led to the crippling of the F.A.E.S. when the employers subsequently launched a campaign to purge the engineering societies of progressives.

The employers' assault proved to be extremely effective in

virtually all the engineering bodies. The only institution of this
nature that throughout the 1920s retained an important number of activists committed to social reform and sympathetic to
trade unionism was the Taylor Society. The members of this
body maintained a continuing, even if hesitant, alliance with
the A.F.L. through the decade and aided the promotion of a
number of its major campaigns. There were, it is true, severe
limits to the extent of this co-operation, for each side retained a
good deal of suspicion of some of the policies promoted by the
other. Whereas the unions welcomed the Taylorists' promotion
of fatigue research, for example, they remained extremely
wary of time and motion studies, arguing that the engineers
tended to adopt a mechanistic and cavalier attitude when dealing with this issue. They insisted, moreover, that all too often
the engineers utilised these tools to raise the level of work intensity to a point where it conflicted with the workers' capacities
to maintain a normal life. They insisted that just as the length
of the workday should be determined "scientifically" to ensure
that workers gained sufficient time to adequately recuperate,
intensity levels should also be set with the whole life needs of
the worker in mind.

Workers have demanded that the pace of work shall not be excessive
and shall be measured by the same criteria which are employed in the
determination of the length of the work week. These should be not
only immediate output but also the long-term rate of production, the
human and economic cost and finally the effects on the health, and
the physical and mental well-being of the workers under present social conditions. (Barkin 1942: 34)

While the labour movement remained critical of some aspects of Taylorism, then, it abandoned its blanket hostility as it
came to realise that, though the scientific core within management science could be utilised against it, this core could also be
utilised by the working class to advance its own interests.

The waste issue

The conviction of the Taylorists that the "indifference of management" was the key obstacle to greater national efficiency
appears to have been justified, given that the planning techniques developed by the scientific managers which were to rev-
olutionise the production process had been widely known and

available for over two decades. It needed the massive stimulus of war and the associated shortage of labour power and state intervention in the production process to impel large numbers of U.S. capitalists to take the steps necessary to begin realising the wider potential offered by systematic planning. For a significant number of firms, however, the war did have this effect, and the postwar competition generated by these leaders in the field, together with fear of unionism, a shortage of skilled labour and state encouragement, proved an adequate substitute impelling many U.S. capitalists to continue the rationalisation process. In the postwar years there was a dramatic increase in the number of firms utilising the techniques of the scientific managers. During the 1920s this expansion developed into an efficiency craze, with firms across the nation achieving enormous success in raising productivity. In the sixteen years 1899 to 1914, for example, productivity growth in manufacturing had expanded by less than 0.5 per cent per year. In the eight years 1919 to 1926, on the other hand, output per worker increased by almost 40 per cent. A rate of productivity growth of this magnitude, Douglas (1927: 20) reported, was "probably unparalleled in the history of the world." Nor was this expansion confined to manufacturing; comparable rates of productivity growth were experienced in mining, transportation and agriculture (Thomas 1928; Durand 1930).

The phenomenal acceleration in the rate of productivity growth amazed observers during the 1920s. As this expansion continued unabated, it began to be realised that something almost unprecedented was occurring. In a series of articles published in 1926 Clague attempted to gauge and analyse the nature of this new phenomenon. His examinations led him to report that the United States was experiencing what was "perhaps the most remarkable advance in productive efficiency in the history of the modern industrial system" (1926: 1). The nature and extent of this advance was such, he concluded, that it had to be considered nothing less than a second industrial revolution.

Through the 1920s numerous scholars joined Clague in his attempt to analyse the nature of this revolution. In general the participants to the debate accepted that whereas the long-term growth in the size of the U.S. economy could be explained by the nation's vast natural resources, availability of capital, advanced political structure and large internal market, these fac-

Table 4.1. *Indexes of employment per unit of ouput*

Year	Manufacturing (1899 = 100)		Agriculture (1900 = 100): gainfully occupied	Railroads (1929 = 100): man-days	Mining (1929 = 100): man-days
	Wage earners	Man-hours			
1919	84	74	84	124	135
1920	78	67	83	120	128
1921	74	61	82	130	130
1922	64	55	81	119	119
1923	65	56	79	114	116
1924	64	53	76	114	118
1925	59	50	74	108	112
1926	57	48	71	105	112
1927	55	47	70	106	108
1928	53	44	68	102	103
1929	51	42	67	100	100

Source: Soule 1962: 122.

tors could not explain the recent rapid increase in the rate of productivity growth. One development which clearly had contributed to this phenomenon was the wider use of electricity in the nation's factories. Between 1919 and 1925 the percentage of total installed horsepower transmitted to machines in this manner increased from 55 to 72. The explanatory value of this factor, however, was limited, given that in the period of low productivity growth, between 1899 and 1919, industrial use of electricity had increased from 2 to 55 per cent. As the debate progressed, it began to be realised that the unique causal factor underpinning the rate of productivity growth was the manner in which the society's resources were coming to be managed at the level of the firm, the industry and the nation. The centrality of this factor was stressed in the report of the Committee on Recent Economic Changes prepared for the president in 1929. Those producing the report offered many partial explanations for the phenomenal productivity growth of the 1920s. In the concluding chapter, however, it was argued that all these answers could be condensed into one.

Since 1921, Americans have applied intelligence to the day's work more effectively than ever before. Thus the prime factor in producing the extraordinary changes in the economic fortunes of the European peoples during the nineteenth century is the prime factor in producing the prosperity of the United States in recent years. The old process of putting science into industry has been followed more intensively than before; it has been supplemented by tentative efforts to put science into business management, trade union policy, and Government administration. (Committee on Recent Economic Changes 1929: 862)

The validity of this conclusion was endorsed two years later by Jevons (1931: 1), who attempted to spell out the significance of what was occurring in the U.S.A. and to highlight its central feature.

The advanced industrial countries of the world are now in the first stage of a sweeping change of the methods and organisation of all their secondary industries, and . . . this new movement is likely to be comparable in its industrial, commercial and social effects with that series of changes which commenced in the latter half of the eighteenth century and is commonly called the Industrial Revolution. The changes are coming about as the result not merely of the application of scientific knowledge to industry, which was, in fact, the last phase of the first industrial revolution, but of the use of the inductive method in the study of an industry, and individual concerns composing it, with a view to gaining facts and generalisations which may serve sooner or later as the basis of the replanning of the productive process and plant. The essence of the new industrial revolution is the search for exact knowledge, and the planning of processes: from the minutiae of manual operations (based on motion study) to the lay-out of the machinery of a gigantic plant – even of a whole industry throughout the country.

Within the firm the rationalisation process took the form of a vigorous application of the techniques of the scientific managers. Particular emphasis was placed on the development of functional management and internal planning (Chandler and Redlich 1966). The central objective of these activities was to give the directors of the firm greater control over what were seen to be the three main factors necessary to attain sustained growth: stabilisation, standardisation and simplification. In manufacturing, for example, stress was placed on the improvement and integration of mechanical devices which could give management greater technical control over both the materials utilised and the processes by which the product was produced. Greater attention was also applied to the utilisation of modern principles of organisation, costing, routing, office procedure, statistics and other refinements of control. Taylorist principles, moreover, were successfully applied to such areas as financial and demand forecasting, advertising and marketing. In the case of the last, rationalisation radically advanced the growth of chain and department stores which enabled retailers to gain significant advantages from standardisation and from large-scale buying. (For data on the spread and development of scientific management within the firm during the 1920s, see Tugwell 1927; Person 1929; Durand 1930; Dent 1935.)

One of the more significant results that also arose from the development of Taylorism, the Committee on Recent Economic Changes reported, was an increase in the capacity of the firm to secure, from large-scale or diverse areas of activity, levels of efficiency that previously could be had only in the small firm working under the direct control of a competent employer owner.

Under the old type of organization there was a gain in efficiency with size, up to the point where the reduction in costs through ability to specialize and functionalize the work of a larger group of workers and the increases in process, purchasing and selling efficiency under larger scale operation, began to be more than offset by a reduced general efficiency due to the inability of the employer owner to maintain close contacts with the members of the enlarged organization. Recent developments in management methods, and in accounting and statistical control, have apparently broken down these former economic limitations on the size of the individual organization or "chain," with the result that practically all types of business and industry are now open to efficient large scale corporate control. (Committee on Recent Economic Changes 1929: 864)

In many industries the desire to reap the benefits of this enhanced capacity to expand led firms to amalgamate their operations. Through the 1920s there was a marked increase in economic concentration. Unlike the wave of mergers that had occurred in the last quarter of the nineteenth century, however, these amalgamations were not undertaken only to limit the degree of competition. They also had as their purpose the attaining of the efficiencies of scale and diversification that the development of scientific management had made possible (Sheldon 1928).

When applying the Taylorists' techniques to the management of the firm, employers often modified Taylor's methods radically. Despite these modifications it is important to note that "in spite of any reservations which might be made it has always to be remembered that the essentials of the efficiency movement, so far as it concerns technology alone, trace directly back to Taylor" (Tugwell 1927: 127). Unfortunately, many scholars have failed to appreciate this link. Radicals such as Richard Edwards (1979), for example, have argued that a "closer analysis" of the practices of the scientific managers suggests that their influence, while not unimportant, has tended to be overstated. Examination of his analysis, however, shows that it is based on a very narrow, one-sided understanding of what scientific management involved. It takes as given the claim that Taylorism was merely a system of labour control with uncompromising principles. It also fails to examine how the movement progressed after 1915. Because of these failings Edwards's assessment does not appreciate the extent of the dissemination and maturation of Taylorism that occurred during the 1920s.

His narrow perspective also leads Edwards to fail to appreciate the extent to which the application of Taylorism moved outside the individual firm. During the 1920s there was a dramatic expansion in the number of bodies established to promote the dissemination of information and co-operation across industries. These industry and trade organisations sought to establish links between individual firms which would enable management to plan its activities more effectively. Their establishment and growth were aided by the activities of Herbert Hoover, the most highly placed exponent of scientific management during the 1920s. This engineer, though an ardent supporter of capitalism, recognised that the market was not a mechanism that always ensured that society's resources were utilised with maximum efficiency. Consequently he believed that the state had a crucial role to play in the economy. For Hoover this did not mean the state should control or regulate industry. He was vehemently opposed to direct interventions of this nature. Rather, what he argued was that the state should adopt policies that limited monopolies and that helped business by showing it how to rationalise itself.

It is obviously not the function of Government to manage business, but to investigate economic questions, to survey economic phenomena and point out the remedy for economic failure or the road to progress, to inspire and assist cooperative action, and to stimulate forces to these ends – surely all these are well within the proper field of public service. (Hoover 1927: 2)

Even before he became Secretary of Commerce in 1922 Hoover's influence was an important factor inducing the spread of scientific management. In November 1920 he used his position as president of the Federated American Engineering Societies to commission a study which aimed to discover the major causes of industrial inefficiency in the United States. Responsibility for undertaking this research he delegated to a committee of seventeen, the great majority of whom were members of the Taylor Society. Hoover was to claim that the subsequent report, *Waste in Industry*, was a major step forward in the transition of scientific management from its prewar devotion to the minutiae of shop and office routine to broad questions of policy making (Metcalf 1975: 64).

The committee defined waste as the difference between the average efficiency of firms within an industry and the most efficient firms in the same class. It was concluded that although the United States was leading the world in the rationalisation of the production process there was still tremendous potential to raise further the general level of efficiency. The conclusion of the committee that elicited the greatest interest from all sections of society, and from capitalists the greatest hostility, was the claim that poor management was responsible for well over half the existing waste, while inefficiency attributable to the workers was less than 25 per cent and even this percentage was largely the result of workers' justifiable fears of how management would respond if productivity was to rise (Committee on Elimination of Waste 1921: 8–10).

The major causes of lost production, the waste report argued, were (1) faulty production control, (2) faulty materials control, (3) lack of cost control, (4) faulty design control, (5) faulty sales policies, (6) faulty labour control, (7) ineffective workmanship, and (8) lack of research. The study examined six major industries and it castigated the established management practices in all of them. Its generalisations as regards conditions in the clothing industry were fairly typical (1921: 12–13).

From shop records it is found that the average loss in clothing factories during running time, not including shut downs, is between 30 and 35 per cent. . . . It is found that at least ten hours per week per man is thrown away on energy-wasting and time-wasting work resulting from lack of shop methods, while an additional two or three hours per man per week are wasted in unnecessary work.

Fixing the value of annual output in the men's ready made clothing industry at $600,000,000 it should be relatively easy to save three quarters of a million dollars a day, an increase of 40 per cent in effectiveness.

If the employers found Hoover's study offensive, the trade unions hailed it with delight. The Taylorists' conclusion that poor management was the major cause of industrial inefficiency was publicised widely by the unions and used by them as a weapon to counter arguments that employers could not afford to pay higher wages or grant reduced working times. Utilising this study, union leaders also attacked employers for their rule-of-thumb methods. To an increasing extent they exhorted capitalists "to analyze production costs, to practice managerial economy, and make 'intelligent efforts to eliminate waste and to establish more efficient methods'" (Nadworny 1955: 121). Rubbing salt into the employers' wounds, they also declared they were eager to co-operate with management to remove the waste the latter's incompetence had caused.

Hoover continued his attempts to promote rationalised production methods after becoming Secretary of Commerce. His strategy involved the establishment of bodies, both public and private, which collated and disseminated statistical and scientific information which both enhanced employers' awareness of the benefits of scientific management and aided its application in an increasing range of areas. On issues such as standardisation, product simplification and the regulation of production to offset the trade cycle, Hoover's department was to take Taylorism out of the workshop and begin applying it at the level of the nation (Metcalf 1975: 61). Unfortunately, however, Hoover's work was only a beginning, a beginning, moreover, which was kept under a very tight rein. Although Hoover was undoubtedly a progressive in many areas, his commitment to capitalism restricted severely the extent to which he would advance the wider application of planning, particularly where this might involve an interventionist role for the state.

A classic example of the limited nature of Hoover's commitment to planning was his response to the development of the American Construction Council. This body was established in 1922 at the inspiration of Hoover's department. Its primary objective was the development of countercyclical policies which could dampen the intensity of the trade cycle in the building industry. The primary means adopted to attain this objective was the collection and dissemination of industrial statistics and the publication of weekly forecasts on construction conditions. By spreading knowledge, it was hoped, builders would be able to plan their activities in a manner which would spread construction into slacker periods. Hoover insisted, however, that the collection and dissemination of the necessary information had to be undertaken by the industry itself. The council was to be an example of self-regulation, not state guidance. He rebuked severely the council's president, Franklin Roosevelt, when the latter had the temerity to suggest that the Commerce Department co-operate by developing a building index.

Hoover's rejection of an interventionist role for the state, it needs be added, was mirrored by most employers in the building industry. While refusing to commit sufficient resources to ensure that the council could be effective, employers in general were hostile to any suggestion that the private sector needed any external assistance. In 1928 the prevalence of these attitudes was to lead Roosevelt to break his connection with the council. At the time he claimed that nothing less than the shock of a depression would be needed to bring about the rationalisation of the industry (Schlesinger 1957: 387). This was an assessment that was soon to be validated.

The rate of profit and economic crisis

The radical acceleration in the rate of productivity growth had a tremendous effect on the U.S. economy during the 1920s. Most important, the improved utilisation and cheapening of resources that the use of Taylorism made possible acted as a massive counterweight to the rising organic composition of capital and the associated tendency for the rate of profit to fall that had characterised U.S. capitalism for the preceding forty years. In his empirical study of the changing nature of the rate of profit Gillman (1957: 58–61) found that in the fifty years prior to 1919 Marx's basic predictions in this area were fairly well sustained. After this period, however, the organic composition of capital tended to remain constant or even to fall while the rate of profit reversed its long-term downward trend and began to rise. With the easing of the 1920–1922 depression, profits in the United States began to grow. Over the next seven years the return on investments grew phenomenally. Profits of industrial corporations increased at an average rate of 9 per cent during the years 1923–1927. For the decade as a whole profits rose by 80 per cent overall while the profitability of financial institutions increased by 150 per cent (Schlesinger 1957: 68).

Through the 1920s, then, scientific management proved to have an enormous capacity to offset the tendency for the rate of profit to fall. By enabling the more efficient utilisation of resources it could generate large increases in productivity without invoking Marx's "general" source of crisis, that is, the tendency for constant capital to rise relative to that utilised for the purchase of labour power. In raising the rate of profit, however, scientific management also created the conditions which, at the end of the 1920s, were to generate economic crisis. For although Taylorism offered a powerful method for offsetting the fall in the rate of profit, as applied in the 1920s it did not resolve the problem of how sufficient demand was to be generated to ensure that the mass of goods produced could be sold and the profits reinvested effectively. The division of the benefits of the 1920s prosperity was heavily skewed in favour of employers. Overall, profits increased at twice the rate that productivity did. As a consequence, the share of disposable income received by the top 1 per cent of the population increased from 13 per cent in 1923 to 19 per cent in 1929 (Holt 1977: 277–280). The severe imbalance between the increase in the rate of productivity growth and the rate of profit created an acute imbalance between people's ability to produce and their ability to purchase. Instability generated by this development was compounded by the high rate of fixed capital investment that high profits encouraged during the 1923–1929 period. In an increasing number of industries this level of investment created excess capacity, with the result that the owners of capital found it difficult to find substantial areas where their profits could be reinvested effectively. Consequently, they began to speculate. In late 1929 this unstable situation generated depression on a massive scale.

The onset of the 1930s depression caught the majority of U.S. employers, politicians and economists unprepared. As in every other boom those committed ideologically to capitalism had soon convinced themselves that prosperity would last forever. Their immediate response to the crisis was to look for scapegoats, with state spending and trade unions being particularly popular. Most economists, for example, initially attempted to exempt employers from any blame. They argued that the crash was the fault primarily of big government and refractory labour and that the only way out of the crisis was to allow greater freedom for the market and for stricter controls to be imposed on government spending and the organised working class. For a minority of observers, however, the facile nature of this assessment was obvious. Indeed, for some the crash was seen as a vindication of arguments they had been promoting for a number of years. As early as 1925 the A.F.L. had warned that in the employers' failure to share more equitably the rewards of rising productivity lay the seeds for disaster. Economists such as Tugwell (1927) and Hobson (1930) likewise had warned that excess profitability generated by the success of the rationalisation movement was creating a serious imbalance in the economy. These individuals argued that it was imperative that the state intervene to increase effective demand. They were later joined by Keynes (1932: 525), who denounced those who were calling for retrenchment and cuts in spending. "This is not a crisis of poverty," he insisted, "but a crisis of abundance." With increasing vehemence the critics argued that the only effective answer to the crisis that Taylorism had engendered was the development of even higher and more extensive levels of planning. Thus, at a special meeting of the Taylor Society held in 1930, Person argued that the crisis had been caused by the failure of the society's economic and political leaders to adequately expand the planning process at the level of the nation. What was required, he argued, was the extension of the principles developed within the firm by the Taylorists to the whole society. "If these were applied to the organization and control of industrial society, conceived as an organic whole, many and perhaps most of the forces which now cause periodic dislocations and distress in industrial life would be eliminated" (cited in Soule 1932: 149–150). The major obstacle preventing the development of national planning, Person argued, was the inconsistency that existed between the basic principles of business enterprise – individual self-interest and intuition – and the basic principle of modern production technology – co-operative integration. If this inconsistency was to be overcome it was necessary for the interests of the individual to be suppressed where these conflicted with the interests of society.

The only force capable of developing the institutional structure that would be needed to control individual self-interest sufficiently, it was realised by the critics, was the Federal Government. Consequently, they called for the establishment of a strong interventionist state that would guide, stabilise and inject some degree of rationality into the national economy. The exact form state intervention should take was a question of intense debate amongst these individuals. Some argued that recovery was impossible with anything less than total socialisation of the means of production. Economists such as Cole (1929), Hobson (1930) and Chase (1932) argued that whereas Taylorism had solved capitalism's production problems, far from saving the social system it had sounded its death knell because those committed to planning had not provided any acceptable means of ensuring that the greatly enhanced capacity to supply commodities was matched by a corresponding demand. Others, however, insisted that institutionalised planning needed to be applied only to certain areas of the economy. As the crisis deepened through 1930–1932 the critics were joined by a growing number of politicians and corporate leaders. In the title of his 1932 book *A New Deal* – which he concluded characteristically with the question "Why should Russians have all the fun of remaking a world?" – Stuart Chase publicised the name this emerging movement was to take, and in 1936 Keynes provided the tools which settled the question of how far planning needed to go to enable capitalism to stabilise.

Taylorism and the need for unionism

Taylor had argued that his main objective when developing scientific management was the removal of the primary "cause for antagonism" between the two major classes. He believed that raising the return obtained from the production process would cause both classes to become more satisfied with their lot. His claim that scientific management could achieve this objective was not to be validated entirely. Conflict between capitalist and worker over the distribution of society's wealth has continued to characterise industrial relations throughout the twentieth century. Taylor's belief in the conciliatory power of high wages and profits, however, was not entirely unjustified. Although it did not remove the primary cause of antagonism between the classes, Taylorism's capacity to raise wages and profits proved a powerful force moderating the intensity of this antagonism.

The years following the 1920–1922 depression saw an abrupt and dramatic easing of overt class conflict in the U.S.A. Over the rest of the decade those who managed to retain a job experienced steadily rising real incomes. By 1929 real wages in manufacturing were 40 per cent higher than in 1914, in electric works 38 per cent, in gas 33 per cent and on the railroads 30 per cent (National Industrial Conference Board 1930: 204). The capacity of this increased income to moderate industrial conflict was made greater by the fact that the rationalisation process created severe divisions within the working class. These splits were particularly acute between those who stood to gain from rationalisation and those whose immediate or long-term interests it was seen to endanger. The divisions, in many cases, destroyed working-class solidarity. Of particular importance was the fact that the growth in real wages was especially high amongst skilled workers.

Differentials based on skill widened considerably through the decade. This development was critical, because the manual sector of the skilled working class constituted the backbone of the U.S. labour movement. These workers had been able to organise effectively because the availability of their particular type of labour power was in limited supply. Consequently, their resistance was not so easily crushed as was that of the mass of unskilled workers. With their incomes rising rapidly, the skilled workers soon lost interest in industrial militancy and class politics. They lost interest, moreover, in the lot of the unskilled, whose numbers were swelled dramatically by an influx of labour from the rural areas and by those displaced by the rationalisation process.

The rising wages of the skilled workers together with the inability or unwillingness of the A.F.L. to play an active role in defending the unskilled and the wide adoption of employer-initiated "welfare" schemes led many observers to assert during the 1920s that trade unions had been made redundant by the rationalisation process. It was claimed that U.S. employers now accepted the Taylorists' argument that the paying of high wages and the reduction of worktimes were not necessarily incompatible with high profits. Bernstein (1960: 180) reports that between 1921 and 1926 the leaders of U.S. industry drastically overhauled their philosophical approach to high wages and industrial reform. He also reports, however, that this apparent conversion was largely "an exercise in verbal gymnastics." Industrialists talked of the need to pay high wages and improve conditions but unless forced to they seldom did. In short, employers needed the pressure of some external force to motivate them to convert their propaganda into practice.

External pressure was necessary even in the case of the most innovative of the bourgeoisie. This was evidenced, for example, by the approach of Henry Ford to the rationalisation of worktime. In 1914 Ford had introduced the endless chain conveyor for final assembly of motor vehicles into his major plants. This method of producing cars, within three months of its implementation, reduced the assembly time for the Ford Model T to one-tenth of the time previously required. The much faster rate of production was brought about partly because the new technology was more efficient in terms of the ratio of physical inputs to outputs. It was also the result of a great heightening of the level of work intensity. This technology gave the employer much greater control over effort standards. The idea that machines could be used as tools for social control was a major element of Taylor's philosophy of organisation (Merkle 1980: 93). It was Ford, however, who took up and fully developed this element of Taylorism.

Taylor's system relied on written records, and the use of management experts for planning, coordination, and experimentation; Ford's assembly line was a nonverbal process in which the timing of the production process was built into the speed of the line; the organization of the work process between machines was invested in the design of the line itself. (Merkle 1980: 95)

The technical form of control involved in mass production, however, was in itself insufficient as a means of intensifying the labour process. For its full value to be realised it was necessary for the workers to be either unable or unwilling to resist the demand for an increased concentration of effort. Failure to appreciate the importance of this factor led Ford to make a serious error when introducing his modifications to the production process. He attempted to shift effort norms radically upward without offering the workers any compensating payment at a time when they could resist because they had alternatives. In order to cut costs he did away with incentive pay and attempted to maintain a high level of work intensity by the use of closer supervision. Wages in his enterprises were frozen at $2.34 a day, the standard rate of pay for the area. The problem for Ford was that the workers in his plants, although not organised, were in a position to rebel. Other jobs paying similar wages but demanding less daily effort were plentiful in the area. Consequently, the workers responded to Ford's action by deserting the company. With the introduction of the production line, Sward (1968: 50–52) has reported, the ranks of Ford's workforce fell apart.

Ford was to admit later that his innovations at this time brought on the outstanding labour crisis of his career. He had a vast factory but not the workers to run it. The company had poured virtually all its innovative efforts into equipment and materials and had all but ignored the fact that unless workers can be compelled or induced to submit to the assembly line it is unworkable. Ford responded to this crisis by announcing, with great fanfare, that he was introducing an 8-hour day into his plants and that he was willing to pay those workers who remained in his employ for a sustained period $5.00 a day. These dramatic changes in wages and conditions in one stroke eliminated Ford's labour-supply problem. He later claimed that the introduction of the $5.00 8-hour day "was one of the finest cost cutting moves we ever made" (Ford 1922: 147).

Ford's innovative strategy was extremely effective as a means of ensuring an adequate supply of high-quality labour power. The very nature of the capitalist market, however, ensured that this advantage was sustained for only a limited period. Ford's competitors were similarly compelled to overhaul their methods of production in order to compete. Thus Ford, by the advantage he obtained, forced the production line on his competitors. The latter, however, by adopting his methods of production, effectively eliminated the relative advantage Ford had gained by being innovative. His novel approach to the wage–effort bargain, though, was far from exhausted.

In 1926 Ford shocked American industrialists and trade unionists by choosing to introduce a 5-day, 40-hour week into his plants. Ford was not the first large U.S. capitalist to introduce this schedule, but no other had applied it on the scale he did. Following the announcement of the new schedule, Ford was lauded by the leaders of organised labour and attacked by most major industrialists as a class traitor (Laue 1926). Despite the criticisms of his peers, the schedule he introduced in 1926 was to become the model adopted by many rationalised industries in the United States over the next decade. By the end of the 1930s it was to receive the force of law at least partly because other capitalists studied Ford's experience and realised the benefits of the shorter week (Labor Research Association 1942: 34–36).

While not denying that Ford had tremendous innovative capacities, we should not give Ford all the credit for introducing the new schedule. Sward reports that Ford took this step to offset a planned unionisation drive in the automobile industry and to offset possible industrial trouble caused by the necessity of having to retrench tens of thousands of workers while retooling for the Model A (Sward 1968: 177). Ford, moreover, had been provided with extensive assistance from the state in that his plant in Detroit had been utilised during the war in a government-funded study of the advantages of an 8-hour day (Florence 1950: 58). The company management was also well aware, from personal experience, that it was possible to reduce the workweek to 5 days without reducing output. During the 1920–1922 depression Ford had been compelled to close his plants. Prior to the close-down he had reduced his workforce by 4,000 and instituted a 5-day week as a way of spreading the available work. The fear of unemployment, however, enabled the management to extract from this smaller number of workers as much work as the greater number of workers had undertaken in 6 days. Output levels, Nevins and Hill (1957: 519) report, were held constant during the shorter week.

Having decided to introduce the 5-day week, Ford became very vocal in his own praise. He reacted indignantly to any suggestion that his reform had been introduced as a measure of philanthropy. It was introduced in order to cut costs. He also became highly critical of those industrialists and economists who continued to insist that a curtailment of worktimes necessarily involved a reduction in output. He castigated German employers, for example, for taking back from the workers the 8-hour day they had won at the end of the First World War.

The hours of the labor day were increased in Germany under the delusion that thus the production might be increased. It is quite possibly being decreased. With the decrease of the length of the working day in the United States an increase of production has come, because better methods of disposing of men's time have been accompanied by better methods of disposing of their energy. (Ford 1926: 13)

Ford had, in other words, no illusions that the maintenance of shorter worktimes was a manifestation of the workers' desire for leisure rather than for greater income. On this issue this capitalist had a much better understanding of economics than those in the universities who teach the subject as an academic exercise.

The hours of labor are regulated by the organization of work and by nothing else. It is the rise of the great corporation with its ability to use power, to use accurately designed machinery, and generally to lessen the wastes in time, material, and human energy that made it possible to bring in the 8 hour day. (Ford 1926: 11)

If so innovative an entrepreneur as Ford needed to be pressured by an acute shortage of labour power or fear of unionism before he would introduce rationalised worktimes, the overwhelming majority of capitalists required a good deal more pressure. When Ford introduced the 5-day week he was denounced by most of his peers. American employers, with few exceptions, continued to deny the validity of the arguments of the Taylorists and the trade unions that productivity might be improved if working times were reduced (Beman 1928). Both the National Association of Manufacturers and the Chamber of Commerce vigorously opposed any reduction in the standard week below 48 hours throughout the 1920s. Even so, worktimes did continue to fall through the decade as the rationalisation movement gathered momentum (United States Bureau of the Census 1976: 168–172; Department of Labor, U.S.A., 1929). This trend can be discerned even in areas where the labour movement remained weak. Thus, in the steel industry the workweek was reduced from 63 hours in 1920 to 54 hours in 1926.

A second factor tending to contract the total time some workers laboured was the expanded adoption of paid holidays. The prevalence of vacation coverage for wage earners increased from approximately 5 per cent in 1920 to 10 per cent in 1930. This expansion, Allen (1969) reports, was a consequence of a growing acceptance by management that there was some validity to the fatigue researchers' claim that vacations could increase overall productivity.

Management initiated the paid vacation movement for employees. It did not do so, however, to compensate employees for their service, nor out of altruistic considerations of social welfare. Employers voluntarily incurred this non-wage labor cost for the purpose of increasing the productivity of the labor force. Individual employers found through experience that annual rest periods for their employees more than paid for themselves in increased employee productivity. (p. 41)

Although it is true that the contraction of time schedules can be discerned even in nonunionised sectors of industry, it needs to be noted that, throughout the decade, it was in those areas where labour could exert sufficient industrial pressure to compel employers to listen to the scientific element in their arguments that the greatest gains were made. In the last half of the 1920s Ford's adoption of the 5-day week had a particularly invigorating influence in this sector. Ford announced the introduction of the 5-day schedule only a few days before the A.F.L.'s national convention. His action staggered the delegates and transformed the question of the 5-day week from a vague, generalised demand of some of the affiliated unions into a national movement. In his coverage of the convention Laue (1926) reports that Ford's action "charged the whole subject with the live current of immediate and concrete possibilities." The unions insisted that if this capitalist could rationalise his production methods in a manner that made the reduced schedule possible, so could all others. The limited coverage of the unions meant that they could not compel the introduction of the 5-day week in most industries. Workers in the highly unionised building industry, however, were able to insist on its adoption to a significant degree. By 1930, 55.5 per cent of building workers were labouring a standard 5-day week. The union in the men's garment industry was likewise able to advance the 40-hour schedule. The Bureau of Labor Statistics in 1928 reported that 33 per cent of the workers in this industry worked a 5-day week.

Union pressure and Ford's example also induced a significant number of other manufacturers to experiment with the 40-hour week. By 1928 some 270 establishments employing 418,700 workers had adopted this schedule on a permanent basis (National Industrial Conference Board 1929: 41). Towards the end of the decade, moreover, there are signs that Ford's success was attracting an increasing number of significant adherents to the new standard. John. J. Raskob (1929), an industrialist prominent in du Pont and General Motors and national chairman of the Democratic Party, for example, argued that the extra rest the 40-hour per week gave to workers would prove a powerful stimulus to production. To those who had studied the question, he argued, it was clear that with the same equipment workers could not only produce as much in 5 days as they could in 6, they could probably produce more. This willingness to display a little entrepreneurial talent, however, was far beyond the capacity of most capitalists. In general, the latter insisted that whereas it was true that the 5-day week had been shown to work in some firms, such examples were unique and their experience not applicable to the majority of enterprises. By 1930 only 5.6 per cent of workers had attained the 40-hour standard. The crisis of the 1930s was to change this situation radically.

The depression and worktime

The important point to heed if one is to comprehend the significance of Taylorism for workers during the 1920s is not that it was a two-edged sword of use to both workers and capitalists. Nor that even entrepreneurs like Ford needed to be pressured into introducing the wage and worktime policies of the rationalisers. Rather, what was of greatest significance at this time was the fact that, because Taylorism reversed the tendency for the rate of profit to decline, capitalists could be so pressured. During the 1920s the American employer had a decidedly fragmented outlook as regards the labour movement. "He was not sure whether to crush organized labor under the American Plan or to woo the workers with welfare capitalism. He did not know whether it was better to seek discord or concord" (Bernstein 1960: 188).

The great value of Taylorism was that it made this choice possible. Rationalisation enabled the generation of an average rate of profit sufficient to pay workers a wage that could buy their co-operation. The importance of profit rates in the promotion of inter-class co-operation was evidenced both in those industries where increased profitability allowed a conciliatory relationship to develop, as with automobile production, and in those such as coal mining where a structural crisis caused profits to fall so low that the owners of the mines could not afford to buy co-operation and turned consequently to the use of thugs, strike breakers and guns.

The importance of the rate of profit was also evidenced by

the offensive launched against the workers during the 1930s depression. Through 1930–1931 President Hoover tried desperately to stem the rising tide of unemployment by continuing to promote the doctrine of high wages. His pleas received some degree of support at first, at least from large-scale industry, but as the crisis deepened and profitability collapsed, wage cuts, layoffs, speed-ups and reductions in the length of time workers were allowed to labour became the order of the day.

The depression brought about an aggregate permanent reduction of basic working times in the United States of approximately 20 per cent. A crucial factor generating this change was the policy adopted by many employers of sharing out what work was available amongst as many workers as possible. This action was supported by Hoover, who considered it more attractive than the alternative of increasing taxes in order to pay unemployment benefits. Ignoring pleas for financial assistance to aid those out of work, the President's Organization on Unemployment Relief initially concerned itself solely with work spreading. It called on both public and private enterprises to share what work was available amongst those workers normally employed in the industry. The reduction of worktime was the principal method utilised for spreading employment. Lessening of the time workers laboured was accomplished in a number of different ways, with the most common method being the introduction of a 5-day week (Barrett 1932: 232).

The work-spreading movement minimised the number of those with no source of income other than charity. By March 1932, 56.1 per cent of all workers and 63 per cent of those in manufacturing were employed part time. Many employers, however, were motivated to adopt work sharing not through any desire to minimise working-class distress but rather by a desire to keep their experienced workforce intact. Evidence of the strength of this factor was provided in late 1932, when a seasonal upturn resulted in employers increasing weekly hours rather than in increasing the number of workers employed. The average hours worked by employees in manufacturing industries increased from 32.3 per week in August to 34.8 in September (*Business Week* 1932). By the first half of 1933 there was a clear tendency for many employers to return to more normal time schedules rather than take on extra staff.

The tendency for capitalists to extend worktimes rather than expand employment, at a time when 25 per cent of the workforce was unemployed, was greeted with dismay by the labour movement and by some employers. It was also met with hostility by many within the state. The Senate responded, in April 1933, by passing the Black Thirty Hour Week bill. This act would have made a 30-hour week compulsory in all industries covered by the legislation. Its passage forced Roosevelt, who had assumed office in March, to take immediate action, and in May he responded by emphasising the importance of worktime reductions in his National Industrial Recovery Act. The N.I.R.A. empowered trade or industrial associations to draw up "codes of fair competition" which, if given approval by the president, were to have the force of law. These codes were to include a minimum wage and a maximum length of time that could be laboured before penalty rates had to be paid. If employers refused to draw up the necessary codes, it was made clear, this would be done for them compulsorily by the state. In the National Recovery Administration Bulletin number 1, of June 1933, Roosevelt made clear the purpose of the worktime provision in his legislation. "The law I have just signed was passed to put people back to work. . . . The idea is simply for employers to hire more men to do the existing work by reducing the work hours of each man's week." In July the president's Re-employment Agreement was put forward as a model of what was expected. This code recommended a 40-hour week for clerical workers and a 35-hour week for those employed in manual work. By this time, however, Code number 1 for the cotton textile industry had already been approved with a 40-hour week. This deviation was allowed because a 40-hour schedule constituted a considerable worktime reduction for the industry. Those formulating the codes, however, saw this development as a precedent and consequently the 40-hour, rather than the 35-hour, week became the standard in most codes.

By 1934 some 22.5 million workers were covered by the N.I.R.A. When it was declared unconstitutional in May 1935, Congress responded by passing the National Labor Relations Act. This legislation strengthened radically the ability of workers to organise and engage in collective bargaining. It did not, however, re-establish maximum-hour laws and consequently the worktimes of many enterprises began to increase. In 1936 the Senate responded to this development by passing the Public Contracts Act, which gave the Secretary of Labor the power to determine wage rates and standard times for all workers em-

Table 4.2. *Worktime standards*

Weekly hours	Codes	Employees covered (000)	Percentage of employees
Under 40	43	2,179	9.7
40	487	12,898	57.2
Over 40	48	7,477	33.1
Total	578	22,554	100.0

Source: Reticker 1936: 74.

ployed on government contracts. The Labor Secretary, Frances Perkins, announced subsequently that no employee undertaking such work was to labour more than 8 hours per day or 40 hours per week. Following the Supreme Court's endorsement of the constitutional validity of the National Labor Relations Act and a sudden upsurge in the level of unemployment in 1937, the Congress continued its intervention in the determination of standard worktimes. In 1938 it enacted the Fair Labor Standards Act, which extended the 8-hour day, 40-hour week to all firms engaged directly or indirectly in interstate commerce. This legislation established a national standard that has been maintained in the U.S.A. to this day.

The maintenance of the forty-hour standard

With the exception of New Zealand, the introduction of a permanent 40-hour week during the 1930s was a phenomenon unique to the U.S.A. Governments in other countries introduced this schedule, but this was either done on a temporary basis, to absorb the unemployed, or its introduction was soon abandoned because of employer hostility. What needs to be explained, therefore, is why the 40-hour standard was retained in the United States.

The explanation for the retention of the 40-hour law has two major elements. First is the greatly expanded strength and militancy of the organised working class. In the second half of the 1930s the A.F.L. and the newly formed Congress of Industrial Organizations (C.I.O.) expanded the spread of union coverage to levels unprecedented in the U.S.A. The former organisation, moreover, abandoned its traditional hostility to state intervention in the labour market, and the latter accepted such intervention as a matter of course. Both organisations became firm advocates of maximum-worktime laws. This enhanced power and change of position would have made it hard for the state to rescind these laws and rescission would have been particularly difficult after 1939, when labour's bargaining power was further strengthened by the elimination of unemployment as Europe went to war.

As important as was the enhanced strength of labour, a second factor of at least equal importance helps to explain why the 40-hour standard was maintained. The second element is the fact that many employers found that this schedule could be adopted at little or no cost. Indeed, many capitalists, either before or shortly after the worktime laws were introduced, came to realise that they stood to gain if a 40-hour standard was imposed universally. Those employers who were both willing and able to rationalise their production methods, so that their employees could undertake as much work under the reduced schedule as they had under the longer, became aware that not only was the 40-hour week more efficient, but its introduction often improved their position vis-à-vis those of their competitors who had difficulty adjusting to the new conditions.

Evidence to support the claim that an increasing number of capitalists were becoming aware of the greater efficiency of the 40-hour schedule was accumulating even before the N.I.R.A. was introduced. In 1931 and 1932 the Bureau of Labor Statistics (1936) undertook two major studies to determine the extent to which the 5-day week had been adopted permanently by U.S. industry. The first survey found that 2.4 per cent of the establishments examined had adopted the 5-day week for all or part of their staff. The number of workers employed by these firms constituted 5.6 per cent of the total workforce of all enterprises surveyed. By 1932 these figures had increased to 5.4 per cent and 8.4 per cent respectively. For manufacturing industries the proportions were considerably higher, being 7.8 per cent and 12.3 per cent. When making its report the bureau emphasised the fact that establishments were listed as having the 5-day week only when this schedule had been adopted on a permanent basis. It did not include those enterprises in which the shorter week had been introduced merely to spread the available work. The point was also made that these figures understated the extent to which time standards had been curtailed. This was, first, because they did not include those cases where weekly hours had been reduced but the workweek was greater than 5 days; second, because they did not include the building industry, where in many trades 90 per cent of the workforce was on 5 days per week or less.

Why the 5-day week had spread so widely in the early thirties, the Bureau of Labor Statistics argued, was explained by the coming together of a number of forces. The primary factor it stressed was the onset of the depression, which had induced employers to reduce worktimes in order to spread the available work. When introducing reduced schedules, they reported, employers concomitantly strove to cut costs by demanding that those employed labour harder during the time they did work. What many of them consequently found was that the reduced schedule enabled workers to maintain a higher level of work intensity, and this fact, combined with the technical changes the workers' enhanced capacity made possible, encouraged the wide adoption of the 40-hour week on a permanent basis.

The extent to which employers attempted to cut costs by intensifying labour time was radically accelerated by the N.I.R.A. Legal restrictions on worktimes, the Women's Bureau reported, resulted in many employers demanding that their employees provide the same output under the reduced schedule as they had under the longer. Different methods for attaining this objective were utilised, the bureau reported, with special mention being made of increased machine speed and an increase in the number of machines each worker was expected to operate (Byrne 1935: 19). Evidence to support these claims was soon abundant. With Code number 1 for the cotton textile industry, for example, the *Daily News Record*, chief organ of the textile trade, reported:

A general speeding up of looms has already gotten under way in the cotton mills of the country. . . . The average cotton manufacturer has planned to get the absolute maximum of productive capacity out of his machinery, under the new restrictions of hours. (Cited by Hutchins 1934: 121)

With the advent of the codes, weavers who had worked sixteen to twenty looms were reported as being jumped to thirty to forty-two looms, and spinners who had worked two frames were compelled to work three. The consequence of such changes in textiles and in many other industries was that employers reported "that workers' output in five days was practically equal to their former output in six days" (Hutchins 1934: 125).

Intra-class divisions

In 1936 the Bureau of Labor Statistics published a report outlining the experience of a number of firms that had adopted the 40-hour week in the early thirties. One of the firms reported as having had great success with this schedule was the Standard Oil Company of New Jersey. What makes this particular case interesting is that the company's president, Walter C. Teagle, was the "national coordinator" of a committee established by the National Industrial Conference Board in 1932 to promote work sharing. The Conference Board had observed that firms engaged in large-scale manufacturing had, in general, been attracted to the idea of work sharing to a much greater extent than had small manufacturers and employers outside this sector. Small producers argued that work spreading was not a viable alternative, given their scale of production, as it significantly increased their costs. This response, however, elicited little sympathy from the large-scale employers represented by the Conference Board. When it began to become clear to the latter that their attempts to promote work sharing by the use of propaganda were having only partial success, they became increasingly enthusiastic about the possibility of enrolling the assistance of the one body that had the power to make the adoption of reduced worktimes compulsory, namely the state.

That the compulsory 40-hour week primarily assisted large, technically advanced firms at the expense of the small, less developed enterprise proved to be one of the major criticisms of the New Deal put forward by its conservative detractors. In the case of worktimes it was argued that those companies that had found they could adopt the shorter schedule at little cost, such as Standard Oil, utilised the act to force this standard on those of their competitors who could less easily adapt. This tactic, it was suggested, was designed both to undermine the latter's competitive position and to impose on them a disproportionate share of the cost of maintaining the unemployed (Douglas and Hackman 1939).

Awareness of the broader ramifications of imposing the reduced schedule on the whole of industry must have been shared by many individuals at the highest level of the state. A number of Roosevelt's associates had an intimate awareness of the relationship among work, time and rationalised production. Frankfurter, Brandeis and Tugwell, for example, were all involved in drawing up the National Recovery Act. Likewise, Frances Perkins had over many years worked closely with those individuals in the Consumers' League who had been part of the worktime struggle. Indeed, even Roosevelt had personal knowledge of the likely consequences of reducing standard worktimes. While Assistant Secretary of the Navy during the First World War, he oversaw the introduction of the 8-hour day in the naval shipbuilding industry. The favourable results attained by this change led him, in 1919, to write to President Wilson urging the adoption of the 44-hour week as a national standard. All these individuals had, at one time or another, gone to some lengths to argue that a reduction in the length of time the worker laboured did not necessarily reduce the amount of work accomplished. They must have been aware, therefore, of how employers would respond if they were compelled to adopt a 40-hour schedule. In case they had forgotten, the point was spelt out by Laird in *The New Republic*. In February 1934, Laird argued that the "spread work" theory behind the shorter hours demanded by the N.I.R.A. ignored the evidence accumulated by the fatigue researchers which indicated that industrial production could be kept up, or even improved, under a 40-hour schedule. By the beginning of 1934, he reported, it was becoming clear that employers were learning this lesson and that they were adapting their production methods accordingly. Consequently, he concluded, it was highly unlikely that many permanent jobs would be created by the introduction of the 5-day week.

It begins to appear that there will be no real spreading of work under the shorter hours of the N.R.A. Human elasticity and new work patterns will step production back to the old level, or even higher, without increasing the number of men at work. There are, to be sure, some minor exceptions to this, retail-store employment, for example, where shortening the hours of the clerks has no perceptible effect on the amount of goods sold . . . but the aggregate of industry will undoubtedly show an equal, possibly rising, production, with no increase in the number of employees. (p. 357)

Given that Roosevelt's administration was aware of how employers would respond if a reduced time schedule was imposed on industry, its decision to proceed with this policy must be explained, first, by the fact that the passing of the Black Act gave it little choice and, second, by its need to take some immediate steps to ease the intensity of the crisis. Whereas Roosevelt may have realised that few permanent jobs would be created by a reduced standard, he clearly hoped, in both 1933 and 1938, that this action would provide some reduction in the level of unemployment even if only during the period it took employers to adapt their methods to the new conditions. That the worktime laws indeed had this effect is attested to by Roos (1971: 145–150), who has estimated that the N.I.R.A. created some two million extra jobs through 1934–1935. He also reports, however, that this improvement was only temporary and that by the end of 1935 the number of people in work was no greater than it had been in December 1933. The claim that the worktime laws provided few permanent jobs is also supported by developments in the manufacturing sector. In October 1939 manufacturing production was about 2 per cent above the level of October 1929. Hours per week and the number of workers employed in 1939, however, were 20.9 per cent and 3.9 per cent fewer respectively.

Why the worktime laws proved ineffective as a provider of long-term jobs is indicated by a study of the bituminous coal industry undertaken by Fisher (1940). In April 1934, he reports, the owners and miners in the Appalachian fields utilised the N.I.R.A. as a means to impose higher wages and reduced worktimes on the whole industry. Maximum weekly hours were reduced from 40 to 35 and minimum wages were increased by approximately 22 per cent. This action undermined the competitiveness of southeastern mines, whose primary means of competing against northern mines which utilised rationalised production methods was to pay lower wages and provide less attractive working conditions.

The introduction of the 7-hour day and higher wage rates increased the total wage bill, per million tons produced in the South, between 31 and 35 per cent. It also resulted in an immediate drop in output of 10 per cent per worker per day. To meet their market requirements the owners were forced both to increase the number of days their mines were worked and temporarily increase the number of their employees. They also responded, however, by utilising the higher prices the N.I.R.A. provided them to overhaul their production methods. Through 1935 the employers invested heavily in mechanical loading equipment. At the same time they took advantage of the enhanced capacity of the workers provided them by the 35-hour week to induce them to labour more intensively. The result of these combined factors was a steady increase in output per worker day and a gradual reduction in the number of workers employed. By 1937, as a result, though production was 7 per cent above that of 1929 the total real wage bill was only 5.5 per cent higher and the number of workers employed had actually decreased by 1.2 per cent.

Conservative critics of the New Deal have argued that the Government's intervention seriously disrupted industry and may even have hampered recovery. Roos, for example, has criticised the administration for "seriously discomfiting" the southern mine owners by compelling them to pay wages similar to those paid in the rationalised sector of the industry. Such criticisms, however, can hardly be taken seriously, particularly when it is realised that forcing backward industries to adopt rationalised production methods not only improved the lot of the worker but also improved the profitability of the industry as a whole. The administration's decision to promote the 40-hour week as a new standard for the United States, after it became clear that it could only provide temporary relief to the unemployed, reflects, then, not only the enhanced bargaining power of labour but also the developments within industry that occurred under the N.I.R.A. Roosevelt's policies prior to 1936 aimed at relief and recovery. After this period they aimed at recovery and reform (Smithies 1964). The resurgence of unemployment in 1937 ensured that this reform programme included a commitment to the 40-hour week, while the positive results many employers had obtained with this schedule under the N.I.R.A. enabled its retention on a permanent basis. The rationalisation of worktimes had, at least temporarily, been achieved in the United States.

CHAPTER 5

The internationalisation of rationalised worktimes

The technical and philosophical approach to management pioneered by Taylor initially attracted interest outside the United States during the last years of the nineteenth century. At first this interest was decidedly muted. In time, however, Taylor's basic methodology became the cornerstone for modern management practice around the globe. This is true of all industrialised nations including those in which ownership of the means of production is socialised. In the years after 1920 the employers of all nations viewed with a mixture of fear and awe the growing industrial power of the U.S.A. Many soon came to realise that they had little choice but to follow the path pioneered by the Americans. This realisation was to accelerate radically the global diffusion of scientific management. In this expansion many of the American movement's concrete or specific aspects were severely modified. Its system, philosophy and method, however, were largely transported undisturbed.

As in the United States, the global application of Taylorism soon moved beyond the resolution of technical problems associated with the workshop. In the early 1920s it merged with industrial psychology, with the result that the rationalisers came to place even greater emphasis on the human factor. At the same time its advocates expanded their horizons to the national and even to the international level as they applied Taylor's planning methods on an increasingly wider scale to such problems as standardisation, marketing, industrial concentration and the systemisation of both private and public bureaucracies. In Europe these developments, by the end of the decade, led many to ask how a "common market" could be organised which would enable European producers to attain the economies of scale Taylorism had made possible. This global diffusion of scientific management in the years to 1930, and more specifically the internationalisation of rationalised worktimes, will now be looked at. It will be suggested that a common path tended to be followed by most industrialised nations during this period. It will also be argued that, as in the U.S.A., the knowledge that working times and wages could be improved without undermining the viability of industry – if the development of the new science was guided in specific directions – acted as a tremendous force aiding workers in their struggle to improve their living standards and reduce the length of time they were compelled to remain at work.

The general course of the movement

Between 1925 and 1927 Paul Devinat, chief of the Employers' Organisation Service of the International Labour Office, undertook a major study of the growth and progress of scientific management in Europe. Devinat (1927: 16) reported: "Generally speaking, the movement would appear to have followed practically the same course everywhere." He suggested that in every country studied, either prior to or immediately after the war, an initial phase could be observed in which certain individuals became convinced of the superiority of Taylorist principles and of the general importance of applying scientific methods to the management of industry. This introductory stage was followed by a second, which he termed the "phase of adaption." Generally, this took the form of expanding and modifying the techniques previously diffused in a rapid attempt to recover from the ravages of the war. During this phase, many of the original characteristics of the movement were changed to fit local or temporary conditions. This second phase, in turn, merged into a third, the phase of "final adjustment" during which a more coherent body of opinion as regards scientific management came to the fore. In this last stage the rationalisers' propaganda became better co-ordinated and methodical while debate was narrowed down to more concrete application and attempts were made to systemise the movement under the guidance of centralised organisations.

Devinat conceded that his divisions were somewhat arbitrary and appeared a little artificial in the case of a number of countries. He also acknowledged that the phases often overlapped to such an extent that it was difficult to tell where one ceased and the next began. Subject to these reservations, however, he insisted (1927: 17) that "this method of subdivision would seem to correspond fairly closely, in general, to the outlines of the movement's development, and in any case it facilitates the historical study of the subject." Examination of the available evidence suggests that Devinat's claims, as to both the existence of these three stages and the utility of his model for historical analysis, have a good deal of validity. Accordingly, his three-stage approach will be utilised in this examination of the international dissemination of Taylorism and rationalised worktimes.

The introductory stage

International interest in scientific management was first kindled when Bethlehem Steel made public the high-speed-tool steels developed by Taylor and White in 1898. Within days of their discovery being made public the two engineers began receiving requests for further information and visitors from all over the world. Taking advantage of this widespread interest, Taylor utilised the opportunity to promote his management ideas. The success his systematic and methodical methods had managed to attain with metal cutting ensured him an audience, and his work was soon recognised by a number of scholars as a major advance on similar management research being undertaken in Europe. This led a number of French and German technicians to begin circulating his ideas through industry. In 1901, for example, following its repetition of his metal-cutting experiments, one of Germany's leading engineering bodies began popularising scientific management amongst its members and began establishing contacts with Taylorists in the U.S.A.

Over the next decade Taylor's works were published throughout Europe. Interest in his methods of organisation, however, was largely restricted to technicians and teachers of technical subjects. These converts invariably attempted to convince others of the benefits that could be gained from applying systematic planning to the management of society's resources. They also undertook sporadic experiments and attempted to apply Taylor's methods within the workplace where they could. In general, where this positive response took place before 1914, however, it was confined to small groups of intellectuals and attracted the attention of few employers. The small number of the latter who did utilise some of Taylor's ideas during the prewar period, moreover, tended to do more harm than good for the popularisation of the movement. With few exceptions, such individuals adopted the same attitude to scientific management as had most U.S. employers. They ignored the wider aspects of Taylor's programme, which necessitated the investment of large sums of capital and effort. They also displayed little interest in the reorganisation of traditional management structures where this involved any undermining of their established perquisites and prerogatives. Instead, they concentrated their attention on the use of the stop watch and incentive wage systems, which they attempted to force workers to accept. Also, like American capitalists, these employers were attracted to "efficiency experts" who offered to sell them cheap time-study and incentive-wage schemes which aimed to extract as much labour as possible from the workers while giving them little in return. These policies elicited the same hostile response from the labour movements of most nations as they had from the American workers. Bricard (cited in Merkle 1980: 153), for example, reports that French employers generally saw in Taylorism merely a new means for speeding up workers, and the latter reacted accordingly:

It (the fundamental principle of Taylor) had been at times misunderstood, notably in the application that had been attempted in one of the great automobile factories in the region of Paris. The principle that the management wanted to adopt was to determine by experience the best method for making a piece. This result once acquired, a special worker would labor as fast as he could for three hours, using the work procedures thus studied. His production would serve as the base for the determination of tasks. This system was not accepted by the workers in the factory who went out on strike until the management returned to its previous practices.

The policy of adopting only those aspects of Taylor's programme which enhanced their control over workers and compelled the latter to increase the intensity of their labour time was implemented whenever and wherever employers had the opportunity to impose their personal preferences. In order for the vast majority of employers to be induced to follow that course which involved effort and cost on their part, it was invariably necessary for them to be placed under significant pressure and for them to be blocked, by the labour movement or the state, from selecting that path that merely meant speed-up. Devinat reports that, in the early years and through the 1920s, the European scientific managers constantly complained that while some employers were willing to accept the costs, partial failure and slow results that the full adoption of Taylor's programme necessitated, many refused even to consider such an approach. Employers usually claimed that Taylor's wider ideas might be suitable for the vast markets of the United States but were not applicable in Europe. Many technicians also reported that even where capitalists could be induced to begin experimenting with Taylor's methods they often abandoned this strategy when positive results were not obtained immediately. The technicians, Devinat (1927: 144) reports,

inveighed against the spirit of routine, the indifference, and the narrow-mindedness which certain owners exhibit as regards any innovation. They sometimes accused them of being more concerned with increasing the output of their workers than with the increase which they might themselves obtain by the introduction of improved methods or equipment, or, to put it briefly, improved management. . . . According to the technicians, who expressed themselves freely to us, the employer, at all events in the case of the average sized undertaking, is not so much a support as an obstacle in the introduction of methods of scientific management.

The inability of the Taylorists to interest employers in their wider ideas prior to the First World War was radically reversed in many countries after 1914. As in the United States, this dramatic change was a direct result of the pressures generated by the conflict and by the economic and political crises that characterised the immediate postwar years. As Devinat (1927: 19) stated, "It is . . . a fact beyond dispute that the war created in every country an atmosphere favourable to the subsequent development of the movement." During the conflict the shortage of labour, the dramatic expansion of mass production and the necessity of employing vast numbers of unskilled workers made the adoption of Taylor's methods a matter of urgency. To make possible the attainment of this objective the state, in all the belligerent nations, actively intervened to direct and accelerate the production of the needs of war. This was done in many cases by utilising Taylorist methods to systematically organise national production and to more closely integrate the army, the workshop and the laboratory. In many instances this policy elicited a hostile response from employers, for it often involved enforced industrial concentration, standardisation and the allocation of raw materials and transport along lines determined by national efficiency rather than by individual profit.

The forces generated by the enhanced demand for the rationalisation of the production process were also aided by the weakened resistance of the workers. Patriotism severely limited the extent to which organised labour was willing to resist the introduction of even those aspects of Taylorism to which they were especially opposed. This factor was particularly significant in the front-line states during the early years of the war. As the conflict continued, however, the ability of patriotism to contain worker hostility began to wane, being replaced, in many states, by resentment and hostility. The subsequent radicalisation of the working class was to influence significantly the character and direction of the postwar development of scientific management.

The stage of adaption

The achievements gained by the use of Taylorism during the war and the immediate consequences of the conflict, most notably the workers' newfound militancy and dramatic fluctuations in the trade cycle, induced the development of a new phase in the rationalisaton movement after 1918. Its principal characteristic was the desire to adapt and present scientific management in a form more suitable to national conditions and to modify it sufficiently to make it more widely acceptable and applicable within industry. Numerous governments attempted in the immediate postwar period to continue the application of Taylorist methods on the scale that had been undertaken during the war. The prestige and power of the state, which had been expanded by the conflict, together with a widespread belief that governments had a duty to ensure the efficient development of industries necessary for military security, encouraged and enabled a number of Taylorists to begin attempting rudimentary economic planning at a national level. These developments were particularly significant in France, Germany and most notably the Soviet Union. The last of these three states was soon to lead the world in developing planning techniques for the scientific management of society. For most other countries, however, resistance on the part of employers to state intervention in the production process limited the Government's ability to engage in macro-economic management.

Given the hostility generated by early employer attempts to utilise limited aspects of Taylorism, the propaganda of the scientific managers was consciously modified, during the adaption stage, to a form which was more acceptable to the labour movement. Much effort was made to convince workers that they stood to gain by abandoning their hostility to the American methods. References to Taylor tended to be deliberately avoided by his supporters, and they increasingly utilised the term rationalisation rather than scientific management. Likewise, those employers who attempted to seriously utilise Taylor's methods tended to de-emphasise their origin for fear of eliciting working-class hostility. Thus, Urwick (1930: 70) reports, it came about that during a period in which increasing use was made of Taylor's ideas and methods his name was seldom used in connection with this work except to insist that it had nothing to do with scientific management. The time-study and wage-incentive aspects of Taylor's programme also tended to be downplayed during the stage of adaption – and this particularly so during the period of the postwar boom. Emphasis instead was placed on the ability of a rationalised production process to deliver improved living and working conditions. Of the latter, stress was placed on the ability of rationalised industry to provide the 8-hour day.

Throughout Europe, in the immediate postwar years the establishment of a general 8-hour day became the primary demand of the labour movement. As Feis (1924: 375) noted, organised labour considered this issue to be much more than merely another industrial reform.

The eight-hour day was to the representatives of these organizations the first and most essential step of a great transformation, required in their eyes to guard the worker's health and energy, to preserve his spirit under the factory routine, and to give him the leisure necessary for the pursuit of his happiness and development.

Labour leaders, therefore, were receptive to the overtures of the rationalisers where these were couched in a form which suggested their work could assist the attainment of this demand. They were especially attracted, moreover, by that aspect of the rationalisers' research which suggested that reductions in working time did not necessarily reduce output. The results of the fatigue research undertaken during the war were widely publicised by the unions and used by them in their struggle for the 8-hour day.

During the period of the postwar boom, the 48-hour standard workweek became the norm in virtually every industrialised country of Europe. In some nations this schedule was adopted as a result of collective bargaining. In the vast majority of cases, however, it was necessary for the state to intervene with some form of enabling legislation. The politicians and state functionaries who supported the compulsory introduction of the 8-hour day generally did so because they feared the radicalised workers. Many of them, however, were also motivated by the belief that the shorter day was a reasonable claim given the evidence accumulated by the fatigue researchers. For these reformers it was generally understood that the concession necessarily involved a quid pro quo. They argued that the workers could have their 8 hours but in return they would have to ensure that they intensified their efforts and did not allow production to be decreased as a result of the reduced schedule. In the words of the British Government's delegate to the Washington convention,

But now, having said so much of what is due to labor, let me by way of another word or preface just say something of what in my opinion is due from labor. There is, in my opinion, due from labor whole-hearted cooperation in the largest possible production of goods. . . . But I submit, fellow delegates, that the way to get that is not by long hours of labor . . . the way to get it, and the only way to get it, is by a better organization of industry, by humanizing the conditions of labor. I believe by carrying out those two principles we can get labor to put its back into its work while it is at it. I hope it will; I believe it will; and I believe further that labor, as well as other classes in the community would benefit thereby. (International Labor Conference 1920: 34)

Employers, on the other hand, generally remained unmoved by the arguments that worktime and output were not proportionally related. In France, for example, the Paris Chamber of Commerce argued that the introduction of the 48-hour week would be disastrous for industry, as it would cause a fall in productivity of 30 per cent. To claims that science had shown that this need not necessarily be the case employers retorted that the traditional nature of French industry made such arguments irrelevant. Despite their hostility, however, French employers did not attempt any serious resistance to the 48-hour law of 1919. It was widely believed within their ranks that it was necessary to make this concession, at least for the moment, if the workers were to be appeased. French capitalists consequently adopted a policy similar to that of their counterparts in the rest of Europe. In other words, they "protested, but in general leading industrialists accepted the eight hours as a dike upon which the radical tide could break" (Maier 1975: 80).

The employers' offensive

The conciliatory attitude maintained by employers during the period of expansion was brought to a sudden halt by the global depression of 1920–1922. By this period the wave of war-induced radicalisation had greatly subsided, swamped by the reforms and prosperity attained during the boom. Conservative governments were returned in many nations, and when the economic crisis had weakened the bargaining power of the workers sufficiently, both the state and the employers counterattacked. Throughout Europe this period saw the workers lose many of the gains they had won during the boom years, and these losses included the renunciation or abandonment of many of the postwar worktime laws.

The employers' offensive against the 8-hour day, it should be added, was not merely a manifestation of their bias against reductions in working time. The much-promised increased hourly output the rationalisers had insisted would result from the worktime laws did not generally materialise. The reduction in the length of the workweek significantly drove up unit costs. Lowe's (1982: 256) description of the consequent response of British capitalists is equally applicable to employers in general.

The failure of the workforce (in the eyes of the establishment) to respond immediately to a reduction of hours with increased productivity stiffened employers' prejudice against "sentimental" social reform which, by adding to the costs of production, was held to decrease international competitiveness and hence increase unemployment.

The reasons why output fell when the 8-hour day was introduced are numerous. Lipmann (1924) has put forward a number of reasons that help to explain this development. He stressed, in particular, the point that it did not follow that if the length of time worked was reduced hourly output would necessarily rise automatically. Certainly there was no reason to believe it would do so to a degree sufficient to fully offset the temporal reduction. If this level of offset was to be attained, active steps had to be taken by both employers and workers.

This fact, he suggested, had not been realised by many in industry. For even though the workers had used the arguments of fatigue researchers to further their claims, all too often they had really fought for the 8-hour day as a means of decreasing unemployment. In reality they had envisaged the introduction of the shorter day as being a work-sharing reform which would increase employment and enhance the bargaining power of labour. Within the labour movement it was widely believed that a 20 per cent reduction in working time, from 10 to 8 hours per day, would mean each worker would undertake 20 per cent less work. In other words, many workers believed, as did the employers, that the 8-hour day was a reform for which labour would not have to bear any cost.

[Workers] accepted the 8-hour day as a free gift, without realising the necessity of making some return for it by increased intensity of work. As a matter of fact, during the period of demobilisation this return was unnecessary; it is only now, when competition in industry has become acute, that the workers must be reminded that with shorter hours increased intensity of work is necessary, and the employers that a reduction in hours does not necessarily mean a decrease in production and that output will not necessarily be increased by increasing hours of work. (Lipmann 1924: 490)

Lipmann's conclusion that both worker and employer had to contribute to the rationalisation of worktimes by raising the intensity of their efforts on the one hand, and by improving the technical and managerial aspects of production on the other, was endorsed by Milhaud (1925: 820; 1926) in his massive study into the global conditions of production undertaken during the 1920s. Milhaud agreed that the effect on output of the passage of the 8-hour laws had not been as positive as had been hoped. He reported that the laws had certainly acted as a stimulant motivating employers and workers to greater efforts, as theory, prewar experience and experimental evidence suggested they should. The response, however, had not been sufficient to totally offset the temporal reduction. He conceded that this failure was partly the result of workers choosing to accept the shorter day as a costless gain. This response had been accentuated by the significant wage increases also won during the 1919–1920 period and by the abolition of piece work in a number of states. As a result of these developments many workers had chosen to reduce the amount of effort they normally undertook, electing instead to enjoy a little more leisure.

Milhaud added, though, that this failure was also the result of employers not adequately carrying through the reorganisation of the production process as the rationalisers suggested was possible and necessary. This was not because they could not do so but rather because, in the immediate postwar period, a number of specific circumstances had existed which had tended to limit the "free play" of those factors which should have ensured they were forced to do so. These were (1) the limited availability of new machinery and equipment relative to the massive demand, (2) the tremendous business boom that followed the war, which resulted in such high profits employers did not need to worry about their increased unit costs, and (3) the acute depression that followed the boom, which severely limited the funds available to firms to finance the necessary technical adjustments. Collectively, Milhaud suggested, the significance of these developments was sufficient to justify the claim that given more normal conditions and a longer period for adjustment, the responses needed from both employers and workers would be forthcoming.

The Americans and the eight-hour day

Milhaud's optimism was soon justified. Indeed, by the time he published his report many of the factors he identified as problems limiting the degree of offset were being or had been dealt with. One of the first to be eliminated was the workers' decision to reduce the amount of effort they were willing to undertake. The unemployment generated by the depression greatly enhanced the bargaining power of the employers. This power, in many cases, was used to drive workers and to compel the introduction of those aspects of Taylorism to which the labour movement was particularly opposed, namely the utilisation of time study and payment by results. In a great number of instances these tools were utilised as a means to intensify labour time, and then rates and bonuses were cut to a level where the higher rate of effort was treated as the new norm.

The employers' return to the form of industrial relations that was normal before the war was characteristic of their general tendency to strive to re-establish the conditions that existed before 1914. Urwick (1930: 60) reports that there was a marked tendency for employers to look back to the norms of this period as a kind of standard to which they should direct their efforts.

The attempt to force the workers to intensify their efforts and accept as much of the cost of the crisis as was possible was the strategy adopted by the vast majority of employers. A significant number throughout the industrialised world, however, did not limit themselves to this method for combating their competitors but also began to experiment with the ideas being developed in the U.S.A. These exceptions were to be found in every industry and, Urwick (1930: 61) reports, their numbers grew steadily through the early 1920s.

The expansion in the number of employers interested in Taylorism is explained, first, by the growing general awareness of what could be gained by applying Taylor's methods and, second, by the increased pressure to overhaul production methods placed on employers by the compulsory reduction of worktime. International awareness of the possibilities inherent in Taylorism was intensified, after 1921, by the tremendous expansion in industrial productivity enjoyed by U.S. industry. Albert Thomas (cited in Devinat 1927: vii), the director of the I.L.O., reported that this development acted as a powerful force compelling European employers to emulate their U.S. counterparts: "In short, the new element [motivating Europeans] is the realisation by many persons in Europe that the economic progress of the United States threatens disaster to the older continent, and that the only way to salvation lies in the rationalisation of production." Through the 1920s a worldwide fascination with what was happening in the U.S.A. developed. This was reflected in the numerous delegations sent to America to study the new methods (Siegfried 1930). It was also reflected in the massive quantity of Taylorist literature that flooded onto the world's markets. Taylor's works were translated into practically every language in the 1920s, and the major part of the debate on scientific management that raged at this time centred on these publications. There was also wide dissemination of the works of a number of Taylor's close collaborators, with the Gilbreths in particular proving popular with some governments and with the labour movement. Hoover's *Waste in Industry* also proved highly influential, particularly in Czechoslovakia, Germany and the U.S.S.R.

One other author whose works were widely read during the 1920s was Henry Ford. Merkle (1980: 193–194) reports that his publications were especially popular in Germany, where they were often taken at face value, with the result that it was widely believed that Ford was as much philanthropist as capitalist. The extent of Ford's influence was also enhanced by the direct experience many industrialists had with his methods, for he not only exported his books, he also exported his plants and his techniques. International dissemination of American production methods was greatly assisted, during this period, by the growth of the multinational corporation. The personal contact brought about, Layton (1974: 381) has suggested, was crucial because of the highly "complex combination of process innovations" involved in these methods.

Like Taylorism, Mass Production represented not merely a few general principles, but a mass of details and orientations, which could be most easily transferred by the movement of people. Ford's international operations provided a mechanism for the transfer of people and for training local technologists in American methods. Thus, the receiving country got not only working examples of the new ideas, but a pool of engineers and others with the new knowledge.

The decision by a growing number of employers to adopt rationalised production methods was also a result of their experiences with 8-hour laws. For many these laws acted as a major stimulant motivating them to overhaul their methods of production. This development, limited in the years immediately after the war, became much more prevalent through the 1920s. Indeed, as early as 1922 the I.L.O. (1931: 96) reports that in Sweden,

in the case of the manufacturing industries, in the strict sense of the term, it would seem that at least a certain degree of compensation for the limitation of hours of work has been found in a greater concentration of labour and an increase in its productivity, secured by technical changes and reforms in organisation. . . . The Eight-hour Day Act, in certain industries at least, has proved a powerful stimulus to these improvements, which are still being extended.

Through the decade, observers in many countries found similar results. The most comprehensive of the studies undertaken of this development was conducted in France between 1922 and 1927 by the Ministry of Labour (I.L.O. 1931: 99). Despite French employers' claims in 1919 that they would not be able to change their production methods, this study reported that the modifications introduced to counter the 8-hour law covered the "whole field of scientific management." Included amongst these changes were improved selection and training of workers, the use of time and motion study, improved working methods, greater specialisation in the division of labour, new forms of work organisation, improved plant and workplace layout and the widespread introduction of payment by results. There was also a great increase in the mechanisation and electrification of the production process. These last factors involved the widespread extension of the use of mechanised equipment for the handling of goods, the use of automatic machines, significant improvements in tools, increases in the speed of machines and the mechanisation of much work formerly done by hand. As part of this process there was also a growth in the size of the enterprise brought on by a wave of amalgamations. This last development enabled firms to scrap much inefficient plant and equipment and gain great efficiencies of scale.

The cumulative evidence gained by observing the way employers responded to enforced reductions in working times during the 1920s led the I.L.O. (1931: 127) researchers to conclude that it was clear that "measures of a collective nature for the reduction of hours of work lead the managers of industry to make efforts to rationalise their undertakings." Having reached this conclusion, these scholars then turned to consider whether rationalisation measures, irrespective of why they were introduced, had an influence on worktime and, if so, what was its nature. To answer these questions the researchers first of all surveyed the various consequences of the rationalisation measures introduced in response to the 8-hour day. This survey led them to conclude that, in the overwhelming majority of cases, the rationalisation measures had enabled output to be increased under the shorter schedule despite the fact that introduction of the 8-hour laws had involved on average a worktime reduction of 20 per cent. They further concluded that the introduction of rationalised techniques, no matter why they were introduced, tended to lead to the introduction or further extension of reduced time schedules. This latter result, it was argued, was brought about by the following factors (I.L.O. 1931: 146).

(1) Certain changes in the nature of the work in rationalised industry. Intensification of effort.
(2) Facilities offered by increased productivity.
(3) Intellectual, moral and social factors.

(4) The importance of spare time in the development of markets.
(5) The progress of the science of labour. The rationalisation of the distribution of work in time.
(6) Factors concerning the technical workings of undertakings.

It was concluded that rationalisation measures encouraged reductions in working time either by consolidating progress already made or by stimulating further progress. In other words, the studies of the 1920s reaffirmed Marx's argument about how capitalists would respond to a compulsory reduction in worktime. The 8-hour laws galvanised employers into applying closer supervision and furthering the adoption of piece work. Moreover, they motivated them to speed up the mechanisation of the production process and improve the quality of the machinery utilised. These developments, in turn, induced increases in the level of work intensity of such a magnitude that old schedules were no longer economically efficient; indeed, in many instances the intensity levels the workers were compelled to maintain were pushed to a point where further reductions in the length of time normally laboured were bound to occur.

The labour movement, the engineers and the psychologists

The loss of or constant pressure from employers to revoke the 48-hour week during the early 1920s shows the difficulty workers invariably face in trying to hold onto a reform the retention of which is based solely on industrial power. The bargaining strength of the working class is too susceptible to fluctuation, because of shifts in political allegiances and changes in the demand for its commodity, to enable major gains to be permanently retained where it is only power that holds them. Indeed, if the gains are of such a magnitude that they place too great a strain on the rate of profit, these advances in themselves will tend to ensure their eventual loss because they will lead to greater unemployment and thus to an undermining of the power upon which they are based. Feis (1924: 644) stressed this point in his analysis of why the I.L.O. proved incapable of securing international ratification of the Washington 8-hour convention:

It seems clear now that no temporary impulse of social justice or even definite ascendancy of organized labor in the economic balance of individual states is sufficient in itself to establish the eight-hour regime *genuinely* and *permanently* in practice. The problem of production will continue to assert itself as persistently in the future as it has in the recent past; and the problem will have to be satisfactorily met before the eight-hour regime is willingly and squarely accepted by international agreement.

This lesson, having once again been driven home to the workers by their losses in the 1920–1922 depression, significantly influenced their tactics in the fight for the shorter week through the rest of the decade. It added a strong negative influence to the positive attractions being held out by those wishing to induce the unions to accept the rationalisation of industry. This combination of force and reward, as in the United States, was to prove too powerful for many unionists to resist. In the period after the crisis, unions around the world began to reappraise their attitude to rationalisation. By the middle years of the decade there was even a growing demand from labour that employers adopt many aspects of Taylorism in their enterprises. Albert Thomas (Devinat 1927: xi) argued that this development was characteristic of all countries. By this period, he claimed, the world's workers had become "warm adherents of the doctrine of rationalisation."

Thomas's assessment tends to overstate the case. Workers did not fully embrace Taylor's programme during the 1920s. Rather, what they did was cease rejecting scientific management as such and become much more selective in their criticisms. In the process they also began to promote the use of certain aspects of Taylorism where they could see these might advance their interests. This strategy was to be particularly common in the area of worktime (I.L.O. 1931: 154).

Very frequently these organisations make a quite general demand for shorter working hours as compensation for the disadvantages of rationalisation or simply on account of the increased productivity to which it leads. Such are the resolutions of the International Congress of Painters, July 1928, the French General Confederation of Labour in 1927 and 1929, the Congress of Polish Socialist Trade Unions, May–June 1929, the Congress of the Hungarian Federation of Trade Unions in March 1930, the Conference of the Railwaymen's Section of the International Transport Federation in Madrid, April–May 1930, and the General Council of the International Federation of Trade Unions at Prague in May 1929.

Increasingly the unions argued that a share of the gains to be had from rationalisation were the rightful due of the workers.

Employers, it was insisted, had to be stopped from trying to raise profitability simply by driving the workers, and they must instead be made to turn to the scientific development of production. This meant they had to be compelled to adopt the most modern methods of organisation, the most modern forms of machinery and the most modern management practices. It was recognised by all that this meant they had to adopt the methods of production pioneered in America.

To the pressures attracting and propelling unions to adopt a more conciliatory attitude towards scientific management were added two further factors in the years after 1922. The first was a revival in their bargaining power which enabled them to have greater influence over the direction and nature of the rationalisation movement. The second was the further coalescing of the opinions of the engineers and the psychologists. Devinat (1927: 34) reports that this latter development had a "particularly fortunate" effect on the labour movement's assessment of Taylorism. The convergence was openly cemented following the publication of a scathing attack on the engineers by the psychologists. In the first edition of the journal *Occupational Psychology*, Farmer (1922) opened the attack by arguing that while time and motion studies were wonderful tools for the scientific examination of the labour process, the attitude of the engineers to these tools was simply not acceptable. He suggested the technicians had been so keen to find new ways to increase output that they had been willing to accept any cost to achieve this objective. They had consequently refused to consider what they were doing to the workers. This was not only immoral, it was also inefficient. A year later the doyen of the industrial psychologists, Charles Myers (1923), took up this attack, criticising in particular the concept of the "one best way." Myers insisted that human variability had to be considered when determining work norms. He castigated the engineers for their mechanistic approach to workers and denounced their failure to adequately collaborate with the labour movement. Workers, he insisted, must be involved in the rationalisation process and they must be involved at the level of the trade union.

Frank and Lillian Gilbreth, representing those engineers who were open to a critique of this nature, replied in 1924. Responding to Myers's paper in particular, they stated that they agreed with the greater part of what had been written by their accusers. Indeed, they suggested all "progressive" industrial engineers had come to recognise and accept that the human factor had to play a major role in scientific management. They conceded that many scientific managers, including Taylor, were open to criticism for the rigidity of some of their early work, but, it was insisted, those who attacked Taylor for driving the workers ought to remember that it was not only the employer that he wished to help, it was the employee as well. In order to distance themselves from Taylor's faults they argued that they and their colleagues, while retaining the essence of their mentor's principles, had moved beyond his position. It was unfair, therefore, to judge them strictly on Taylor's application of scientific management. They defended, moreover, the idea of the "one best way" but in doing so they reformulated the concept. From being the one standard all workers had to maintain, the term was redefined as "the One Best Way at the time, under the specific conditions, and with the particular individual, considering his psychological and physiological differences" (Gilbreth and Gilbreth 1924: 41). It was insisted that the concept was an ideal derived from studying the best worker available – not necessarily the fastest method, but the best when all factors were considered. If one allowed for individual differences, they asked, what was wrong with attempting to determine the most efficient way to undertake a task and then setting this as the model for other workers to emulate?

Having made these concessions, the Gilbreths went on to make it clear that they agreed with the suggestion that the engineers and the psychologists had to work together. They suggested, however, that the engineer had centuries of experience in industry while the psychologist was a relative "newcomer" who was traditionally more at home in the laboratory. Consequently, the psychologists had not only to co-operate with the engineers, but if they wished to be successful in the industrial sector they also had to acknowledge the latter's greater experience in this arena. Given the concessions made by the engineers, this was to prove a stipulation the psychologists were more than willing to concede if this was what it took to gain acceptance from employers. Over the next two years the intensity of their criticisms of the engineers subsided dramatically. By the second half of the decade it was even possible for the psychologists (Miles 1926; Myers 1932) to concede that their criticisms of Taylor might have been unjustly harsh, given the size of his contribution to the rationalisation process.

The coming together of the engineers and the psychologists enabled the former to gain valuable information upon which they could base effort norms and the design of equipment. It also lessened the danger that the engineers would inadvertently drive intensity levels beyond the workers' capacities. This last benefit was further aided by the fact that those scholars primarily concerned with the human factor, moreover, continued their attempts to expand the importance of this issue. Myers (1932), for example, continued to remind the engineers that there remained serious unresolved human problems with the rationalisation process brought on by the low skill and monotony of many of the jobs it created. He pointed out that rationalisation often transformed the employee from a manual to a machine worker whose labour tended to be more mechanical, monotonous or unnatural and thus mentally more strenuous. Collier (1943: 133) likewise, while lauding the greater productivity that the utilisation of Taylorism engendered, warned that much of this improvement had been attained by increasing the intensity of the workers' labour time. This was not necessarily a cause for alarm during the initial stages of the rationalisation process, because of the slackness and inefficiency that characterised traditional production methods and because this stage was usually accompanied by increased wages and reductions in standard worktimes. He argued, though, that there was good reason to fear that in their enthusiasm for ever higher levels of intensity employers and their engineers might push these levels too high and thus create new "hidden costs" and wastage.

The newly established affinity between the engineers and the psychologists was also important for the labour movement. It lessened the workers' fear of what scientific management necessarily involved. Unions consequently began to utilise the arguments of the rationalisers to an even greater extent. They were now able to argue that the engineers and the psychologists agreed that the maximisation of efficiency demanded not only the payment of high wages and significantly improved working conditions but also the reduction of worktime. From this period, Devinat (1927: 39) reports, there was a clear "tendency, both among the workers and among the employers, to appeal to scientific management to supply a rational basis for the eight-hour day."

The phase of final adjustment

In Devinat's description of the internationalisation of scientific management his third phase involved the application of Taylorist principles to the resolution of the general problems of industry and government. This stage was characterised by a tendency for the state and progressive industrialists to work together to co-ordinate the scattered activities associated with rationalisation. It also witnessed a growing awareness of the need to establish institutions which would be responsible for the development and dissemination of scientific knowledge in all areas of industry. Consequently, through the 1920s numerous government and semi-government scientific bodies were established which had as their purpose the exploitation of those aspects of Taylorism which were compatible with their societies' social systems. This development was particularly significant in Czechoslovakia, Germany, Italy and the U.S.S.R. The period also saw the formation of national and international standards associations, the development of national campaigns for the elimination of waste, the further extension and development of national planning, attempts at extending international co-operation and a radical increase in economic concentration. Urwick (1930: 19) reports that the outstanding aspects of this phase of the rationalisation movement included efforts

to improve the General Organisation of Production and Distribution on national and international lines by elimination of waste, simplification and standardisation, horizontal and vertical combinations, industrial agreements, action by Governments and Public Services, and by organisations of employers and workers, mass production and distribution, forecasting of business movements, and by the statistical study of the general world conditions bearing on these issues such as the supply of raw material and of labour, markets, transport, and power.

The publication of *Waste in Industry* in 1921 acted as a powerful goad stimulating the development of this third stage. Of greatest importance was the fact that it made clear to many the great potential inherent in the scientific management of the production process. If Hoover's report on the level of waste within the United States was correct, it was reasoned, how much greater must be industrial inefficiency in those nations only setting out on the Taylorist path.

The national and international nature of the issues involved in the phase of final adjustment invariably necessitated an interventionist role for the state. In many nations it was necessary for the Government to take a leading role in promoting the movement, the state being compelled, by the indifference or hostility the Taylorists continued to meet in many quarters, to actively exhort, bribe and compel both capitalist and worker to accept the value and urgent necessity of systematic planning. Even where employers and organised labour came to accept the need for rationalisation, moreover, differences of opinion as to precisely what form the process should take ensured that state power remained a factor of crucial importance. As in the U.S.A., the fact that the interests of the two major classes were not homogeneous was also a source of intense disputation and conflict. Serious divisions, for example, emerged between those workers who stood to gain from rationalisation and those whose immediate or long-term interests it was seen to endanger. These divisions, in many cases, led to severe splits in the solidarity of the working class. When the state or the employers moved to impose a rationalisation strategy on specific sectors of the class, or failed to defend the interest of those adversely affected, these divisions often resulted in the disadvantaged sector finding itself isolated.

Similarly, with employers the question of precisely whose interest the state was to serve in its drive to rationalise industry created intense divisions. Exactly how the state behaved in such circumstances depended on a tremendous number of diverse factors, precise policies being specific to individual nations. By the end of the 1920s, however, the factor common to all the industrialised states was government recognition that the techniques pioneered in America had to be adopted. The question that remained was how this was to be done.

Not the least important of the ways rationalisation was promoted by the state were the provision of funding for scientific research and the convening of national and international congresses the purpose of which was to co-ordinate and systemise the growth and direction of the movement. Thus, in 1921 and 1924 congresses were held in Moscow designated the All-Russian Scientific Management Conference. In 1923 and 1924 similar congresses were held in France. Also in 1924 the First International Scientific Management Congress was held in Prague. This meeting was attended by delegates from six European nations, Australia and the United States. Amongst other things, those at this conference unanimously endorsed the 8-hour day. A further congress was held in Brussels in 1925 at which ten nations were represented, and a third took place in Rome in 1927.

The Rome congress showed clearly the extent to which interest in rationalisation was spreading internationally. It was attended by 1,400 delegates representing forty-five nations. In 1927 the I.L.O. and the Twentieth Century Fund responded to this expanding interest by establishing the International Management Institute at Geneva. This body was to act as a clearing house where information on scientific management from all over the world could be collated and classified. It was also to strive to bring together individuals from all countries who were interested in management questions. Finally, also in 1927, the League of Nations convened an International World Economic Conference in Geneva with the twofold purpose of preparing the way for international economic rapprochement and of improving the state of the global economy. This conference, the I.L.O. (1931: 5) reported, was dominated by the idea of rationalisation.

The resolutions on international trade were inspired by the ideal of the rational distribution of work between nations. The resolutions on agriculture placed in the foreground the idea of the rational organisation of the relations between agricultural producers and industrial consumers. Finally, the various industrial questions were studied from the standpoint of rationalisation, particularly the question of international industrial agreements, this part of the programme being headed by the problem of rationalisation.

The importance of this conference, it must be added, should not be dismissed because of the collapse of international co-operation during the 1930s. Certainly, the depression and the war set back the progress of many aspects of the rationalisation movement, but in the postwar period the ideas developed at this time were to underpin the reorganisation of the capitalist world undertaken during the years of the long boom. A primary reason for calling the conference, for example, had been the recognition by many Europeans that if they were to compete with the Americans they needed to construct a home market, comparable in size to that of the United States, which would allow the development of large-scale rationalised production. To realise even Taylorism's limited potential within capitalism, in other words, the Europeans realised that they had to have a common market.

Rationalised worktime in Germany

The history of the German experience with working times and rationalisation will now be looked at briefly, in order to give greater substance to what has been argued in this chapter and to provide an example of how a major capitalist nation handled the issue. The German experience is particularly important because within Europe Germany became a model and a leader in the race to adapt American production methods to local conditions.

As it became clear, towards the end of 1918, that Germany had lost the war, the major German industrialists desperately began constructing bulwarks that could withstand the expected political upheaval. It was recognised that the petty bourgeoisie and the discredited Junkers alone did not have sufficient strength to hold back those demanding radical social change and an accounting for the conflict. Consequently, the industrialists turned to the conservatives within the trade unions affiliated to the Social Democratic Party. In return for their support against the radicals it was agreed that the employers would renounce company unionism and support universal suffrage, the establishment of unemployment and health insurance, and the introduction of the 8-hour day.

The adoption of the 8-hour day reduced the average workweek by 6 to 12 hours for the majority of workers, and in some cases this went as high as 18 hours. These new standards were implemented by means of Demobilisation Orders which were valid for five years, the supposition being that they would be made permanent once appropriate legislation could be processed. The Government, in fact, did prepare three bills covering manual, salaried and domestic workers. These were submitted to the National Economic Council, a body composed of employers and workers which considered proposed industrial legislation prior to its introduction in the Reichstag.

The employers' delegates on the council, however, put up numerous objections to these laws. It was argued that the introduction of the 8-hour day had led to a considerable reduction in output and increased costs at a time when reparation obligations made the maximisation of production a matter of national urgency. Labour delegates, on the other hand, replied that their empirical investigations had led them to conclude that the productive capacity of the individual worker was on the whole greater under the 8-hour day than it was under any longer schedule. In support of their claims the unions cited examples of large-scale rationalised enterprises which had successfully adopted this standard. They also utilised a major economic study, commissioned by the Frankfurter Zeitung, which concluded that the introduction of the 8-hour day had generally produced favourable results. The study had conceded that production had contracted in some areas. Where this had occurred, however, it was argued that this was generally not because of any failing inherent in the 8-hour schedule itself. Rather, it was the result of the unstable political situation and the lowered physical vitality of the workers brought on by the war-induced decline in their living standards. The unions insisted, finally, that industry's productive capacity was not being utilised anywhere near as efficiently as it could be. It was wrong, therefore, to demand more of the workers' time when the reduction of costs and the expansion of output could be more effectively attained by improved management.

The trade unions think that there is still room for vast improvements in the German organization of production, and they are of the opinion that a more organic connection of work processes and concentration and rational exploitation of labor power will increase production immeasurably. In the view of the trade unions the shorter workday has led already to considerable technical improvements and commensurate increases in production, and it is altogether desirable to insist upon the maintenance of the eight hour day in order to effect even more extensive improvements. (Frankel 1924: 332–333)

The conflicting positions of the workers and the employers on the proposed worktime laws delayed their progress until well into 1923. By this period the postwar radicalism had passed and the economy was reeling under hyperinflation and mass unemployment brought on by the French occupation of the Ruhr. Once convinced that these factors had sufficiently weakened the workers' ability to resist, the employers launched a co-ordinated assault on many of the conditions won during the postwar years. Amongst their demands was the general intro-duction of piece work and the right to insist on overtime. Fran-kel (1924: 327) reports that the employers generally dismissed the union claim that longer working hours did not necessarily produce lower labour costs. Rather, most agreed with the in-dustrialist Stinnes, who declared that, given the state of the economy, German workers would have to labour a 10-hour day for the next ten to fifteen years. The overtime provisions they insisted on, therefore, were designed to effectively abrogate the 8-hour day, and the result was the widespread restoration of 9- and 10-hour days.

During the 1923–1924 crisis, then, the employers' primary means of maintaining profitability was the cutting of wages, the raising of intensity levels and the extension of worktime. As the crisis eased through 1924, however, their capacity to ensure an adequate return on their investments by these methods waned significantly. Limitations in the supply of skilled labour became a particularly acute problem, and this difficulty was com-pounded by a lack of liquidity, excess fixed capital and a short-age of future profit prospects. Blocked in their attempts to resolve these problems by further increasing the rate of abso-lute surplus value, they turned or, in many cases, returned to rationalisation as the means by which profit rates could be im-proved and efficiency enhanced without necessitating the in-vestment of exorbitant amounts of capital.

The German rationalisation movement had a similar origin to its counterpart in the United States. With the onset of the period of decay that began in the 1870s, German employers and workers soon abandoned any attempt to maintain the prin-ciples of laissez-faire. Unlike the British, who remained com-mitted to free-market policies, or the Americans, who at least maintained the fiction that they were, German industrialists abandoned even verbal support for the idea that the market should be allowed to remain unrestricted. They strongly sup-ported the monopolisation of industry, and their cartels were actively encouraged by the state, which gave their agreements the force of law. Besides having the common experience of a definite trend towards monopolisation after 1870, German in-dustry was also similar to its American counterpart in that em-ployers had a practical commitment to the use of science in industry. Consequently, there was fertile ground for Taylor's ideas when these began to become known internationally at the turn of the century. German technicians, while conceding the advanced nature of Taylor's research, recognised that his work had many similarities to their own. Very soon, therefore, they began publicising his ideas, and many of his techniques were introduced into German industries.

Where attempts to adopt Taylorism occurred prior to the world war, they invariably elicited intense resistance from trade unions because of the crude and often harsh way this was done. Even so the movement made significant progress, and this was radically accelerated after 1914 by the success achieved by Richard von Moellendorff, who applied Taylor's methods on a vast scale to the planning of war production. The postwar period saw the continued growth of the movement, though it underwent a certain "nativisation" which tended to camouflage its antecedence. Taylorists encouraged this latter process both to overcome the hostility to Taylor's name in the labour movement and to lessen the resistance scientific management often met because of its foreign origins. Finally, from 1924, the movement flowered into a national campaign, under the guidance of the state and major industrialists, which aimed at the reconstruction of the national economy by the systematic development of planning at the level of the firm, the industry and the nation.

It was at this time that the term rationalisation came into popular use, being initially applied to the process of "rationing" production which the cartels organised in the overexpanded heavy industries. This process involved the dividing up of the market amongst the various producers. By thus adjusting supply to demand, the firms involved were able to save themselves from bankruptcy. The problem with the system, however, was that it resulted in all firms having to operate at a point way below that of maximum capacity. Overhead costs per unit of output consequently rose significantly. In other words, German industry faced an acute version of the situation that had given rise to Taylorism in the U.S.A. at the end of the nineteenth century. As the immediate German problem was to bring down prices to a point compatible with an impoverished market, it was not possible to respond to the lack of demand by further tightening monopolistic controls or raising prices. The response adopted consequently involved the systematic mass restructuring of industry along Taylorist lines. This reorganisation involved the realignment of technically related industrial units, increased plant specialisation, the closing down of inefficient sectors and the scrapping of obsolete plant and equipment. As this initial "negative" phase of the rationalisation process neared completion, it progressed into what became known as "positive" rationalisation, that is, the systematic introduction of the scientific method into all aspects of production and distribution.

Throughout the various stages of Taylorism's development in Germany, the state played a crucial role in its promotion and regulation. Indeed, particularly in the 1920s the breadth and intensity of the state's commitment went far beyond that undertaken in the United States. Governments in the U.S.A. at least retained the anti-trust laws even if they did not attempt to enforce them. They severely restricted, moreover, the extent to which they intervened in the economy. German governments, on the other hand, positively encouraged, indeed in some cases forced, the establishment of cartels and undertook a much more active role in the economy. At a very early stage it was widely recognised in Germany that planning was the essential element in scientific management and that even the narrow technical problems with which Taylorism was initially concerned were bound up with major social issues. Brady (1974: vii) has made this point well:

The primary emphasis of the movement was, at the outset, technical. In a multiplicity of ways it helped to lay bare the engineering and organizational limitations of, as well as the paradoxes inherent in, the postwar German economic system. But, very soon, a need for the arts of organization became manifest, and thence it was an easy, if inescapable, step to consideration of larger questions of social policy. Thus throughout the entire range of rationalization activities there are to be found the directing concepts of plan, order, system, foresight, control, and rational guidance. In detail and at large *rationalization is planning*, and planning calls for the full mobilization of all scientific information and the rational utilization of unscientific criteria as to means.

The state's involvement with planning was particularly significant in the ministries of Traffic, Labour, Economics, and Food and Agriculture. It took on its most concrete form in 1925 with the establishment of the National Economic Advisory Board.

This institution was charged with the promotion of scientific management throughout the economy.

The success achieved by the rationalisation process amazed the rest of Europe. In the six years 1924–1929, Brady (1974: xi) reports, the rationalisation campaign enabled Germany to recover from a condition which experts believed had crippled the country for fifty years. Indeed, by 1930 even the Americans were becoming worried by the German achievements. In its 1931 study *Rationalization of German Industry*, the National Industrial Conference Board reported that Taylorism had been able to progress much further in Germany than it had in the U.S.A. because the state actively assisted the rationalisation process not only by providing technical assistance, as it did in America, but also by enabling industrialists to freely compete or combine in whatever form they wished. The unity of the state and the rationalised sectors of industry, the N.I.C.B. reported, had enabled the development of a system of "planned economy" in some of the nation's major industries which contrasted greatly with the "planlessness" of industrial life in those countries in which unrestricted competition was still believed to be indispensable for progress and prosperity. The extent of the German success, the N.I.C.B. warned, would prove a serious threat to the U.S. economy unless a similar unity of state and corporation was attained.

The utilisation of Taylorism as a weapon to combat one's opponents, it needs to be stressed, was not a tactic that was adopted only by German employers and the Weimar state. In the early 1920s a great deal of scientific research on working conditions was undertaken within the republic. Trade unions enthusiastically endorsed this research and collaborated with the rationalisers' attempts to improve lighting, safety measures and working arrangements in industry. They worked closely, moreover, with scholars such as those at the Wilhelm Institute for Labour Physiology who undertook extensive studies into the nature of fatigue. The scientific support such institutions provided the labour movement induced many labour leaders, in the middle years of the 1920s, to seriously reappraise their attitude towards scientific management. This reappraisal, in turn, led many of these individuals to become much more positive in their attitude towards the rationalisers. The positive reassessment was particularly pronounced among social democrats, though even the communists acknowledged that there was much the working class could gain from rationalisation. For the latter, however, this would necessarily have to mean socialist rationalisation, as was being developed in the U.S.S.R., not the limited version offered by capitalism which they believed invariably meant greater exploitation of the working class.

The communists' hostility to any form of collaboration with the employers which might assist the further development of capitalist rationalisation led them to denounce as class traitors those labour leaders who were willing to negotiate on this issue. Their criticisms, however, became increasingly ineffective as the rewards of the rationalisation process began to be shared by increasing numbers of the working class. By the last years of the decade social-democratic theoreticians were arguing that rationalisation had made possible the establishment of a planned, stable capitalist economy which, in time, could gradually be transformed into socialism (Hilferding 1927; Hertz 1928). Taking up this cue, many union leaders began to demand that capitalists accelerate the pace at which those Taylorist production methods which enhanced productivity, lowered prices or improved working conditions were introduced. Under this new policy, it was insisted, employers must be compelled to adopt the more positive aspects of rationalisation while at the same time they must be stopped from using the rationalisers' techniques in a manner which merely led to increased unemployment, speed-up and greater exploitation. They must be compelled, moreover, to accept that the benefits of rationalisation did not belong solely to the employers. The latter's claim that gains from rationalisation did not have to be shared with the workers or consumers, as it was management that had introduced the new methods, was savagely condemned. Repeatedly, the unions warned that this policy was a recipe for disaster. Ten years before Keynes published his *General Theory* the German unions, when opposing an employer demand for a general cut in wages, beseeched the employers to accept that there was a major problem with demand management, a problem which was greatly accentuated by limited rationalisation.

Rationalisation is necessary. It is a task both for separate concerns and whole industries. Its aim must be a reduction in the costs of production and lower prices, together with a simultaneous increase in wages.

Only by means of an increase in mass purchasing power created in this way can the workless become re-employed. The method, often practised at present, of rationalising without simultaneous lowering of prices and raising of wages must produce a crisis of over-production. (Cited by Meakin 1928: 214)

Another vital factor in the unionists' reappraisal of Taylorism was the issue of the 8-hour day. The argument that the use of the rationalisers' methods would make this schedule economically viable was increasingly forced by the unions to the attention of the employers as the crisis of 1923–1924 eased. For many capitalists the validity of these claims was made clear when they personally experienced the effect on output of maintaining longer time schedules together with the higher levels of work intensity their use of Taylor's techniques made possible. By May 1924 there was a marked tendency for the length of the workday, in many industries, to return to 8 hours. The growth of this trend accelerated through the rest of the year as the economy revived, and it continued to develop at an increasing rate as the higher levels of intensity induced by the rationalisation process spread through industry. Indeed, so pronounced was the effect of increasing intensification the German unions soon began to link their demands for reduced worktimes with the question of the "culturally admissible intensity" of work. There was a serious danger, they argued, that rationalisation would force up intensity levels to a point where workers would be so exhausted, even with a reduced schedule, that they would be unable to engage in any social or cultural activities that required sustained effort.

There is an intensity of work which is not "culturally admissible" because it does not leave room for culture or thought, just as there is an intensity of land cultivation which is not admissible. Rich life is as important as rich soil. . . . Workers should not have to expend all their capacity for fatigue upon work; other interests demand attention if they are to live human lives. Here is a demand which rationalisation must meet. And the fact that it is put forward in those countries where rationalisation has gone furthest proves that it is a modern problem which cannot be brushed aside. (Fox 1929: 686)

The establishment of the 8-hour schedule did not spread evenly across industry. To a significant degree its adoption was dependent on whether the workers had the capacity to induce the employers to take the steps that would make the schedule viable. This, in turn, largely depended on the average level of skill required within an industry. Thus, Bonig (1980) reports, in those areas where the quality of human input largely determined productivity outcomes, such as in the machine technical industry, certain parts of metal manufacturing and the fine mechanical trades, there were introduced those rationalisation techniques designed to reorganise the production process in a manner which would enable a greater concentration and intensification of effort within a reduced working time. In sectors such as textiles and certain parts of the chemical and steel industries where the average level of skill was low, on the other hand, unemployment amongst unskilled workers made it difficult to induce employers to adopt those aspects of Taylorism favourable to the workers' interests.

The differing nature of their experiences with rationalisation was to have serious effects on the solidarity of the workers. Those with few skills and little bargaining power primarily experienced greater insecurity, unemployment and higher effort norms. Conversely, skilled workers tended to fare much better, achieving higher wages and greater security together with improved working times. These differing experiences not only divided the workers within the workplace but also affected their political consciousness, with the communists gaining the bulk of their support from the unemployed and the unskilled workers, while the skilled continued to support the social democrats. As Peterson (1982) has shown, this division had serious repercussions when the major employers, in November 1928, launched an offensive against their employees when the latter attempted to use the power of the state to enforce the introduction of the payment of higher wages and the reintroduction of the 8-hour day.

Like their American counterparts, then, German unions utilised Taylorism as a tool to combat the employers and advance their own interests. In passing, it needs to be stated that this provisional support for scientific management in the late 1920s was not unique to the German and American labour movements. Their reappraisal, rather, was replicated around the world at this time. Indeed, even in Britain, a nation which was particularly slow at taking up the possibilities offered by Taylorism, labour leaders seriously began reconsidering their attitude to this issue towards the end of the decade. Thus, the 1929 Trades Union Congress endorsed the claim, put forward by

Ben Tillet, that the advance of rationalisation was inevitable and that not only could it not be halted, it should, if adequate safeguards were offered the workers, be welcomed (Fox 1929: 683). Nor were British union leaders in any way confused as to what the term rationalisation meant, as was made clear by Arthur Pugh, the secretary of the Iron and Steel Trades Confederation.

Rationalisation involves Scientific Management; a much misunderstood term. This does not mean the regimentation of labour, a sort of goose step to the time of the machine; it means the science of good management, good government in industry, applied to the workshop, winning the co-operation of labour for the elimination of waste in human effort, material and organisation, and in getting the best results in productive enterprises and services. Combined with this is the acceptance of the principle that, in the science of good management, cutting down wages and extending hours of labour is the last and not the first resource. (Cited by Urwick 1930: 74)

Again, it needs to be stressed that, in arguing that labour leaders became increasingly enthusiastic as to the possibilities inherent in Taylorism, it is not suggested that this attitude was held without reservation. Unions everywhere continued to oppose those aspects of scientific management of which they disapproved (Lawley 1929). Their enthusiasm, moreover, was to be short-lived. It was to be retained only while the workers had sufficient industrial power to guide and limit the freedom with which capitalists could utilise Taylor's techniques. Workers' experience of how systematic planning could be used if employers were given a free hand was, during the depression, once again to make Taylor's name a synonym for the worst forms of exploitation. It is also emphasized, however, that this experience did not lead the world's working class to embrace Luddism and abandon all support for the rationalisation process.

With the coming of the depression in 1929, opinion seems to have returned to the earlier position. As the depression continued the mood tended once more to become distinctly hostile. Yet with comparatively few exceptions the charges brought against rationalization have had to do not with the movement as such but with its use for purposes of exploitation of the laboring class. Rationalization that lightens and simplifies labor, increases its productivity, grants to labor a hand in management, shortens hours, increases wages and purchasing power, and betters the status of the workers has been approved almost without exception. (Brady 1974: 328–329)

The belief of the German trade unions that it was possible "to pull out the 'poisonous teeth' carried by the monster imported from America and to turn its powers of destruction into service of the common weal" (Brady 1974: 330) was to be ground into dust by the depression and fascism during the 1930s. Likewise, throughout the world once the working class lost the capacity to influence the pace and direction of the rationalisation process few capitalists chose to emphasise those aspects of Taylorism the labour movement found attractive. This was certainly the case with reduced worktimes. With the rationalisation of industry not having developed to the extent that it had in the United States, the alliance among labour, the state and rationalised industry that made possible the permanent introduction of the 40-hour week in the U.S.A. was not able to be replicated elsewhere until after the Second World War. Consequently, many of the productivity-inducing capacities of Taylorism were not to be realised outside of the United States until the 1950s. For most of Europe, for example, it was only when the massive oversupply of labour power, induced by the destruction of the war, began to ease in the mid 1950s that capitalists were again to turn seriously to the all-round rationalisation of industry including the rationalisation of working time. This was to mean that it was not until this period that these states were to fully experience the capitalist regeneration that Taylorism had made possible.

A new historical epoch?

In his paper "Americanism and Fordism," written during the depression, Antonio Gramsci (1971) discussed the effect the introduction of Taylorist production methods in Europe was having on society and on the social and political attitudes of the various classes. Like Lenin, Gramsci firmly supported the rationalisation of production. He opposed the greater exploitation of the workers that the use of Taylorism often made possible but at the same time he recognised that the working class had much to gain from the application of science to the problems of management. He noted that while workers strenuously opposed some of the specific forms Taylorism could take, if capitalists were given a free hand they were not opposed to rationalisation as such (Gramsci 1971: 277, 292–293). Rather, he suggested, at least in Europe the major source of opposition to the new methods came not from the workers but rather from "parasitic" elements left over from feudalism such as the small landlords and their attendants, civil service personnel, the church, the army and a reactionary intelligentsia "stuffed with myths about its cultural heritage and unable to accept its own uselessness and impending supercession by more vital forces" (p. 278). He believed that in time the development of Taylorism throughout Europe would destroy the last vestiges of feudalism and would raise capitalism to a new high point based on planning, high profits and high wages. The last of these, he suggested, was necessary so that workers could enjoy a mode of living that would enable them to sustain the high-intensity work demanded by rationalised industry.

One of the basic questions Gramsci attempted to resolve in his discussion was whether rationalised capitalism would constitute a new "historical epoch" in which the social system would be radically changed by a process of gradual evolution or whether the forces and contradictions generated by the widespread adoption of Taylorism would produce a revolutionary "explosion." At no stage in his discussion does Gramsci explicitly answer this question, but as Hoare and Smith (Gramsci 1971: 279–280) have noted, it is clear throughout that he believed that, in the face of the capitalist regeneration made possible by scientific management, those committed to the revolutionary overthrow of capitalism were everywhere in a phase of retrenchment and retreat. Consequently, the forthcoming changes would invariably take place within an evolutionary rather than a revolutionary scenario.

For the communist Gramsci, this was clearly a pessimistic position to adopt. However, it did not mean he believed rationalisation had permanently resolved the basic contradictions of capitalism. He argued that the competitive advantage Taylorism had given American industry would in time be eliminated as the new production methods became generalised. As soon as this possibility was realised and the potential for regeneration exhausted, the contradictions inherent within capitalism would again manifest themselves in crisis, making it both necessary and possible for capital to begin taking back the advances made by the workers. In other words, like Tugwell, Gramsci argued that capitalism's capacity to gain sustenance from the use of planning was severely limited, that private ownership of the means of production created insurmountable barriers to the

realisation of the possibilities inherent in the scientific management of society's resources. Once the productivity-inducing
capacities of Taylorism that capitalism could utilise had been so
exploited that gains from further rationalisation ceased out-
weighing the forces tending to lower the rate of profit, capitalists would once again be forced to turn on the workers. The
Taylorist epoch was thus to be of a decidedly limited nature.

Gramsci's understanding of the capacity of the American
production methods to raise productivity, profits and wages
and the consequent effect this capitalist regeneration would
have on the revolutionary movement has certainly been realised in the time since he wrote. The techniques and ideas associated with rationalisation proved a tremendous stimulant to the
rate of economic growth and the rate of profit in the capitalist
nations. The capacity to expand production by the use of these
methods has been far greater than that attainable from the
greater accumulation of physical capital and indeed from all
other sources (Denison 1980: 220).

Gramsci's belief that the rejuvenation of capitalism would
have a debilitating effect on the revolutionary movement has
also been proven justified. In societies characterised by high
growth rates and rising standards of living the call to revolution
appeared increasingly ludicrous and fell to an ever greater extent on deaf ears. The improved living standards rationalisation made possible, in other words, undermined the communists' primary justification for demanding the abolition of
capitalism, namely that the capitalist system necessarily involved the ever greater immiseration of the working class. It
also undermined the primary source of the revolutionary
movement's recruitment base, the workers who were forced to
suffer the poverty and degradation of capitalism in decay.

To conclude that Gramsci's assessment of the potential of
rationalisation to rejuvenate capitalism and counter the revolutionary challenge has been validated by historical events leads
one to ask, What of his forecast that Taylorism would in time
prove increasingly ineffective at sustaining the vitality of
capitalism? To attempt to tackle this problem in this volume
would involve moving too far outside the question of worktime
and the associated problems with which this work has attempted to come to grips. Consequently, comment on Gramsci's prediction is limited to observing that, as Rostow (1983:
10–17) has shown, the postwar global boom was largely based

on the falling price of raw materials and the global exploitation of the production techniques pioneered in the U.S.A. prior to the Second World War. Further, as he notes, it was the European and Japanese delayed exploitation of these techniques that largely explains the higher growth rates in these countries in the period 1950–1973. As the potential of these techniques that capitalism is able to utilise has been realised, these countries have, one after another, followed the path again pioneered by the United States since the mid 1960s. In short, since 1966 there has been a sustained decline in the rate of productivity growth and a subsequent fall in the rate of profit (Nordhaus 1974; Baily 1981, 1984; Harrison 1982; Sachs 1983). To what extent capitalism's limited ability to realise the potential in the rationalisation process is a cause of this deterioration is an issue that at this stage is unresolved. Given the nature of the sources of growth during the postwar boom, however, it is not unreasonable to suggest that the deteriorating situation may well be explained by this factor. This is an explanation many have found impossible to accept because of its tremendous ramifications. The response to the crisis in the U.S.A. has been typical.

As the trusted formula of high volume, standardized production has ceased to deliver prosperity, America has been ready to embrace any explanation but the most obvious: The same factor that previously brought prosperity – the way the nation organizes itself for production – now threatens decline. Everywhere America has looked, it has seen the symptoms of its economic impasse, but the nation has been unable to recognize the problem because its roots are deeply embedded in the organization of America's business enterprises, labor unions and government institutions. (Reich 1983: 119)

Finally, what of Gramsci's claim that as capitalism moved once again into a stage of decay the bourgeoisie would be compelled to begin taking back the gains won by the workers during the period of expansion? With the end of the "long boom," one can fear that this prediction is also proving to have a good deal of substance. As growth and profit rates have declined, the depth of cyclical crises has intensified and unemployment has risen, employers and the state throughout the capitalist world have moved to offset the fall in profit rates by unleashing what Rostow has termed a barbaric counter-revolution. This offensive has involved the cutting of wages and welfare spending, the undermining of working conditions, the driving up of the rate of exploitation and, in general, the growing spread of immiseration amongst the working class. This strategy, particularly if it is combined with fiscal and monetary policies which place pressure on employers to innovate, restructure and exploit what potential still exists in the market system, does have the ability to raise the rate of productivity growth and the rate of profit at least temporarily. If this process is to be sustained, however, what is needed is some new element that can provide capitalism with an acceptable rate of productivity growth and rate of profit. The boost to productivity, moreover, must be in a form that does not necessarily drive up the organic composition of capital. If this is not forthcoming, capitalists will be forced to compete by increasing investments in high-technology, low-employment areas. Along this path, however, lies the spectre of Marx's ultimate "general" source of capitalist breakdown, the tendency for technical and nature-imposed restraints to productivity growth to drive up the organic composition of capital and consequently for the rate of profit to fall (Lebowitz 1982).

To put forward the hypothesis that the capacity of Taylorism to sustain capitalism may be approaching exhaustion is not to suggest that this social system has necessarily reached any final stage of development. Apologists for capitalism have always been overly eager to rush forward, with every sustained boom, to announce that the inherent instability of this social system has at last been overcome. Marxists, likewise, have too often been overly eager to suggest that the development of capitalism has finally reached its limits. Whether or not this is the case is, at this stage, simply not known. For it might well be the case that new ways to exploit the potential inherent in scientific planning, compatible with capitalism, will yet be devised. Likewise, there might yet be unexploited possibilities in other areas. In many ways we appear to be in a situation similar to that described by Engels in 1886 when it became apparent that the stimulus provided by the first industrial revolution was subsiding and that capitalism had entered a period of sustained decay.

The decennial cycle of stagnation, prosperity, over-production and crisis, ever recurrent from 1825 to 1867, seems indeed to have run its course; but only to land us in the slough of despond of a permanent and chronic depression. The sighed-for period of prosperity will not come; as often as we seem to perceive its heralding symptoms, so often do they again vanish into air. (Cited by Hansen 1985: 37)

Like many of his contemporaries, Engels was aware that the depression was a unique moment in the development of capitalism. Likewise, it has become clear to many observers today that we are now in some form of hiatus. Where the present situation differs from Engels's last days is that by the early 1890s there were sufficient signs for him to suspect the potential inherent in a regulated, managed capitalism. At the moment it is difficult to see possibilities of comparable significance in contemporary capitalism. While acknowledging that a revival may come, therefore, it should not be presumed that this will occur. Given that an ever more serious decline is possible, it is imperative to develop a viable, democratic alternative and to begin preparing for the next step in the creation of a rationalised society: the abolition of "business" and the establishment of a planned economy.

Conclusion

Capitalist industrialised nations are characterised by a tendency to reduce the length of time employees normally spend at their place of employment. Over the last century standard paid worktimes have contracted by approximately 40 per cent. This temporal contraction has had very little influence on the level of employment or on labour costs. The primary objective of this volume has been to explain why the contraction occurred and why it had so little impact in these important areas. It has been argued that the crucial factor propelling the continuing curtailment of worktime has been the tendency for the demands of the production process to periodically come into conflict with the innate and social needs of human beings. This development, which is brought about by the competitive nature of capitalist economies, creates inefficiencies which reductions in schedules can help to alleviate both by allowing the worker greater time to recuperate and by increasing the need for employers to ensure that they utilise their resources with greater efficiency.

Changes in the level of the demands placed upon the worker, it has been argued, may emanate from both the paid workplace and the domestic sector. The demands of each of these arenas acts as a tax on the amount of effort the individual has available to utilise in the other. Thus, workers may find that their ability to cope with a given balance of work intensity and length of worktime is severely undermined if the effort they are able to put into this schedule is reduced by, for example, their spouses taking on paid employment and consequently requiring greater assistance within the home.

The increasing demands the production process tends to place on individuals, it has been argued, are both a cause and a consequence of the temporal shift. Increasing pressures create the conditions that make it possible and necessary to periodically reduce time standards, but such reductions, in turn, enhance the workers' capacity to labour more intensively and place new pressures on employers to ensure that this greater capacity is tapped. Central to the argument that has been advanced is the issue of human social and innate psycho-physiological capacities. Human capacities are elastic, it has been shown, but there are limits to this elasticity. If the demands placed upon the employee either at the workplace or within the domestic sector continue to rise while the length of time provided for recuperation remains fixed, there must come a point where these pressures come into conflict with the individual's limited abilities. It is the continuing re-emergence of this contradiction, generated by forces inherent in the very nature of capitalist economies, that ensures that the issue of worktime is a perennial source of industrial disputation.

The contemporary significance of the worktime issue stems from the re-establishment of mass unemployment as a normal characteristic of developed capitalism. With the end of the long boom the question of what effect the reduction of standard time schedules has on the availability of jobs has again become an issue of immediate and significant concern. The history of the literature outlined in this work has shown that the question of whether more jobs can be created by curtailing time standards has invariably been raised whenever paid employment has become scarce. At such times working-class leaders have repeatedly put forward the argument that time standards should be further reduced in order to spread what work is available amongst a greater number of individuals.

The present crisis has proved no exception to this general phenomenon. In the early 1970s trade unions in many nations advanced the argument that, as the market economies were proving incapable of producing enough jobs to replace those lost by technological advance and population growth, it was necessary to reduce the supply of labour power coming on the market. One of the most effective means of achieving this objective, it was insisted, was the reduction of time standards. It has been argued throughout this work that were time schedules to be reduced for this reason, employers would invariably respond by restructuring the production process in a manner which both decreased the demand for labour power and took advantage of the workers' newfound capacity to labour more intensively. For this reason, plus the fact that were it to prove impossible to offset the temporal reduction by these means then production costs would rise and industry's competitiveness be undermined, it must be concluded that the hope that the further curtailment of time standards will expand the availability of jobs will not be realised.

The validity of the claim that worktime curtailment is at best merely a short-term palliative for unemployment has increasingly come to be accepted by the international labour movement. This shift in labour's position is explained by the failure of those worktime reductions which were introduced in the decade 1976–1985 to produce any substantial increase in employment. It is also a consequence of the fact that a number of the economists who have entered the revived worktime debate have been able to advance convincing theoretical arguments to support the claim that reductions in standard times will not create jobs. These scholars have, in essence, utilised the production-cost argument pioneered by Senior and his colleagues in the 1840s. By this means they have been able to convince many within the labour movement that reduced time standards will have a deleterious effect on costs and consequently on inflation, on the balance of trade and perhaps even on the level of employment.

Whereas the conclusion of marginalist members of the economics profession that few jobs can be created by the manipulation of time schedules may well have validity, this work has shown that they should take no pride in their ability to present such a case. Given the enthusiasm with which, during the years of the long boom, they promoted the argument that worktime reductions necessarily involved forgone production and income, the marginalist tradition must surely be assigned a good deal of the blame for the re-emergence of the belief that reduced time standards would create more jobs. The history of the literature suggests, moreover, that the enthusiasm with which some marginalist economists have shifted the worktime debate away from the individual's preference for income and leisure and towards production cost needs to be treated with more than a little suspicion. Effectively, they have responded to labour's demand for further cuts in time standards in a manner very similar to their peers in the 1840s and the 1890s who, when they realised that the individual-rights argument had become an embarrassment to the buyers of labour power, quickly laid this argument aside for another day.

The suspicion that many marginalist scholars have been

more concerned with protecting the profitability of investments, rather than seeking to understand the true nature of the political economy of worktime, is strengthened by their continued tendency to inflate the likely increases in costs that further reductions in time standards are likely to generate and by their general failure to analyse the implications of the production-cost argument. If it is the case that worktimes cannot now be reduced because this would raise costs and undermine the competitiveness of industry, surely scholars should have asked how it was that this was not an insurmountable problem in the past. They might also have considered the implications for preference theory of their newfound awareness that workers tend to respond to reductions in the length of time they labour by increasing the effort they put into the time they continue to work.

These questions have not been examined by marginalist scholars. Nor has the fact that they have discovered, once again, that worktime reductions tend to lead to increases in the intensity of work led them to consider the implications of this response for the wellbeing of the working population. The labour movement might well ask why this has not been done and might be justified in suspecting that such research has not been undertaken because along this path there is a good case for further reductions in standard times. For such curtailments can be justified on the grounds stressed by scholars such as Rae, Florence and Goldmark; that is, on the need to protect the working class from the damage inflicted upon it by the production process and on the need to ensure that direct producers maximise the rewards this process is potentially capable of providing them.

It is on health and safety grounds and on the need to ensure that workers gain the greatest mass of free time and income potentially available to them that unions should advance the demand for further cuts to standard times. As did their forebears in the 1840s and the 1890s, in other words, labour needs to take up the production-cost argument and show that the claim that giving the workers more free time necessarily involves increased costs is simply not valid. At the same time they should insist that the individual-rights argument must not be allowed to be laid aside simply because it has now become an embarrassment to the employers. It should be taken up, and it should be insisted that workers, in fact and not merely in theory, must have the right to freely determine the division of their own time and efforts between income and leisure.

To conclude that most postwar marginalists have failed to deal adequately with the worktime issue is not to imply, it needs to be reiterated, that Marxists have done any better during this period. Marxist contributions relevant to the worktime issue have tended to treat the subject as one solely shaped by the nature of working-class collective action. Worker resistance to the demands of the employers and workers' willingness and ability to engage in industrial struggles have been treated as if they were the sole significant factor relevant to the question of how and why worktime change occurs. The political primacy and voluntarism inherent in this form of analysis is inadequate because it fails to come to grips with the economics of the subject. It also fails to deal adequately with biology and the necessary conclusion inherent in Marx's worktime theory that biological factors often play a major part in shaping human action.

This is a claim many Marxists have found unattractive, particularly since the rise of the "new left" in the late 1960s with its intense aversion to biology and its implicit or explicit acceptance of cultural determinism. During this period Marxists have tended to treat human capacities as if they were infinitely malleable. Marx's argument that human capacities are elastic, in other words, has been accepted, but his insistence that there were often innate limits to this elasticity inherent in the biology of human beings has been effectively ignored. Suspicion of arguments which suggest that human development is shaped by innate factors contained within a fixed human nature are justified. Biological determinism is all too clearly a form of argument favouring the retention of the status quo. To ignore biology, however, and to accept implicitly or explicitly that humans are only a product of their culture is equally fallacious. Human psycho-physiological limits, this work has shown, have played a major role in shaping not only the direction of worktime change but also the pattern this movement has tended to take. If the Marxist theory of worktime is to be further developed, it is necessary for scholars sympathetic to Marxism to throw off their fears of biology and adequately integrate this factor into their analysis. This integration of biology into the Marxist worktime literature will need to be accompanied by a reconsideration of the relationship between politics and economics. What is needed, it is stressed, is not the acceptance of some form of economic or structural determinism but rather a more rigorous application of the dual emphasis Marx placed on both working-class collective action and the structural determinacy of the capitalist production process.

The failure of most Marxist contributions to the postwar worktime debate to adequately emphasise both class struggle and structural factors resulted in radical scholars coming to accept a very one-sided understanding of the political economy of this issue. The data put forward in this volume, it is suggested, must also lead one to conclude that an equally gross imbalance exists in much of the radical literature on scientific management that has been published since the late 1960s. Those who pioneered the development of Taylorism, it has been shown, strove to develop systematic planning tools which would expand the capacity of management to control the utilisation of a firm's resources. The Taylorists recognised that this was a two-sided process involving both the management of things and the management of people. On one side they sought to establish costing systems which would make it possible to specify areas of waste, the cost of separate processes and the profitability of individual areas of production. By systematically analysing methods of production, rather than relying on tradition or rule of thumb, the Taylorists were able to develop tools which greatly aided the flow of resources both within the firm and across the various sectors of industry. Their methods, moreover, enabled the further development of large-scale production, which necessarily requires systematic co-ordination and co-operation if it is to function effectively.

Taylorism's second task involved providing employers with greater control over labour by concentrating knowledge in the hands of management and by developing methods of work and systems of reward and punishment which would enable the latter to regulate the mass of effort workers normally undertake. It is this second aspect of the way management science has been utilised that has been the primary source of industrial disputation.

Employers have continuously striven to utilise the tools provided them by the Taylorists to increase the rate at which surplus labour is extracted from their employees. Workers consequently have been compelled to wage a continuing campaign of resistance which aims to counter these strategies and which maximises their own level of control over the processes of production. In doing so they too have made great use of many of the techniques and insights developed by scientific managers. By utilising these tools to systemise the management of their own organisations, by using knowledge generated by management research in their various campaigns and by promoting those aspects of Taylorism – not least the introduction of more rational worktimes – which employers have found unpalatable but which have the capacity to significantly improve the well-being of employees, the working class has not only been able to make significant advances in a wide range of areas, but it has also made a major unacknowledged input into the development of management science. This contribution has helped to shape the pace and direction the growth of Taylorism has taken, and thus the working class must be accorded a good deal of the credit for developing this element so vital to advanced forms of production.

That the Taylorists aimed to enhance management's control over both people and things has been recognised by many of the radical scholars who have contributed to the debate on the history of management science. Most of these individuals, however, have chosen to discuss only the first of these two elements. This narrow, one-sided perspective has seriously limited the value of most of their contributions and has proved a major obstacle to the development of the so-called labour-process debate. The extreme importance of the issue of labour control has not been denied in this work. What has been argued is that to separate out the labour-control aspect of Taylorism and to attempt to analyse this factor independently of scientific management's other dimensions, as so many of these scholars have done, produces a radically one-sided, myopic perspective which conceals more than it reveals of the real nature of the rationalisation process. Because of the harm the promotion of this perspective has caused, it has been necessary in this work to place primary emphasis on bringing out the point that labour control was only one aspect of Taylorism and that scientific management does have a scientific productive essence which has been of great value to the working class. That employers have also advanced their interests by the use of management science should not be allowed to obscure this fact.

By conceiving of Taylorism merely as a form of labour control, radical scholars have been led to deny the labour movement the credit it deserves for aiding the maturation of management science. They have also been led to seriously underestimate the influence Taylorism had on the development of the forces of production and on the continued viability of capitalism. Where Gramsci, Tugwell and Jevons, writing at the depth of the 1930s depression, had the ability to recognise Taylorism's potential for revitalising this social system, most of those who have engaged in the labour-process debate, despite the fact that they lived through this period of revitalisation, have not been able to develop the level of understanding achieved by these scholars. They have, rather, accepted as valid the limited conception of scientific management that employers initially attempted to adopt and have confined their contribution merely to criticising some of the ways in which employers and the capitalist state utilised Taylorism. In the process they have helped to disarm the working class by undermining its ability to consciously utilise management science and have effectively allied themselves with those conservative political forces committed to besmirching the positive role played by the planning mechanism through the twentieth century. They have also failed to highlight the extent to which the application of industrial, economic and social planning underpinned the postwar boom and have thus helped to prevent the labour movement from being able to capitalise politically on these achievements, as Tugwell hoped would be possible when the impetus given to capitalism by the utilisation of those aspects of planning compatible with private ownership of the means of production began to wane. Consequently, the Margaret Thatchers of the world have been able to successfully promote the claims that state intervention in the economy is the primary cause of our present malaise and that market freedom rather than systematic planning has the most to offer the working class.

Failure to understand why scholars such as Lenin believed that scientific management contained a number of the "greatest scientific achievements" of capitalism has also led those who have engaged in the labour-process debate to fail to comprehend the socialist potential inherent in the rationalisation movement. The possibility of building socialism within the U.S.S.R., Lenin recognised, required the Soviet Government to combine its political power with the most advanced technical achievements of capitalism. These achievements included those capitalist planning tools which could be suitably modified to suit the needs of a socialist society. The establishment of a national economy based on planning rather than on the tyranny of the market, the Bolsheviks soon realised, requires the use of the most highly sophisticated management techniques. It needs to be added that this was not a matter of choice, for freedom of choice lay only in the use to which these techniques were put and the extent to which they were modified to suit the needs of socialism.

If human beings are to gain any significant degree of control over the market, it should surely be clear to all but the most utopian of individuals that the "economics of feasible socialism" make it imperative that humans be able to effectively plan the utilisation of society's resources. Planning at this level cannot be undertaken effectively without the science of management. Historically, one of the most effective criticisms of the socialist objective was the observation that no matter how attractive might be the idea of a society based on planning rather than on the vagaries of the market, a national economy was too complex a phenomenon to plan effectively. The development of scientific management through the twentieth century, in both the socialist and capitalist nations, has forged a powerful tool which, while still very far from perfect, has already developed sufficiently to greatly undermine the validity of this argument. In short, the development of management science has greatly enhanced the capacity of human beings to construct a society based on democratic and effective planning.

Throughout the early years of the rationalisation movement's development Taylorists constantly complained that the hostility or lack of interest they received from most employers was one of the major obstacles hampering the advancement of their work. Conservatism and risk aversion rather than the entrepreneurial spirit, they discovered, were the norm in turn-of-the-century capitalism. In time, however, the very nature of the relations of production inherent within this social system ensured that the development of management science was able to break through these barriers, with competition gradually forcing an increasing number of employers to take up those aspects of Taylorism which they found were necessary to enable them to continue to engage in the accumulation process. Governments likewise came to accept that if they were to fulfil their dual functions of legitimation and accumulation effectively they had to accept the need for a degree of economic and social planning.

Capitalist relations of production, in other words, acted as a positive influence compelling the acceptance and further development of this new element in the material forces of production. The property relations of capitalism, however, severely limit the extent to which this social system can realise the potential inherent in the planning mechanism. Thus, though capitalism gave birth to the rationalisation process and enabled it to develop within its framework, its property relations limit the extent to which this material productive force can mature. From being a positive influence inducing the maturation of the rationalisation process, capitalist property relations may have now become a major fetter to its further development. If this is the case – and the economic crisis that has bedevilled the capitalist nations since the late 1960s suggests that it is – the time may have come for these fetters to be removed.

References

Addison, J.T. and Barnett, A.H. (1982), "The Impact of Unions on Productivity," *British Journal of Industrial Relations*, Vol. 20, No. 2, pp. 145–162.

Allen, Donna (1969), *Fringe Benefits: Wages or Social Obligation?* Cornell University, Ithaca, N.Y.

Alluisi, Earl A. and Morgan, Ben B. (1982), "Temporal Factors in Human Performance and Productivity" in Earl A. Alluisi and E.A. Fleishman, *Human Performance and Productivity: Stress and Performance Effectiveness*, Lawrence Erlbaum Assoc., Hillsdale, N.J., pp. 165–247.

Baily, Martin Neil (1981), "Productivity and the Services of Capital and Labor," *Brookings Papers on Economic Activity*, No. 1, pp. 1–65.

Baily, Martin Neil (1984), "Will Productivity Growth Recover? Has It Done So Already?" *American Economic Review, Papers and Proceedings*, Vol. 74, pp. 231–241.

Baldamus, W. (1961), *Efficiency and Effort: An Analysis of Industrial Administration*, Tavistock Publications, London.

Barkin, Solomon (1942), "Labor Views the Working Day," *Advanced Management*, Vol. 7, pp. 32–37.

Barrett, W.J. (1932), "Present Plans for Spreading Employment," *Congressional Digest*, Vol. 11, pp. 232–233, 255.

Bastin, G.S. (1981), "The Implementation of the 39-Hour Week in the Engineering Industry," M.A. thesis, University of Warwick.

Becker, Gary S. (1985), "Human Capital, Effort, and the Sexual Division of Labor," *Journal of Labor Economics*, Vol. 3, No. 1, pp. 33–58.

Beman, Lamar T. (ed.) (1928), *Five Day Week*, The H.W. Wilson Co., New York.

Bernstein, Irving (1960), *The Lean Years: A History of the American Worker, 1920–1933*, Houghton Mifflin Co., Boston.

Bienefeld, M.A. (1972), *Working Hours in British Industry: An Economic History*, Weidenfeld and Nicolson, London.

Blaug, Mark (1958), "The Classical Economists and the Factory Acts – A Re-Examination," *Quarterly Journal of Economics*, Vol. 72, pp. 211–226.

Blyton, Paul (1985), *Changes in Working Time*, Croom Helm, London.

Bonig, Von Jurgen (1980), "Technik, Rationalisierung und Arbeitszeit in der Weimarer Republik," *Technikgeschichte*, Vol. 47, No. 3, pp. 303–324.

Bosworth, Derek L. and Dawkins, Peter J. (1981), *Work Patterns: An Economic Analysis*, Gower Publishing Co., Aldershot, Hants.

Bowen, J.C. (1923), "The 48-Hour Week in Industry," *Monthly Labor Review*, Vol. 17, pp. 1305–1326.

Brady, Robert A. (1974), *The Rationalization Movement in German Industry: A Study in the Evolution of Economic Planning*, University of California Press, Berkeley and Los Angeles.

204

Brandeis, Louis D. and Goldmark, Josephine (1908), *Women in Industry*, National Consumers' League, New York.

Braverman, Harry (1974), *Labor and Monopoly Capital: The Degradation of Work in the Twentieth Century*, Monthly Review Press, New York.

Brentano, Lujo (1894), *Hours and Wages in Relation to Production*, Swan Sonnenschein and Co., London.

Bronson, David W. (1968), "Soviet Experience with Shortening the Workweek," *Industrial and Labor Relations Review*, Vol. 21, No. 3, pp. 391–399.

Brown, C.V. (ed.) (1983), *Taxation and Labour Supply*, George Allen and Unwin, London.

Burawoy, Michael (1985), *The Politics of Production*, Verso, London.

Bureau of Labor Statistics (1936), "Movement Toward the Shorter Workweek Prior to the National Industrial Recovery Act," *U.S. Bureau of Labor Statistics Bulletin*, Vol. 616, pp. 1062–1070.

Business Week (1932), "Work-Spreaders Will Make Jobs Now, Face the Issues Later," *Business Week*, Oct. 12, pp. 13–14.

Byrne, Harriet (1935), *The Health and Safety of Women in Industry*, Bulletin of the Women's Bureau, No. 136, Govt. Printing Office, Washington.

Chandler, Alfred D. and Redlich, Fritz (1966), "Recent Developments in American Business Administration and Their Conceptualization" in Stanley Coben and Forest G. Hill (eds.), *American Economic History*, J.B. Lippincott Co., Philadelphia, pp. 539–562.

Chapman, S.J. (1909), "Hours of Labour," *Economic Journal*, Vol. 19, pp. 353–373.

Chase, Stuart (1932), *A New Deal*, Macmillan, New York.

Clague, Ewan (1926), "Index of Productivity of Labor in the Steel, Automobile, Shoe and Paper Industries," *Monthly Labor Review*, Vol. 23, No. 1, July, pp. 1–19.

Clarke, Allen (1899), *Effects of the Factory System*, G. Richards, London.

Cleaver, Harry (1979), *Reading Capital Politically*, The Harvester Press, London.

Coats, A.W. (1958), "Changing Attitudes to Labour in the Eighteenth Century," *Economic History Review*, Vol. 11, No. 1, pp. 35–51.

Cole, G.D.H. (1928), *The Payment of Wages*, George Allen and Unwin, London.

Cole, G.D.H. (1929), *The Next Ten Years*, Macmillan, London.

Collier, Howard E. (1943), *Outlines of Industrial Medical Practice*, Edward Arnold, London.

Committee on Elimination of Waste (1921), *Waste in Industry*, McGraw-Hill Book Co., New York.

Committee on Recent Economic Changes (1929), *Recent Economic Changes*, McGraw-Hill Book Co., New York.

Committee on Work Periods in Continuous Industry (1922), *The Twelve-Hour Shift in Industry*, McGraw-Hill Book Co., New York.

Copley, Frank B. (1969), *Frederick W. Taylor: Father of Scientific Management*, Augustus M. Kelly, New York.

Cuvillier, Rolande (1984), *The Reduction of Working Time: Scope and Implications in Industrial Market Economies*, International Labour Office, Geneva.

Denison, Edward F. (1967), *Why Growth Rates Differ: Postwar Experience in Nine Western Countries*, The Brookings Institution, Washington.

Denison, Edward F. (1980), "The Contribution of Capital to Economic Growth," *American Economic Review*, Vol. 70, No. 2, pp. 220–224.

Dent, Arthur George (1935), *Management Planning and Control*, Gee, London.

Department of Labor, U.S.A. (1929), "Union Scales of Wages and Hours of Labor, 1913 to 1929: Preliminary Report," *Monthly Labor Review*, Vol. 29, pp. 644–667.

Department of Labor, U.S.A. (1947), *Hours of Work and Output*, Bulletin No. 917, Govt. Printing Office, Washington.

Devinat, Paul (1926), "The American Labour Movement and Scientific Management," *International Labour Review*, Vol. 13, No. 4, pp. 461–488.

Devinat, Paul (1927), *Scientific Management in Europe*, International Labour Office Studies and Reports, Series B (Economic Conditions), No. 17, Geneva.

Douglas, Paul H. (1927), "The Modern Technique of Mass Production and Its Relation to Wages," *Proceedings of the Academy of Political Science*, Vol. 12, No. 3, pp. 18–42.

Douglas, Paul H. (1957), *The Theory of Wages*, Augustus M. Kelly, New York.

Douglas, Paul H. and Hackman, Joseph (1939), "The Fair Labor Standards Act of 1938," *Political Science Quarterly*, Vol. 53, pp. 491–515, and Vol. 54, 1940, pp. 29–55.

Doyal, Lesley (1979), *The Political Economy of Health*, Pluto Press, London.

Drury, Horace B. (1921), "The Three-Shift System in the Steel Industry," *Bulletin of the Taylor Society*, Vol. 6, No. 1, pp. 2–49.

Duncan, G. and Stafford, F. (1977), "Pace of Work, Unions, and Earnings in Blue Collar Jobs," mimeograph cited by Charles Brown and James Medoff, "Trade Unions in the Production Process," *Journal of Political Economy*, Vol. 86, No. 3, 1978, pp. 355–378.

Durand, Edward Dana (1930), *American Industry and Commerce*, Ginn and Company, Boston.

Edholm, O.G. (1970), "The Changing Pattern of Human Activity," *Ergonomics*, Vol. 13, No. 6, pp. 625–643.

Edwards, Richard (1979), *Contested Terrain: The Transformation of the Workplace in the Twentieth Century*, Basic Books, New York.

Edwards, Ron (1982), "The Campaign for Shorter Working Hours in Manufacturing Industry: The Pursuit of Trade Union Objectives Through Collective Bargaining or Legislation," M.A. thesis, University of Warwick.

Elger, Tony (1979), "Valorisation and Deskilling: A Critique of Braverman," *Capital and Class*, No. 7 (Spring), pp. 58–99.

Evans, Archibald A. (1975), *Hours of Work in Industrialised Countries*, International Labour Office, Geneva.

Fabian Society (1895), *Eight Hours by Law*, Fabian Tract No. 48, The Fabian Society, London.

Fahey, Walter S. (1981), "Some Reactions to the Proposed 39 Hour Week in the Engineering Industry," M.A. thesis, University of Warwick.

Farmer, Eric (1922), "The Economy of Human Effort in Industry," *Occupational Psychology*, Vol. 1, No. 1, pp. 18-22.

Farquar, H.H. (1924), "Positive Contributions of Scientific Management" in Edward Eyre Hunt (ed.), *Scientific Management Since Taylor*, McGraw-Hill Book Co., New York.

Fawcett, Henry (1872), *Essays and Lectures on Social and Political Subjects*, The Macmillan Press, London.

Fawcett, Henry (1873), *Speeches on Some Current Political Questions*, The Macmillan Press, London.

Feis, Herbert (1924), "The Attempt to Establish the Eight-Hour Day by International Action," *Political Science Quarterly*, Vol. 39, No. 3, pp. 373–413, and No. 4, pp. 624–649.

Feldstein, M.S. (1968), "Estimating the Supply Curve of Working Hours," *Oxford Economic Papers*, Vol. 20, No. 1, pp. 74–80.

Filipetti, George (1946), *Industrial Management in Transition*, Richard D. Irwin Inc., Chicago.

Finegan, T. Aldrich (1962), "Hours of Work in the United States: A Cross-Sectional Analysis," *Journal of Political Economy*, Vol. 70, No. 5, pp. 452–470.

Fisher, Waldo E. (1940), "Union Wage and Hour Policies and Employment," *American Economic Review*, Vol. 30, pp. 290-299.

Flanders, Allan (1964), *The Fawley Productivity Agreements*, Faber and Faber Ltd., London.

Florence, P. Sargant (1924a), *Economics of Fatigue and Unrest and the Efficiency of Labour in English and American Industry*, George Allen and Unwin, London.

Florence, P. Sargant (1924b), "The Forty-eight Hour Week and Industrial Efficiency," *International Labour Review*, Vol. 10, No. 5, pp. 729–758.

Florence, P. Sargant (1950), *Labour*, Hutchinson's University Library, London.

Ford, Henry (1922), *My Life and Work*, William Heinemann, London.

Ford, Henry (1926), "The 5-day Week in the Ford Plants," *Monthly Labor Review*, Dec., pp. 10–14.

Fox, R.M. (1929), "The Repercussions of Rationalisation," *Nineteenth Century*, No. 633, pp. 683–691.

Frankel, Emil (1924), "The Eight-Hour Day in Germany," *Journal of Political Economy*, Vol. 32, pp. 315–334.

Frankfurter, Felix and Goldmark, Josephine (1915), *The Case for the Shorter Workday*, National Consumers' League, New York.

Friedmann, Georges (1955), *Industrial Society: The Emergence of the Human Problems of Automation*, The Free Press, New York.

Gilbreth, Frank B. G. and Gilbreth, Lillian (1916), *Fatigue Study*, Sturgis and Walton, New York.

Gilbreth, Frank B.G. and Gilbreth, Lillian (1924), "The Efficiency Engineer and the Industrial Psychologist," *Occupational Psychology*, Vol. 2, No. 1, pp. 40–45.

Gillman, Joseph M. (1957), *The Falling Rate of Profit: Marx's Law and Its Significance to Twentieth-Century Capitalism*, Dennis Dobson, London.

Goldmark, Josephine (1919), *Fatigue and Efficiency: A Study in Industry*, Russell Sage Foundation, New York.

Goldmark, Josephine and Hopkins, Mary D. (1920), *Comparison of an Eight-Hour Plant and a Ten-Hour Plant: Report on an Investigation by Philip Sargant Florence*, Govt. Printing Office, Washington.

Gompers, Samuel (1911), "Machinery to Perfect the Human Machine," *Federationist*, Vol. 18, p. 117.

Gompers, Samuel (n.d.), *The Eight-Hour Workday: Its Inauguration, Enforcement, and Influences*, American Federation of Labor, Washington.

Gramsci, Antonio (1971), *Selections from the Prison Notebooks of Antonio Gramsci*, edited and translated by Quentin Hoare and Geoffrey Nowell Smith, Lawrence and Wishart, London.

Greenberg, David, Moffitt, Robert and Friedmann, John (1981), "Underreporting and Experimental Effects on Work Effort: Evidence from the Gary Income Maintenance Experiment," *Review of Economics and Statistics*, Vol. 63, No. 4, pp. 581–589.

Grinstein, Alexander (1955), "Vacations: A Psycho-Analytic Study," *International Journal of Psycho-Analysis*, Vol. 36, pp. 177–186.

Grossman, Philip (1970), "Hours and Output: The Reduction in the Soviet Workweek, 1956–60," Ph.D. thesis, The American University, Washington, D.C.

Haber, Samuel (1964), *Efficiency and Uplift: Scientific Management in the Progressive Era 1890–1920*, The University of Chicago Press, Chicago.

Hadfield, P.A. and Gibbins, H. de B. (1892), *A Shorter Working Day*, Methuen, London.

Hansen, F.R. (1985), *The Breakdown of Capitalism*, Routledge and Kegan Paul, London.

Hardie, Colin (1978), "Struggles for Shorter Hours," B.A. thesis, University of Sydney.

Harris, Jose (1972), *Unemployment and Politics: A Study in English Social Policy 1886–1914*, Clarendon Press, Oxford.

Harrison, John (1982), "The Profit Squeeze, Unemployment and Policy: A Marxist Approach" in Angus Maddison and Bote S. Wilpstra (eds.), *Unemployment: The European Perspective*, Croom Helm, London.

Hart, Bob (1982), *Working Time: A Review of Problems and Policies within a Collective Bargaining Framework*, International Institute of Management, Berlin.

Harvey, David (1982), *The Limits to Capital*, Basil Blackwell, Oxford.

Hertz, Paul (1928), "Labour and Rationalisation in Germany," *Labour Magazine*, Vol. 6, pp. 463–466.

Hicks, J.R. (1963), *The Theory of Wages* (1932), The Macmillan Press, London.

Hilferding, Rudolf (1927), "The New Capitalism," *Socialist Review*, Vol. 19, pp. 22–30.

Hobsbawm, E.J. (1964), *Labouring Men: Studies in the History of Labour*, Weidenfeld and Nicolson, London.

Hobsbawm, E.J. (1977), *The Age of Capital*, Abacus, London.

Hobson, John A. (1894), *The Evolution of Modern Capitalism*, George Allen and Unwin, London.

Hobson, John A. (1930), *Rationalisation and Unemployment*, George Allen and Unwin, London.

Holt, Charles F. (1977), "Who Benefited from the Prosperity of the Twenties?" *Explorations in Economic History*, Vol. 14, pp. 277–289.

Hoover, Herbert (1927), *Thirteenth Annual Report of the Secretary of Commerce*, Dept. of Commerce, Washington.

Horner, Leonard (1845), "Reports of the Inspectors of Factories," *British Sessional Papers* [639], Vol. 25, p. 431.

Horner, Leonard (1852), "Reports of the Inspectors of Factories," *British Sessional Papers* [1439] [1500], Vol. 21, pp. 353, 377.

Hutchins, Grace (1934), *Women Who Work*, International Publishers, New York.

Hyman, Richard (1975), *Industrial Relations: A Marxist Introduction*, The Macmillan Press, London.

I.L.O. (International Labour Office) (1931), *The Social Aspects of Rationalisation*, Studies and Reports, Series B (Economic Conditions), No. 18, Geneva.

Industrial Health Research Board (1942), *Hours of Work, Lost Time and Labour Wastage*, Emergency Report No. 2, His Majesty's Stationery Office, London.

International Labor Conference (1920), *First Annual Meeting, Washington, 1919*, Govt. Printing Office, Washington.

Jacoby, Sanford M. (1983), "Union–Management Cooperation in the United States: Lessons from the 1920s," *Industrial and Labor Relations Review*, Vol. 37, No. 1, pp. 18–33.

Jeans, J. Stephen (1894), *The Eight Hours Day in the British Engineering Industry: An Examination and Criticism of Recent Experiments*, Ballantyne Hanson, London.

Jevons, Stanley H. (1931), "The Second Industrial Revolution," *Economic Journal*, Vol. 41, pp. 1–18.

Jevons, W. Stanley (1894), *The State in Relation to Labour*, The Macmillan Press, London.

Jevons, W. Stanley (1965), *The Theory of Political Economy*, Augustus M. Kelly, New York.

Keeley, Michael C. (1981), *Labor Supply and Public Policy: A Critical Review*, Academic Press, New York.

Kelly, John E. (1982), *Scientific Management, Job Redesign and Work Performance*, Academic Press, London.

Keynes, John Maynard (1932), "The World's Economic Outlook," *Atlantic Monthly*, Vol. 149, pp. 521–526.

Killingsworth, Mark R. (1981), "A Survey of Labor Supply Models: Theoretical Analysis and First-Generation Empirical Results," *Research in Labor Economics*, Vol. 4, pp. 1–64.

Killingsworth, Mark R. (1983), *Labor Supply*, Cambridge University Press, Cambridge.

King, J.E. (1972), *Labour Economics*, The Macmillan Press, London.

Knight, Frank H. (1921), *Risk, Uncertainty and Profit*, Houghton Mifflin Co., Boston.

Labor Research Association (1942), *The History of the Shorter Work-Day*, International Publishers, New York.

Laird, Donald A. (1934), "Shorter Hours – Bigger Output," *New Republic*, Vol. 77, pp. 356–357.

Laue, J. Charles (1926), "Five-Day Week Becomes a Vivid Issue," *New York Times*, Oct 17, Section 9, pp. 1, 9.

Lawley, F.E. (1929), "Why Fear Rationalisation?" *Socialist Review*, pp. 13–17.

Layton, Edwin (1971), *The Revolt of the Engineers. Social Responsibility and the*

210   **References**

American Engineering Profession, Case Western Reserve University Press, Cleveland, Ohio.

Layton, Edwin (1974), "The Diffusion of Scientific Management and Mass Production from the U.S. in the Twentieth Century," *Proceedings of the 14th International Congress of the History of Science*, No. 4, Tokyo, pp. 377–386.

League of Nations (1927), *The World Economic Conference: Final Report*, Geneva.

Lebowitz, Michael (1982), "The General and the Specific in Marx's Theory of Crisis," *Studies in Political Economy*, No. 7, pp. 5–25.

Leibenstein, Harvey (1966), "Allocative Efficiency vs. 'X-Efficiency,'" *American Economic Review*, Vol. 56, No. 3, pp. 392–415.

Lenin, V.I. (1947), "The Immediate Tasks of the Soviet Government" in *Selected Works*, Vol. 2, Foreign Languages Publishing House, Moscow, pp. 312–341.

Lewis, Alan (1982), *The Psychology of Taxation*, Martin Robertson, Oxford.

Linder, Staffan Burenstam (1970), *The Harried Leisure Class*, Columbia University Press, New York.

Lipmann, Otto (1924), "Hours of Work and Output," *International Labour Review*, Vol. 9, No. 4, pp. 481–506.

Litterer, Joseph A. (1963), "Systematic Management: Design for Organizational Recoupling in American Manufacturing Firms," *Business History Review*, Vol. 37 (Winter), pp. 369–391.

Louden, J.K. and Deegan, J. Wayne (1959), *Wage Incentives*, Second Edition, John Wiley and Sons Inc., New York.

Lowe, Rodney (1982), "Hours of Labour: Negotiating Industrial Legislation in Britain, 1919–39," *Economic History Review*, Vol. 35, No. 2, pp. 254–271.

Macarov, David (1982), *Worker Productivity: Myths and Reality*, Sage Publications, Beverly Hills, Calif.

McKelvey, Jean Trepp (1952), *AFL Attitudes toward Production, 1900–1932*, Cornell University Press, Ithaca, N.Y.

Maier, Charles S. (1975), *Recasting Bourgeois Europe: Stabilization in France, Germany, and Italy in the Decade After World War I*, Princeton University Press, Princeton.

Margolis, Bruce L. and Kroes, William H. (1974), "Work and the Health of Man" in James O'Toole (ed.), *Work and the Quality of Life*, The M.I.T. Press, Cambridge, Mass., pp. 133–144.

Marshall, Alfred (1890), *Principles of Economics*, Vol. 1, The Macmillan Press, London.

Marshall, Alfred (1927), *Industry and Trade*, The Macmillan Press, London.

Marx, Karl (1969), *Wages, Price and Profit*, Foreign Languages Press, Peking.

Marx, Karl (1976), *Capital*, Vol. 1, Penguin Books, Harmondsworth.

Mather, William (1894), *The Forty-eight Hours Week: A Year's Experiment and Its Results at the Salford Iron Works, Manchester*, Guardian Printing Works, Manchester.

Meakin, Walter (1928), *The New Industrial Revolution: A Study for the General Reader of Rationalisation and Post-War Tendencies of Capitalism and Labour*, Victor Gollancz Ltd., London.

Meiksins, Peter F. (1984), "Scientific Management and Class Relations: A Dissenting View," *Theory and Society*, Vol. 13, No. 2, pp. 177–209.

Merkle, Judith A. (1980), *Management and Ideology: The Legacy of the International Scientific Management Movement*, University of California Press, Berkeley and Los Angeles.

Metcalf, Evan B. (1975), "Secretary Hoover and the Emergence of Macroeconomic Management," *Business History Review*, Vol. 49, No. 1 (Spring), pp. 60–80.

Michael, Robert T. (1985), "Consequences of the Rise in Female Labor Force Participation Rates: Questions and Probes," *Journal of Labor Economics*, Vol. 3, No. 1, pp. 117–146.

Miles, G.H. (1926), "The Uses and Abuses of Time Study: A Reply," *Occupational Psychology*, Vol. 3, pp. 145–146.

Milhaud, Edgard (1925), "The Results of the Adoption of the Eight-Hour Day: The Eight-Hour Day and Technical Progress," *International Labour Review*, Vol. 12, No. 6, pp. 820–853.

Milhaud, Edgard (1926), "The Results of the Adoption of the Eight-Hour Day: The Eight-Hour Day and the Human Factor in Production," *International Labour Review*, Vol. 13, No. 2, pp. 175–209.

Mill, John Stuart (1859), *On Liberty*, Second Edition, John W. Parker, London.

Mincer, Jacob (1980), "Labor Force Participation of Married Women: A Study of Labor Supply" in Alice H. Amsden (ed.), *The Economics of Women and Work*, St. Martin's Press, New York, pp. 41–51.

Ministry of Labour (1981), *Employment Gazette*, Vol. 89, No. 10, p. 426.

Muensterberg, Hugo (1913), *Psychology and Industrial Efficiency*, Houghton Mifflin Co., Boston.

Munro, J.E.C. (1891), "The Probable Effects on Wages of a General Reduction in the Hours of Labour," *Report of the Sixtieth Meeting of the British Association for the Advancement of Science*, John Murray, London, pp. 472–485.

Muscio, Bernard (1917), *Lectures on Industrial Psychology*, Angus and Robertson, Sydney.

Myers, Charles S. (1920), *Mind and Work: The Psychological Factors in Industry and Commerce*, University of London Press, London.

Myers, Charles S. (1923), "The Efficiency Engineer and the Industrial Psychologist," *Occupational Psychology*, Vol. 1, No. 5, pp. 168–172.

Myers, Charles S. (1932), *Business Rationalisation*, Isaac Pitman and Sons, London.

Nadworny, Milton J. (1955), *Scientific Management and the Unions 1900–1932: A Historical Analysis*, Harvard University Press, Cambridge, Mass.

Naschold, Frieder in co-operation with Funke, Hajo, Hildebrandt, Eckart, Rinderspacher, Jürgen and Watkinson, Christof (1979), *Worktime and Stress and Strain – The Importance of Resisting Work Intensification Within the Framework of Worktime Reduction Policy*, International Institute for Comparative Social Research, Berlin.

National Industrial Conference Board (1920), *Practical Experience with the Work Week of Forty-eight Hours or Less*, Research Report No. 32, New York.

National Industrial Conference Board (1929), *The Five-Day Week in Manufacturing Industries*, New York.

National Industrial Conference Board (1930), *Wages in the United States, 1914–1929*, New York.

National Industrial Conference Board (1931), *Rationalization of German Industry*, New York.

National War Labor Board (1918), *Memorandum on the Eight-Hour Working Day*, Govt. Printing Office, Washington.

Nelson, Daniel (1980), *Frederick W. Taylor and the Rise of Scientific Management*, The University of Wisconsin Press, Madison.

Nevins, Allan and Hill, Frank Ernest (1957), *Ford: Expansion and Challenge 1915–1933*, Charles Scribner's Sons, New York.

Newmarch, William (1862), "On the Extent to Which Sound Principles of Taxation Are Embodied in the Legislation of the United Kingdom," *Report of the Thirty-first Meeting of the British Association for the Advancement of Science*, London.

Nordhaus, William D. (1974), "The Falling Share of Profits," *Brookings Papers on Economic Activity*, No. 1, pp. 169–217.

North, D.T.B. and Buckingham, G.L. (1969), *Productivity Agreements and Wage Systems*, Gower Press, London.

O.E.C.D. (Organisation for Economic Cooperation and Development) (1975), *Theoretical and Empirical Aspects of the Effects of Taxation on the Supply of Labour*, Paris.

Oliver, Thomas (1902), *Dangerous Trades*, E.P. Dutton & Co., New York.

O'Toole, James (1973), *Work in America*, The M.I.T. Press, Cambridge, Mass.

Owen, Robert (1815), *Observations on the Effect of the Manufacturing System*, Richard and Arthur Taylor, London.

Person, H.S. (ed.) (1929), *Scientific Management in American Industry*, Taylor Society, Harper and Bros., New York.

Peterson, Larry (1982), "Labor and the End of Weimar: The Case of the KPD in the November 1928 Lockout in the Rhenish–Westphalian Iron and Steel Industry," *Central European History*, Vol. 15, No. 1, pp. 57–95.

Pigou, A.C. (1928), *A Study in Public Finance*, The Macmillan Press, London.

Pigou, A.C. (1962), *The Economics of Welfare*, Fourth Edition, Macmillan, New York.

Pollard, Sydney (1965), *The Genesis of Modern Management*, Edward Arnold, London.

Pollard, Sydney (1978), "Labour in Great Britain" in Peter Mathias and M.M. Postan (eds.), *The Cambridge Economic History of Europe*, Vol. 7, Part 1, Cambridge University Press, Cambridge, pp. 97–179.

Poper, Frank J. (1970), "A Critical Evaluation of the Empirical Evidence Underlying the Relationship Between Hours of Work and Labor," Ph.D. thesis, New York University.

Popper, Karl R. (1972), *Objective Knowledge: An Evolutionary Approach*, Oxford University Press, London.

Rae, John (1894), *Eight Hours for Work*, The Macmillan Press, London.

Ramsbottom, J.S. (1914), "Suggestions for an Inquiry into Industrial Fatigue," *Economic Journal*, Vol. 24, pp. 393-402.

Raskob, John J. (1929), "What Next in America?" *North American Review*, Vol. 228, No. 5, pp. 513–518.

Reich, Robert B. (1983), *The Next American Frontier*, Times Books, New York.

Reticker, Ruth (1936), "Labor Standards in NRA Codes," *Annals of the American Academy of Political and Social Science*, Vol. 184, pp. 72–82.

Reynolds, Lloyd G. (1974), *Labor Economics and Labor Relations*, Sixth Edition, Prentice-Hall, Englewood Cliffs, N.J.

Rice, M.J. (1980), "The 1979 National Engineering Dispute," M.A. thesis, University of Warwick.

Robbins, Lionel (1929), "The Economic Effects of Variations of Hours of Labour," *Economic Journal*, Vol. 39, pp. 25–40.

Robbins, Lionel (1930), "On the Elasticity of Demand for Income in Terms of Effort," *Economica*, Vol. 10, pp. 123–129.

Robertson, John M. (1899), *The Eight Hours Question* (1893), New Edition, Swan Sonnenschein and Co., London.

Robson, Ann P. (1985), *On Higher than Commercial Grounds: The Factory Controversy 1850–1853*, Garland Publishing, New York.

Roos, Charles F. (1971), *NRA Economic Planning*, Da Capo Press, New York.

Rostow, W.W. (1983), *The Barbaric Counter-Revolution: Cause and Cure*, University of Texas Press, Austin.

Rothschild, K.W. (1960), *The Theory of Wages*, Basil Blackwell, Oxford.

Sachs, Jeffrey D. (1983), "Real Wages and Unemployment in the OECD Countries," *Brookings Papers on Economic Activity*, No. 1, pp. 255–289.

Schlesinger, Arthur M., Jr. (1957), *The Crisis of the Old Order*, William Heinemann, London.

Schoenhof, Jacob (1892), *The Economy of High Wages*, G.P. Putnam's Sons, New York.

Schultz, Duane P. (1978), *Psychology and Industry Today – An Introduction to Industrial and Organizational Psychology*, Second Edition, Macmillan, New York.

Senior, Nassau W. (1837), *Letters on the Factory Act: As It Affects the Cotton Manufacture*, B. Fellowes, London.

Sheldon, 0. (1928), "The Significance of Rationalization," *Harvard Business Review*, Vol. 6, pp. 264–269.

Siegfried, André (1930), "The Mechanization of Culture," *Fortnightly Review*, Vol. 77, pp. 770–784.

Slichter, S., Healy, J. and Livernash, R.E. (1960), *The Impact of Collective Bargaining on Management*, The Brookings Institution, Washington.

Smith, Adam (1964), *The Wealth of Nations*, Everyman's Library, London.

Smithies, Arthur (1964), "The American Economy in the Thirties" in Gerald D. Nash (ed.), *Issues in American Economic History*, D.C. Heath and Co., Boston, pp. 393–408.

Soule, George (1932), *A Planned Society*, Macmillan, New York.

Soule, George (1962), *Prosperity Decade*, Holt, Rinehart and Winston, New York.

Sward, Keith (1968), *The Legend of Henry Ford*, Russell and Russell, New York.

Tanner, J.M. (1969), "The Meaning of Physical Fitness," *Proceedings of the Royal Society of Medicine*, Vol. 62, pp. 1192–1193.

Taylor, Frederick Winslow (1903), "Shop Management," *Transactions of the American Society of Mechanical Engineers*, Vol. 24, pp. 1337–1480.

Taylor, Frederick Winslow (1917), *The Principles of Scientific Management*, Harper and Bros., New York.

Thomas, Woodlief (1928), "The Economic Significance of the Increased Efficiency of American Industry," *American Economic Review Supplement*, Vol. 18, No. 1, pp. 122–138.

Thompson, E.P. (1967), "Time, Work-Discipline, and Industrial Capitalism," *Past and Present*, No. 38, pp. 56-97.

Thornton, William T. (1971), *Over-Population and Its Remedy*, Irish University Press, Shannon.

Tsujimura Kotaro (1980), "The Effect of Reductions in Working Hours on Productivity" in Shunsaku Nishikawa, *The Labor Market in Japan: Selected Readings*, The Japan Foundation, Tokyo, pp. 67–83.

Tugwell, Rexford Guy (1927), *Industry's Coming of Age*, Harcourt Brace & Co., New York.

Tugwell, Rexford Guy (1928), "Experimental Control in Russian Industry," *Political Science Quarterly*, Vol. 43, No. 2, pp. 161–187.

Tugwell, Rexford Guy (1932), "The Principle of Planning and the Institution of Laissez-Faire," *American Economic Review Supplement*, Vol. 22, No. 1, pp. 75–92.

Tugwell, Rexford Guy and Banfield, E.C. (1951), "Governmental Planning at Mid-Century," *Journal of Politics*, Vol. 13, pp. 133-163.

United States Bureau of the Census (1976), *The Statistical History of the United States*, Basic Books, New York.

Urwick, L. (1930), *The Meaning of Rationalisation*, Nisbet & Co. Ltd., London.

Veblen, Thorstein (1921), *The Engineers and the Price System*, Viking Press, New York.

Vernon, H.M. (1921), *Industrial Fatigue and Efficiency*, George Routledge and Sons Ltd., London.

Webb, Sydney and Cox, Harold (1891), *The Eight Hours Day*, Walter Scott, London.

Wells, David A. (1889), *Recent Economic Changes*, D. Appleton & Co., New York.

White, Michael (1981), *Case Studies of Shorter Working Time*, Policy Studies Institute, No. 597, London.

White, Michael (1982), *Shorter Working Time Through National Industry Agreements*, Research Paper No. 38, Department of Employment, London.

White, Michael and Ghobadian, A. (1984), *Shorter Working Hours in Practice*, Policy Studies Institute, No. 631, London.

Yamaguchi Koichiro (1980), "Prospects for Shorter Hours and a Five-Day Workweek," *Japan Labor Bulletin*, Vol. 19, No. 8, pp. 5–8.

Index

215